Developing the Whole Student

Developing the Whole Student

New Horizons for Holistic Education

Clifford Mayes

ROWMAN & LITTLEFIELD
Lanham • Boulder • New York • London

Published by Rowman & Littlefield
A wholly owned subsidiary of The Rowman & Littlefield Publishing Group, Inc.
4501 Forbes Boulevard, Suite 200, Lanham, Maryland 20706
www.rowman.com

6 Tinworth Street, London, SE11 5AL, United Kingdom

Copyright © Clifford Mayes

All rights reserved. No part of this book may be reproduced in any form or by any electronic or mechanical means, including information storage and retrieval systems, without written permission from the publisher, except by a reviewer who may quote passages in a review.

British Library Cataloguing in Publication Information Available

Library of Congress Cataloging-in-Publication Available

ISBN 978-1-4758-5558-6 (cloth)
ISBN 978-1-4758-5560-9 (electronic)

To Evy and Liz
"Das ewige Weibliche zieht uns hinan." —Goethe

Contents

	Acknowledgments	ix
Introduction	Holistic Education in a New Key	xiii
PART A	**A Primer of Integrative Theory**	
Chapter 1	On Subjectivity and Objectivity in Integrative Educational Theory	3
Chapter 2	Features and Advantages of an Integrative Model	9
Chapter 3	The Hierarchic, Item-and-Process, and Pie-Chart Models	15
Chapter 4	The Integrative Option	23
PART B	**The Integrative Curriculum: Theory, Practice, and Issues**	
Chapter 5	The Growth and Consolidation of the Ego: Domains 1 to 4	45
	Domain 1: The Organismic Curriculum	45
	Domain 2: The Emotional Curriculum	52
	Domain 3: The Empirical-Procedural Curriculum	63
	Domain 4: The Legal-Procedural Curriculum	67

Chapter 6	The Emergence and Fruition of the Self: Domains 5 to 7	103
	Domain 5: The Phenomenological Curriculum	103
	Domain 6: The Immanent Curriculum	133
	Domain 7: The Ontological Curriculum	147
PART C	**An Exercise in Integrative Teacher Reflectivity**	
Chapter 7	A Study in Integrative Reflectivity with Dr. Martin Kokol	161
	References	177
	Index	195
	About the Author	205

Acknowledgments

I wish to begin by thanking those people who must be the alpha and omega of a teacher's professional life—his students. Mine at Pacifica Graduate Institute between 2018 and 2019, when I was writing this book, offered profound insights into and practical critiques of sections of this book which I invited them to read and comment on if they wished in addition to their already rigorous reading and writing schedule. Daniel Culbertson, Ben Edwards, Kyle Jankowski, Vanessa Jankowski, Kevin Kell, Dr. Donald Marks, and Susan Persing were especially helpful in this regard and have gone on to become my personal friends since my days there. I also would like to thank my chairman at Pacifica, Dr. Keiron Le Grice, whose support of this work while I was writing it was genuine and kind. His groundbreaking studies in archetypal cosmology informed certain elements of this study and will continue to influence me in future work.

Dr. Tom Koerner, vice president of Rowman & Littlefield, has not only been my "boss" in my various projects with this wonderful publishing house over the last fifteen years but has become a dear friend, too. So much of my career has depended on his faith in me and his seasoned advice. Ms. Carlie Wall and Ms. Naomi Minkoff, my editors at Rowman & Littlefield, shepherded this book with a professionalism and tact that cannot be surpassed, equaled only by Ms. Wall's kind and expert labors on my behalf in my other books at Rowman & Littlefield—a publishing house of true excellence that is near and dear to my heart.

Dr. Pamela Blackwell, a sister and mentor of thirty years and a psychotherapist of the rarest abilities, also offered her intuitive understanding of transpersonal theory that rivals any scholar's theoretical formulation of it. She does not merely read but lives the truths embodied in the wisdom of the best of transpersonal theory, and she brings it all to her practice to bless beyond measure those who have been guided to her sacred consulting room.

Fr. David Mayer (*Societas Verbum Divini*) has been my spiritual advisor since I met him at Nanzan University in Nagoya, Japan in 1982, where we both taught. As a literary scholar, poet, and writer of short stories, Fr. Mayer's comments and criticisms regarding my work have made me a better writer. As a physician of souls, he has made a better man even out of such unpromising material as I am.

I wear two hats. One is as an academic psychologist, the other as a curriculum theorist. The following people have been key in my educational research and writing. Dr. Robert Bullough, one of the premier scholars in the history of the twentieth-century U.S. curriculum, showed me how to parse a curriculum as essentially a world-historical text that encodes the whole spectrum of a culture's psychosocial problems and prospects. Dr. Stefinee Pinnegar's work in narrative theory, especially her prodigious labors of love with teachers about their sense of calling and the existential roots of their *praxis*, has helped transform teacher education in the United States, and would do so even more if policymakers and university and college administrators had the good sense to listen to her more, and more carefully. Dr. Robert Carson, creator of the *Ourstory* approach to the curriculum, offers in it a vision of the curriculum that is more capacious, daring, and simply more intellectually dazzling than any other theory of the curriculum I have ever encountered in my forty years of studying it. Dr. Joseph Matthews, veteran principal and much-admired scholar of the principalship, taught me, both by example and in his work, that in school leadership, as in everything, balance and humor are all. Dr. Vance Randall, who was my most influential chairman at Brigham Young University during my twenty-two years there, is one to whom everyone who has ever been in a position of academic leadership might well look as an example of that perfect blend of care and demand that characterizes the most memorable and creative leadership.

I would be ungrateful, indeed, if I did not acknowledge the singularly important work of Ken Wilber. Because he does not have all the academic credentials that gain entry into standard academic discourses, he is not taken nearly as seriously as he deserves to be. Mr. Wilber is not only deep; he is, in my view, a visionary and one of the most significant thinkers of my generation. I hope that this book is a means of honoring him and his iteration of holarchic theory. Often enough, I disagree with him. But that I owe him an enormous debt of intellectual gratitude I gratefully affirm here and throughout the book.

My father-in-law, Raymond Gemal, is simply the wisest man I have ever known. With a native intelligence honed by his personal studies, his devotion to Judaism, and a lifetime of adversities in the twentieth-century Diaspora that would have undone most men, my father-in-law's words and example make me a better Jew and therefore a better person.

Above all, I stand all amazed at God having blessed me with my wife, Evelyn, and my daughter, Elizabeth. The acute yet tender intelligence they carry humbly within them but will egolessly share if asked, the compassion-in-action they lavish upon all who fall within their circle of care, and their breathtaking patience with and love for me—I, more their servant, I hope, than even their husband and father, for they are both queens who deserve to be served—are what keep me moving on and trying to live a life that will, notwithstanding my many weaknesses, somehow prepare me to be with them forever in a heaven that would be no heaven without them.

Introduction

Holistic Education in a New Key

Since my orientation as an educational psychologist is holistic, I want to present a new taxonomy, or classification, of the curriculum that, as holistic taxonomies do, honors the physical, psychological, cognitive, sociocultural, ethical and spiritual aspects of teaching and learning. What I hope to show is that the taxonomy I advocate for, the *Integrative Curriculum*, has much to add to the terms and structures typically employed in making and evaluating curricula holistically. Before turning to that model, let us first look at the major taxonomies that currently are used in curriculum theory.

I have found that there are three major types of classifications, three different "heuristics" (or "interpretive lenses") generally employed in classifying curricula in curriculum studies (Mayes, 2017b, 2016, 2015, 2012, 2005b). In this, there is little difference between standard curriculum theory and holistic curriculum theory. They both categorize curricula by using the following three means of classification.

1. *Hierarchical taxonomies*. Represented in figure A, these taxonomies classify curricula as rungs on a ladder or layers of a pyramid. I will refer to them as Hrc (for "hierarchical") taxonomies: I will also refer to them as "Hierarchic," "Ladder," or "Pyramid" taxonomies. How high on the ladder the curricularist has placed a curriculum tends to reflect his judgment about the overall worth of that curriculum, for that is what ladder-hierarchies are designed to do.

Figure A

Figure B

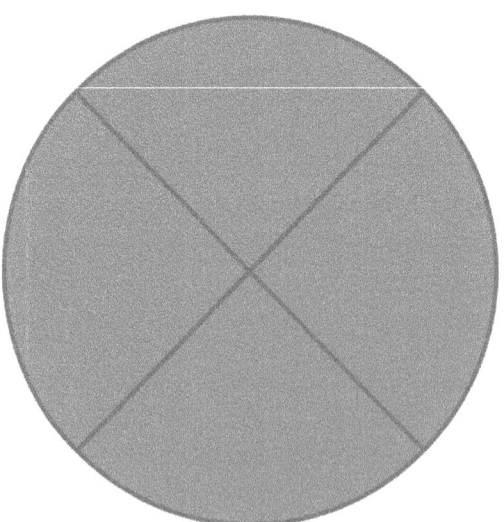
Figure C

2. *Item-and-process taxonomies.* Represented in figure B, these taxonomies classify different curricula as *items processing* along on a conveyer-belt. I will refer to them as *IP* (for "item-and-process") taxonomies. Conveyer-belt taxonomies reflect the curricularist's judgment about how far along on the conveyor-belt, how fully "realized," how close to attaining an overall development "goal" a curriculum is; for, that is what IP taxonomies are meant to do.
3. Discrete-units (PC) taxonomies. Although this is a third way of classifying curricula, it is not as common and thus will not figure into this study. It will also not be included because a Pie Chart is merely descriptive and does not carry the meaning of "higher" or "more developed." It simply reports the prevalence of a certain type of curriculum. There is no "value judgment" of the slices that make up the pie. And since it is the idea of "value judgments" in the holistic classifying of curricula that I wish to both celebrate and problematize in this study, I will not examine this third taxonomical category. Also, because a major purpose of this study is to examine how much or how little the different categories may synergistically interact with each other, the PC curriculum is ruled out since there is generally no interaction of its categories, merely its fixed use of categories for static descriptive purposes. A curricularist may assign values and interactive potential to a PC, but these things are not inherent elements in a PC.

The higher something is in a hierarchy (figure A) *compared against* the position of other things on that ladder, or the farther along it is on a conveyor belt (figure B) *compared against* the position of other things on that belt, then the "better" that thing is considered to be. It is often esteemed superior to everything below or behind it. Even if that may not be the intention of the person classifying the curricula, it is inevitably and rather deeply inscribed in that model itself and will be present at some level of consciousness or subconsciousness in the person who is examining the curricularist's classification.

This can be a problem for holistic theory, which is supposed to be about integrating all components of a system as equally valuable. In other words, Hrc and IP models, so useful in so many ways, can rest on assumptions and send messages that are inimical to the radically egalitarian assumptions and goals of holistic theory that all elements of a system are equally valid and valuable. It is that inconsistency that I aim to address in this study and to offer an answer to it.

For, even in a holistic hierarchy, which prizes "integrality," or the harmonious interaction of all elements in a system as equally valuable members of that system, there is sometimes the subtext and always the possibility that one will ascribe some sort of deep psychological or ethical difference just on the basis of someone's or something's position on the ladder. This happens even when it is not relevant to do so—if only because of the psycholinguistic tendency to subconsciously "metaphorize" prepositions and invest them with semantic weight: "Ahmed is above the class-average score in American history"; "Maria is way beyond me in understanding physics."

Small linguistic units can kickstart a subconscious process that ends in the nuclear explosion of a moral judgment when only simple description is or should be the purpose for the classification. With this, we may wind up morally esteeming one rung or stage as being "more important" in life than another and, even more damagingly, one person as being more valuable than another. Such things threaten the democratic, radically egalitarian assumptions on which holistic theory must rest and which it must also advance.

Naturally, there are certain contexts when such classifications are appropriate, even necessary: "Who should be awarded this scholarship?" "Who should sit as first violin in our orchestra?" "Who should have priority receiving this vaccine that we've only been able to produce limited quantities of?" But there are many times when it is not appropriate and may even do harm. Yet it is always the impulse when assessing something that presents itself as an ascending scale or an advancing process. In other words, the taxonomical models that holistic approaches employ may not be totally consistent with what holistic approaches wish to accomplish and may sometimes run quite contrary to it.

This kind of categorization can wreak psychosocial damage and ethical harm to the person or group of people being "evaluated" in both holistic and non-holistic approaches to education (Jones, Jones, and Hargrove, 2003).

Thus, it is that linguistic particles as small as morphemic opposites like *sub-/super-* and *pre-/post-*, which, in a certain context, should be serving only the functional purpose of describing a person's performance regarding a particular task or clearly delimited goal can now come to inappropriately serve an existential purpose of rendering judgment on a person's entire being (Lakoff, 1987, p. 181). This potentially hurtful and even unethical category-error may be a vestige of our evolutionary past (Renfrew, 1984). To be physically higher or farther down the path than another animal or to arrive at a place of conflict before or after one's opponent, often undoubtedly had physical survival value.

The ethical problem arises when, for whatever reason(s), we extrapolate from a person's specific performative ability to his general moral and social value on such flimsy grounds as, for example, his standardized test scores. It's no secret that such scores, especially on high-stakes testing, can, and often do, dramatically and even tragically shape the person's sense of self-worth and others' judgment of her. Test results have even been known to be a prelude to suicide.

Despite these inherent difficulties, the Hrc and IP model each has its merits and undoubted uses. Still, they must be handled with care, for they share the problem of objectifying the individual by means of numbers and diagnostic categories that can shatter lives, or at least hobble the potentials of those lives.

To offer a model that not only identifies but can often help us move beyond this widespread problem is primarily why I have written this book. The other reason is ideological. The model advanced in this study is the one whose ethos is most egalitarian and therefore, I maintain, most consistent with the spirit of democracy, especially as outlined by Dewey (1916) in *Democracy and Education*.

The model that I propose as another taxonomical option in holistic educational theory rests on the idea of the *Holarchy*, which I will occasionally refer to as *Hlc*. The idea of a *holarchy* goes back in the Western tradition at least as far as Plato, and Lao Tzu in the Eastern tradition. It is certainly present in Spinoza and Schopenhauer. The idea of a holarchy gives rise to what I will call *Integrative Curriculum Theory,* which, with major modifications, draws on Ken Wilber's *Integral Theory* (2000, 1999) in his evolutionary model of the development of consciousness at personal, cultural, and ontological realms.

Integrative Curriculum Theory will, I hope: 1) Prove a useful addition to the holistic repertoire of systematic and, above all, *humane* terminologies and "technologies" for making and evaluating specific curricula as well as for theorizing the curriculum at a time when "scientistic," "technist," and profit-driven views of education have commandeered the podium, policy, and *praxis* (Cremin, 1988; Rury, 1989; Spring, 2002; Watras, 2002) and 2) address some areas of concern that I have with certain holistic models of education based on my own researching and writing in holistic education over the last thirty years (2017b, 2016, 2010, 2005a,b, 2004, 2001, 1998), and 3) address what I believe are some problems in Wilber's *integral model* of psychological, cultural, and spiritual evolution.

Following Koestler's (1969) and Wilber's (1999) lead, I will deploy the holarchic model of seven perpetually expanding concentric circles, like those generated by a pebble dropped in a lake, as taxonomic categories, or *domains* as I prefer to call them. These I will use to produce a holarchic taxonomy of the curriculum, represented in figure D below. As we will see later, all of the circles interact with each other in every possible permutation. For reasons of simplicity and convenience, I will offer below a visual of a holarchy consisting of only four domains, however, in figure D, since there are 24 permutations possible (4 factorial = 4! = 24), whereas there are 7! = 5,040 permutations in a 7-domain holarchy, which would be unnecessarily difficult to portray here. And to make matters even more difficult to render visually, the number actually would be 8 factorial (8!) or 40,320 permutations since, for reasons I discuss presently, the seventh circle is divided into two categories. A holarchy of 4 rungs must therefore suffice in giving the reader a sense of the combinatory possibilities or a hierarchical model before they branch out into so many permutations that, for all practical purposes, the number of them is functionally infinite. A holarchy of 10 rings, for instance, would be 10!—or 3,620,800 combinations. Even if only a single article was done on the educational implications of each the different permutations by every educational researcher alive, it would take generations upon generations to produce even that first article in each

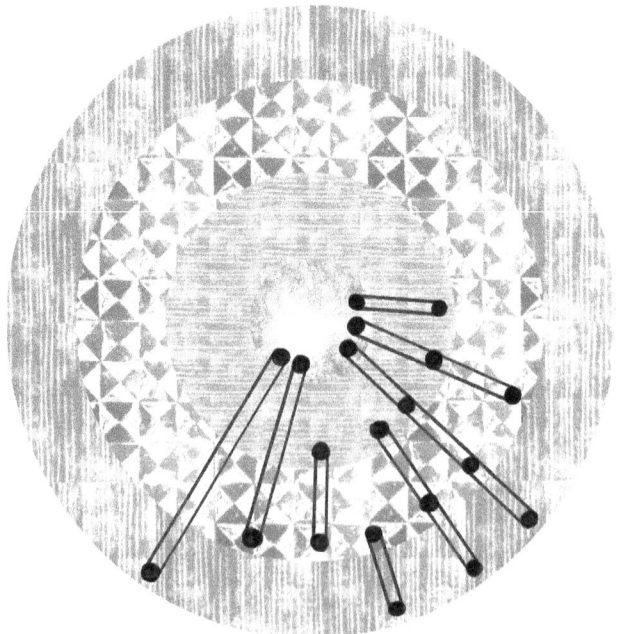

Figure D

combination. In other words, the possibilities of holarchic educational theorizing and practice are endless.

The discussion of the seven domains will occur in the following chapters of this book. For now, one observes that starting with the innermost circle and moving outward, they are: 1) organismic, 2) emotional, 3) empirical-procedural, 4) legal-procedural, 5) phenomenological, 6) immanent, and 7) ontological $7^{m/d}$ Wilber uses other terms to describe similar categories, although I, again, sometimes differ from him in how he conceptualizes a certain domain and envisages the type and scope of its reach. Also, I have found that students in even doctoral-level seminars in curriculum studies find Wilber's terminology opaque, overly exotic, and even biased in a certain spiritual direction and thus more than a little off-putting if they do not share his worldview in this respect. This is my major point of disagreement with Wilber, and I should therefore now say more about it and how I have tried to address it in this study.

In our (post-)postmodern times, what is needed is *dialogue* among spiritual traditions. This requires a mature affirmation of the virtues of the other's worldview and a willingness to be *educated* by them. Dialogical processes effect change (or at least a workable agreement to disagree) with a minimum of pain and a maximum of creativity if both sides enter into dialogue in a generous spirit of teaching the other and the humble spirit of being taught by that other.

I have attempted to do that in this book by dividing the final and most advanced reaches of human experience and hope as consisting of monistic *and* dialogical spirituality—*co-regnant* in that sphere and in constant, mutually edifying conversation, not with one structurally and philosophically positioned over the other as Wilber does (2000, 1999). This is my biggest disagreement with Wilber and it is a crucial one since the outermost sphere of a holarchy is, as it were, that system's "guidance system" and current realization of all that it can be or become in an evolutionary sense.

For these and other reasons that I make clear as this study develops, I both gratefully acknowledge my indebtedness to Wilber's wonderful work but also indicate major points of disagreement with him by speaking of the model used in this book as *integrative*, not *integral*. By doing this, I also want to indicate that I consider my work firmly in the holistic tradition but also that that tradtition stands in need of some updating, which I believe Wilber's model helps with. I have seen no need to disavow holistic theory but rather to loyally situate myself unapologetically within it and perhaps to lend a hand in expanding it.

Another large point of disagreement with Wilber's *integral theory* relates to my other major theoretical orientation as a scholar. It is Jungian, based on the work of Carl Jung and his "Analytical Psychology." My (2005a) *Jung and Education: Elements of an Archetypal Pedagogy* is credited as being the first book-length study of the pedagogical implications and applications of Jungian psychology. I am told that my subsequent books along these lines (Mayes, Grandstaff, & Fidyk, 2019, Mayes, 2017, 2016 a,b, 2015, 2007, 2005b) have formed a foundation for a "school" of pedagogical and curricular theory called "Archetypal Pedagogy." I mention this to explain why Jungian themes will therefore weave in and out of this present study since I see Jungian psychology as being quite holistic, especially in the central Jungian concept of "individuation," which is integration of all parts of the personality. Similarly, I see holistic theory as being quite Jungian in the holistic emphasis on integrating universal aspects of human nature and action-in-the-world (archetypes) within the individual in order to nurture the growth of a deeply humane and creative person. This is my second major point of disagreement with Wilber. His treatment of Jung is lopsided and dismissive.

Wilber reduces Jungian theory to only a marginal manifestation of the spiritual domain—a Maya-web of quasi-spiritual illusions that must be "grown out of" in order for the individual to enter to more properly called "spiritual realms" of Buddhist philosophy and practice. This is a *fiat* that Wilber makes on the basis of his own personal preferences. He is quite free to do so for his own purposes. It is a beautiful choice. But he is not free to assume that as a universal truth and for it to go unmentioned. I am mentioning it.

I am also asserting that for some of us, the opposite is the case. The closer we move to and live in the archetypal realm and the fuller our experience of the Ground of Being grows in that context, the closer we move to an understanding of and personal communion with what we believe to be the Divine Person.

It is to evidence due respect for the psychological and spiritual beauty that each approach possesses as well as to encourage dialogue between the two, that I have divided the outermost circle of my holarchic interpretation into two interacting and equally honored, equally empowered territories at their most developed reaches: The Buddhistic *monistic* domain and the Judeo-Christian *dialogical* domain. East *can* meet West, as a body of literature and the rise of many spiritual practices in the last half-century especially attest to.[1] Wilber's *integral* model tends to foreclose that possibility. I wish the *integrative* variation on it to open it up even more. As Ferrer has suggested, it is useful to picture religious truth as an eternal ocean that contains many different islands of salvation in the life that awaits us (2002).

Note

1. Ajaya, 1985; Coward, 1985; Epstein, 1995; Gellert, 1994; Herrigel, 1971; Jung, 1969a; Kawai, 1996; Mocanin, 1986; Rama, Ballentine, and Ojaya; 1976; Sovatsky, 1998; Spiegelman & Mokusen, 1984; Spiegelman and Vasavada, 1987; Suzuki, 1964.

PART A

A PRIMER OF INTEGRATIVE THEORY

CHAPTER ONE

On Subjectivity and Objectivity in Integrative Educational Theory

In later chapters, we will look in depth at how many more new theoretical and practical areas of holistic educational inquiry and practice open up for us to explore when we are guided by a holarchic map as compared to hierarchical and process model maps. Indeed, a major thesis that will be developed throughout this study is that a radical shift of imagery changes not only *what* one thinks about something but *how* one thinks at all fundamental epistemological levels.

For now, let Kant's (1781/1997) argument in *The Critique of Pure Reason* be noted that we have two basic epistemological functions, two ways of "processing" *reality*—which, in and of itself (reality *per se* in Latin or *an sich* as he wrote in the original German) we can never know with certainty. Those are: 1) our rational, syllogistic, empirical ways of knowing, as in math, and hence our *mathetic* ways of knowing and 2) the equally-valid and equally-limited *other* way of knowing: our intuitive, imagistic, and value-laden epistemological capacity: the *poetic*. We cannot know, Kant averred, which way of knowing corresponds best to reality as it really is: the objective mathetic way or the subjective poetic way.

One of those two epistemological modes may correspond with fidelity to reality *per se* while the other may not at all. Or, one may correspond better than the other, although both play a role. (This was Jung's view, by the way, with him strongly favoring the poetic mode, as I make clear in a recent study [Mayes, 2017a]). Or, both may play an equal role. Or, both may be totally "off" and not correspond to what is *really real* and *truly true*. Or, there may not even be such a thing as an ultimate reality. We simply cannot know with certainty which of these possibilities best captures the nature of existence, Kant says. All we can say is that we have two epistemological capacities: an "objective" one (so called not because it is more true but simply because it concerns itself primarily with the nature of *objects*/things) and a "subjective" one (so called not because it is less true than "objective" but simply because it concerns itself primarily with people's/*subjects*' inner *experiences*).

In all of this existential ambiguity, which it is simply the human condition to live within and there is no way around that, one thing is clear: Images and concept are profoundly interwoven. They may even be physically interwoven in the form of neural nets. They are *both* involved in human knowing and it is impossible to have a "thought" without it bring some admixture of both the mathetic and poetic shaping that thought. This theme and its many implications for education suffuse this present study.

Hence, as I will discuss throughout this study regarding many educational issues, the *image* we use to represent an idea is crucial, as conceptual-change theorists have found over the last several decades (Pintrich, Marx, and Boyle, 1992; Nussbaum, 1985) and as psychoanalytic educational theorists have insisted for almost a century (Mayes, 2009). And as I, in the spirit of transparency, have already discussed, the view that guides this book is that *the image precedes the thought*. Subjectivity is existentially prior in what follows, although the enormous importance of objectivity is given its due respect throughout. In other words, I take a "blended epistemology" approach among those possibilities listed above, in which both subjectivity and objectivity are at play in the formation of thought, but the subjective dimension is privileged *above* the objective but not to the *exclusion* of the objective.

The physicist and historian of science Thomas Kuhn (1970), whom we will discuss in more depth presently, makes the same point and takes the same stance in *The Structure of Scientific Revolutions* that scientific paradigms undergo major shifts (the term "paradigm shift" comes from Kuhn) when there is a general worldhistorical shift in cosmological imagery, poetic tropes on the grandest scale, that then instantiate a new cultural and worldhistorical attitude, orientation, and set of protocols in the "sciences" in determining what counts as evidence, where to look for it, what protocols to engage in to determine its probative value, and what rules of abstraction and association should guide one in making a "theory." According to Kuhn, even in what we have believed to be that most "objective" of things—the physical sciences—it is the subjective component of knowing that gets the determining vote in which paradigm prevails at a certain time and place in history, not the objective.

I mention all of this now merely to adduce it as one reason I will in this book advocate for *the image of concentric circles* as a way of categorizing educational processes, for it imagistically generates many different conceptual possibilities and interpretive nuances which standard holistic interpretation sometimes misses with its typical Hrc and IP categorizations.

"Every way of seeing is also a way of not seeing," Kenneth Burke (1989) famously proclaimed. Hierarchical and Item-and-Process models certainly buy us things in holistic theorizing and practice—allow us to "see" a great deal. But the integral/integrative model of expanding concentric circles, each relatively sovereign in its own domain but also radically and extensively interwoven with all other domains in degrees of complexity and differentiation (that might be likened to interwoven neural networks) can often buy us a great deal more scope, intricacy, and depth.

This is precisely the kind of thing that sets holistic educational theory apart from standard scholarship in curriculum and instruction, which usually moves along only one or two lines of analysis. It is the greatly magnified degrees of complexity, nuance, and scope that recommends holistic theory in general—virtues that are markedly enhanced by the introduction of integrative theory/imagery into our theorizing and practice. Integrative Curriculum Theory is not a challenge to Holistic Theory except insofar as it is a call to extend and expand its ways and means of conceptualizing holism and thereby grow even more "holistic." As mentioned before, the integrative approach does not necessitate a departure from the holistic movement but instead offers an elegant means of reinforcing it and expanding it in an educational environment that has never been especially friendly to it and (especially in conservative environments) has tended to be hostile to it (Forbes, 2003).

At any rate, it is the position taken here that our imagistic, value-laden, "primary" and poetic grasp of an idea comes before, and indeed is at the core of, our "secondary" expression in the form of a "concept" (Croce, 1953). This is one of the major theses of this study and it will be mined throughout for its educational significance.

Closely related historically and ideologically to standard holistic models, the Integrative model is also a significant departure from them in its: 1) semantically richer—or "polysemous"—rubrics, 2) structure, which *itself* carries as much semantic significance as its classificatory terms do, 3) attendant imagery, which provides poetic bases for new lines of thought, experimentation, and practice in education.

Before offering an *integrative* taxonomy of the curriculum, however, it will prove helpful to first gain a more rigorous purchase on what in general is meant by a *taxonomy*—the types of taxonomies that presently are most used in educational studies—and then to juxtapose those against the idea of an integrative taxonomy to stress the latter's unique nature, special advantages, and exciting new possibilities in the study of the curriculum—standard as well as holistic.

The second half of the theoretical introduction more fully states the case for integrative taxonomies as—*at a bare minimum*—an important addition to the currently most popular structures of categorization in both holistic and non-holistic curriculum theory and arguably a generally more serviceable one.

In chapters 5 and 6—the heart of this study—I look in greater detail at each of the seven categories, or "domains" as I call them, of the integrative curriculum. Those domains are: 1) organismic, 2) affective, 3) empirical-procedural, 4) legal-procedural, 5) phenomenological, 6) immanent, and $7^{m/d}$) ontological, which is a combination of Eastern/monistic spirituality (7^m) and Western/dialogical spirituality (7^d).

These chapters also offer my own example of what an integrative taxonomy of the curriculum might look like, not as a theoretical possibility but as a worked-out, first attempt in the curricular literature. I do this by delving into each of the seven integrative rubrics—or "domains" as I call them—in sequence, followed by a presentation of which aspects of the theorizing and classifying curricula and the actual making and delivering of a curriculum that that domain best answers to. This study is a first pass at an integrative parsing of the curriculum and as such is not meant to be prescriptive in any way.

Indeed, another curricularist might: 1) interpret the integrative rubrics differently than I do, 2) devise different rubrics, 3) categorize curricula differently than I have done using the same rubrics, and 4) see connections between categories that I do not, which is highly probable since, as we just saw, there are 5,040 possible connections in a 7-element integrative model, and this is not even considering the multiplier effect of the fact that each category is itself a highly complex organization with all sorts of intra-domain permutations that raise the number of combinations to an asymptotic approach to infinite.

Here, complexity becomes super-complexity—offering worlds upon worlds of research possibilities that even the most current holistic models and non-holistic models do not.

In sum, chapters 5 and 6, in addition to their theoretical purposes, equally delve into an array of practical pedagogical, historical, and policy-oriented points in education.

The conclusion of this study, "Calling and Commitment in the Classroom," is an eminently practical and elegantly wrought essay—a felicitous blend of theory and practice, which Dewey saw as being educational research in its best mode. In that culminating chapter, my colleague Dr. Martin Kokol —an educational scholar at various universities, an engaging essayist, and a passionate master high-school teacher and administrator of four decades— favors us with his reflections on his distinguished career in the classroom, deploying integrative terms to do so.

CHAPTER TWO

Features and Advantages of an Integrative Model

An integrative taxonomy can be used by a practitioner to construct a curriculum that evidences concern for a teacher or student in every domain, from the biological to the spiritual.

This integrative model of the curriculum may also be marshaled by the theorist as a means of classifying curricula *diachronically*—(i.e., in terms of the history of education) by locating the category in which any given curriculum falls, as well as *synchronically* (i.e., seeing a given curriculum or approach to the curriculum in terms of the types of curricula being discussed and used *now*). A synchronic analysis shows how that curriculum compares and contrasts with other curricula currently "on the market."

"Holarchies 101"

The Px2 Advantage. In chapters 5 and 6, I place different theories and types of the curriculum in their most suitable integrative and holarchic categories, although each type of curriculum may (and generally should) ramify and intertwine with a curriculum in another category, with curricula in various categories, and even with other curricula in its own category since each category is itself an organic system in addition to being a component in a larger organic system. This opens up worlds of holistic, deeply systemic analyses that holistic theory has yet to explore.

All this a holarchic model does with special force and subtlety because of: 1) the *permeability* of the boundaries of each domain, which are like a very fungible membrane for each domain, and also because of 2) the *permutability* of the domains among themselves and also within themselves (since each domain is an organic whole with permeable and permutable elements too) in an integrative model. I call it *The Px2 Advantage* of integrative systems and discuss it throughout this book. The Px2 Advantage evidences the radically synergistic nature of integrative systems, more than standard holistic models do.

After examining the structural preferences of current holistic theory—the strengths and weaknesses of the models that are presently being used—I will turn to a detailed analysis of what a holarchy is and discuss its unique usefulness in both extending our inquiries in holistic theory and avoiding some of the problems inherent in the models we currently tend to favor.

For now, I will simply make some prefatory observations about holarchies before going more deeply into them theoretically in this introduction and then presenting them in more descriptive detail with the focus squarely on educational issues. The result will be a first attempt at a theoretically grounded integrative taxonomy of curricula.

The image of the rippling pond: Holding the tension between egalitarianism and gradation. The first thing to observe is that the holarchy employed in this book is a system of circles nested within circles, all on one plane, no circle "above" another one.[1] This is the emergence of ever broader circles radiating out of circles, radiating out of circles, all emanating concentrically from the point in the pond where a stone was initially dropped in an act of creation. This is to indicate that each circle, each "domain," is essential to the functioning of the complete system of circles within circles, and thus no circle is "more important" than another. Rupture one of the rings of concentric circles in a pond and the entire system breaks down.

Politically, this answers to the pivotal principle in a democracy that no citizen is intrinsically more entitled than any other citizen in terms of civil rights and processes or in having his sphere of interests and hopes honored and nurtured. It also attends to the postmodern imperative not to "privilege" one person or group over another by means of what are ultimately linguistically complex ruses, semantically disguised power-politics, that both cover and legitimate anti-egalitarian contradictions in a system that advertises itself as being democratic but in fact is not, or is inadequately so.

Yet, the circles *are* concentric. This is meant to indicate—in the imagistic trope that I am developing to guide this discussion, following Koestler and Wilber—that each larger circle *is* a more complex "emergence" from the preceding circle. It possesses a broader, more evolutionarily extended "reach." The more "outer" a circle, therefore, the more "articulated" it is and the more "advanced" its epistemological and ontological scope and teleological realization.

This answers the instrumental *and* ethical human need to assess the relative "value" of something or someone in specific contexts and for specific purposes. Without *that*, an individual or group falls into ethical disarray and the epistemological crisis of what Gebser (1985) has called the "aperspectival madness" of "adualism."

Aperspectival madness is the inability to say that anything or anyone is better than anything or anyone else in any situation or for any purpose or by any standard. Down that road lies a systemwide disorientation, even an epistemologically-based psychosis (Wilber, 2000). It is the sophistic specter that haunts postmodernism's deconstruction, at its most extreme, of virtually everything at every "linguistic turn" (Rorty, 1992).[2]

Hence, a holarchy aims at protecting the radically *egalitarian* arrangement of units in a system. All elements are on the same plane and have equal *rights*. Yet holarchic theory also understands the evolutionary necessity of affirming and cultivating *gradations* within that system; for, different domains have differential structural articulation and teleological *reach*. The pivotal difference here regarding the categories in the *holarchic* (Hlc) model as opposed to the IP model is that *the Hlc model's evolution is not defined and determined by mere human agency but is a function of the cosmos itself as it evolves*. An IP model's directionality, on the other hand, is determined by a person or persons in all of their limitations, biases, and interests. An IP model moves toward a necessarily delimited goal. The Hlc model moves to the rhythm of the stars and the intelligence of the Timeless. Or rather, the Hlc model does have one teleological imperative. It is this. It is that a domain does not become more privileged to the degree that it is more advanced. On the contrary, *that more advanced domain has greater responsibilities under the pull of the ideal of the servant-leader, to dedicate oneself to the service of others*. This is the ultimate rationale and achievement at the seventh and most advanced sphere of development captured in the image that emblemizes the seventh domain—that of the Buddha-Christ (Hanh, 1997).

The ethics of evolutionary advancement. This is a theme will be developed as we move on, especially in chapters 5 and 6: *The greater the evolutionary advancement, the greater the ethical duty to serve others*. Appealing to the systematic theologies as well as the mystical literature of virtually every major religious tradition, it will be taken as axiomatic that the teleological goal of all spirituality is the increase of love, compassion, and self-sacrifice.

It is crucial to note pragmatically that the advancement of the outer circles benefits the whole system by drawing each and every element of it forward as a single organism. Again, this does not make the broader circle "better" in a *structural, jurisprudential, or axiological* sense. But it does make it more "advanced" in *functional, epistemological, and ontological* terms.

Holarchies are admirably suited to holding and even being energized by this creative tension between 1) *egalitarianism*, which admits of no intrinsic privileging of individual A over individual B in terms of *rights* and structural *importance* and 2) *evolutionary responsiveness* to the need to make valid distinctions between A and B based on degrees of their respective ability to guide a system towards its evolutionary growth and teleological unfoldment.

In other words, *a holarchy is politically and ethically egalitarian but existentially and functionally gradated.*

This is a delicate balance to be sure, but one that is inherent in the very idea of a liberal democracy in an evolutionary context (Dewey, 1916; Lasch, 1996; MacIntyre, 1981). There is nothing else for it, if one's political purposes are the advocacy of liberal democratic discourse, except to not only hold this tension but to tap into it as a productive dialectical tension. Anything else is destructive of democracy (*The Atlantic*, October, 2018, 322[3]. *Is Democracy Dying?*).

For, the alternatives are unacceptable: Succumbing, on one hand, to crass populism (egalitarianism but with no standards of judgment), or, on the other hand, to effete-judgmentalism (aristocratic "standards" of judgment lacking compassion, justice or any humane moral center because they are about the maintenance of privilege, not the good of one's fellow beings).

Finite versus Nonfinite Systems. In this study, the holarchic model is also referred to as a "non-finite/open-ended system." This is the holarchic model's premier advantage over simple holistic models, which tend to be "finite/steady-state systems," where each of its categories is self-contained, is dealt with as a unitary phenomenon (a "single thing" and thus generally not very complex), and where complex cross-fertilizations within, between, and among categories, are undertheorized and come much less naturally (if they come at all) than to an integrative model.

Finite/steady-state models generate a limited number of possibilities. Nonfinite/open-ended systems generate infinite possibilities—or they may be "functionally infinite" in that the possibilities are more than can ever be practicably explored. As we will see, standard holistic models tend to be finite/steady-state. In integrative models, by contrast, complex and effectively inexhaustible permutations of relationships both within and among domains are key to the whole organism staying and remaining whole but ever in new permutational clusters. They provide virtually endless possibilities in research and practice.

My task in this book is, therefore, necessarily preliminary. Building upon it, further research will, I hope, be inclined to 1) continue to explore the theoretical bases of and case for a holarchic educational project, laid out as a first iteration here; 2) begin to specifically examine the practicability of various of its inexhaustible number of synergistic permutations and permeabilities (that Px2 Advantage again) as a non-finite/open-ended system; and 3) get down to "cases" in specifically describing as well as reflectively[3] and critically examining the efficacy and efficiency of the holarchic model in action with specific teachers in their classroom in action-research (Bullough and Gitlin, 1995).

Such research would be especially amenable to qualitative methods such as phenomenological and life-history interviews, self-reflectivity, clinical interviews, case studies, and focus groups (Patton, 2002).

The Supreme Court of the Classroom

However integrative educational theory—or any educational theory for that matter—plays out can, at last, only be adjudged in that court of last appeal: The *praxis* of the teacher and the growth of the student, each in his[4] many roles and inevitable guises, each with his own needs and directions, situation-by-situation, site by site, and including, to be sure, but by no means limited to the classroom-in-the-world; but rather, affirming the classroom-*as-a*-world and finally the world-as-a-*classroom*—indeed, the cosmos itself as a "universal schoolhouse" (Moffett, 1994).

That is another reason that the curricular taxonomy being proposed here is especially useful. Its categories and unique structure provide us with a taxonomy of the curriculum that helps us understand any curriculum as a symbolic "site" where many worldhistorical forces have come together to construct the very idea of a "teacher," a "student," and a "school."

Moreover, the assumption everywhere guiding this book is the heartfelt conviction that wherever and whenever a moment of any existential gravity is taking hold between individuals, there, also, is an educative site coming into being. There and then, in that place and at that time, is constelled a classroom, where, if the teacher's concern is deep and the student's intentions are true (and we are all, alternately, the teachers and the taught), then the lessons given and taken, in time, point (given enough time) beyond themselves. Maybe it is true that we master the many curricula of mortality. But much more does a larger template master us, until, prepared at last for the classroom of the cosmos, the valediction to *this* one on our concluding lips, we graduate into a new course of study—in and as the Timeless. That belief informs this book.

Notes

1. See Wilber (2000), who, like Koestler (1969) before him, proposes this image as a developmental paradigm.

2. See also Best and Kellner (1991) and Paglia (1992) for trenchant critiques of postmodernism.

3. See Mayes, Grandstaff, and Fidyk (2019) and Mayes (2001, 1998) for examples of my attempt over the last two decades to introduce depth psychology and Jungian psychology, especially in the literature on teacher reflectivity as means of expanding and deepening the ways that teachers may reflect upon their practice as their narratives of their professional lives are implicated in the larger narratives of their lives as psychospiritual beings.

4. I have adopted the increasingly popular convention to satisfy the need for grammatical gender-equity by using the pronoun that fits the author's gender-identity as the general third-person singular pronoun. That said, I also from time to time use my opposite-gender pronoun as the general one to duly evidence sensitivity about this politically fraught and stylistically challenging topic.

CHAPTER THREE

The Hierarchic, Item-and-Process, and Pie-Chart Models

This is a study in "the human sciences" as that field is understood in a distinctly qualitative (Patton, 2002), broadly narratival (Clandinin and Connelly, 2000), and organically emergent (Strauss and Corbin, 1990) sense, with special reference to the emotional, ethical, and cultural complexity of educational processes. It is Polkinghorne's approach (1988) in *Narrative Knowing in the Human Sciences*, not the positivist and computational sense that prevails in much research in the human sciences today.

For, the organizational-behavioral and cognitive-behavioral orientations generally commit the category-error of misapplying the ontological assumptions, terms, and procedures of the physical sciences to the infinitely more complex existential nature and needs of the human being, which positivist approaches are simply unable to capture in their subtlety or fullness (Slife, 1993). To try to understand the complexity of the human condition by means of the positivist sciences is like trying to perform surgery while wearing boxing gloves.

Soon we will turn our attention to holarchic theory in general since the holarchic taxonomy—that is, the *Integrative Taxonomy*—speaks to and resolves what I hope to show are some problems in Hrc and IP curricula despite the valuable functions they serve. But this entails a closer look at those problems.

Ladders, Conveyer Belts, and the Anglo-Germanic Rhetoric of Privilege

To appreciate both the usefulness and pitfalls of the first two taxonomic patterns, in figures A (Hrc) and B (IP), consider the two reigning (and sometimes only) composition patterns taught to incoming university freshmen in Composition 101 classes each spring every academic year (Mayes, 2012). These are the two basic, even archetypal, forms that the student is now taught to punctiliously attend to in discovering and communicating what, by implication, is true and valuable.

We all know the drill: 1) Figure A: Ascend step by step, with impressive pieces of evidence under your arms that you will leave at each level, to bear witness to your having conquered that level, until you finally reached the top, declared it your own and planted your argumentative flag on it, or 2) Figure B: Move like phalanx-in-oneself itself, step by step, in parade-ground precision, armed with the ordnance of examples, until you blow your dialogical opponents away with the main force of your rhetorical order of battle. (Figure C: The pie chart does not really figure into this discussion as it is primarily descriptive, not evaluative.)

Note that IP is really Hrc turned on its side to form a straight horizontal line, with the top of Hrc as the point farthest right on the vertical IP axis. IP conveys a sense of superiority with a metaphor of time (the conveyor belt) and Hrc accomplishes the same thing with a metaphor of space (ladder).

Hrc is *a spatiality of privilege* and IP is a *temporality of privilege*. These two models, Anglo-Germanic in origin and still ruling the rhetorical roost, therefore dominate time-space assumptions, imagistically turning time-space into an arena of battle.

As I have contended in other work, this inevitably has *sub*-ordinating effects on students who come from other cultural worldviews and psychological/aesthetic predispositions that do not "fit" the cosmological assumptions about what it means to be "in" a "normative" classroom (hierarchies of authority and modes of interaction) and how things are "done" in that classroom (ways of interpreting the curriculum and its texts and also procedures of accomplishing tasks in that classroom) (Mayes et al., 2016).

Although these two rhetorical and epistemological forms have educational limitations in terms of understanding and catering to both the deep psychodynamics of concept-formation/change (Mayes, 2017d, 2009a) and culturally diverse epistemologies (Mayes, 2016, 2007b), they can for all that still be enormously efficient and effective in all matters cognitive and procedural, from baking a cake to forensic accounting to putting a human being on Mars.

These two basic linear patterns are at the heart of Western philosophy, which is, of course, not the case with classical Asian philosophy, which favored spiral/circular rhetorical patterns, or Semitic philosophy, which preferred parallel and chiastic rhetorical structure, or Romance-languages' breaking off of the linear rhetorical track to tell illustrative stories or even just anecdotes that arise by colorful and humanizing associations and then return to the main line of argumentation (Connor, 1996).

In a brief but charming article, Au and Kawakami (1986) noted that when South Pacific Islander students were allowed to "talk-story" during reading instruction, they learned to read quickly and well. When they were not allowed to talk-story, they did not.

Talk-story is an amiable free-for-all discourse pattern in South Pacific Islander conversation that consists of interjecting personal tales, overlapping with others' tales, in a friendly cacophony of personal narratives. To the unaware teacher, this looks like disorderly, even rude, behavior. To the teacher who understands this discourse pattern for what it is—an expression of interest in, even excitement about, the matter at hand by participants, and a way of bonding with other participants around it—allowing "talk-story" and even channeling its energy leads to educational success with Polynesian students.

On the other hand, the clarity of linearity, the lure of abstraction, discourse itself as an order of battle, these are the gold-standard of argumentation in the Western tradition, which tend to educationally disprize, even punish, alternative modes of expression.

For example, Gee, Michaels and O'Connor (1992) provided a deft analysis of how a young African American girl's show-and-tell narrative was judged an utter failure by her white teacher but, when closely analyzed by the authors in terms of the child's story-telling conventions of her community-of-discourse, was nothing less than a narrative *tour de force* by this brilliant six-year-old girl.

And yet, on the *other* other hand, though they have been much maligned by some postmodern theorists (who, nevertheless, were born of that cultural tradition and employ it frequently), we have reason to thank our lucky stars that our Western legacy abides. For, despite the historical catastrophes that Enlightenment and post-Enlightenment reason and empiricism have visited on us, they have also liberated us.

In the last century and this one, which has seen the stunning, almost inconceivable, growth of information, people live longer and healthier lives than ever before. Even the poor in our culture have access to certain goods and services that kings and queens could never have even dreamt of just a few hundred years ago (which is, of course, no excuse for not attempting to continue to address the many injustices that remain).

We can communicate with each other, even see each other, in "real time" across the world with just the tapping of a brightly colored icon on what the ancients might have called a lustrous diamond seer-stone but that we just call a cellphone. We can move through the sky to be with each other in a usually safe and comfortable way that the ancient Greeks saw only as the prerogative of the gods. These are miracles that have been made everyday realities by the historically unprecedented wealth of information and the symbolic systems and concrete technologies that not only enrich our epoch but define it.

The Western dedication to hierarchical and linear discourse and action are the two crucial cognitive and proactive capacities, the twin venerable vehicles, we have ridden to produce much of what is best and most constructive in us. And yet, it is these we now drive with reckless abandon, racing them, pedal to the metal, and go careening off the cliff in them into the fatal free-fall of planetary oblivion (Gellert, 2001; Giddens, 2001).

The order and productivity that these two models—hierarchical and linear processing—have given the world is great and undeniable. However, as such luminaries of sociology as Sir Anthony Giddens (2000), Peter Berger (1967), and Brian Fay (2000) have gone to great pains to warn us, we are living in a world-historical epoch of political and ethical disarray—a "runaway world" (Giddens, 2000). Its plight, largely caused by "technical rationality" (Schon, 1986) run amok, now needs reason restored and humbled to bring that runaway world under control (Giddens, 1991. See also: Best and Kellner, 1991; Fay, 2000, 1987).

Hierarchical and Item-and-Process models assert the idea of values, which, culturally variable though they may be in their cosmologies, rites, daily practices and so on, *do* have with surprising constancy, a purer reason, perhaps, at their conceptual core (Giddens, 1991; Fay, 2000) and even at an archetypal core (Adams, 1995; Gray, 1996; Henderson, 2000; Singer, 2000). For as Jung, drawing on Kant, declared, morality is itself an archetype and epistemologically fundamental to the human being—and to being human.

Giddens thus notes a universal logic and gradation of values that are the infrastructure of most cultures. These include prohibiting sexual relations between close relatives, the existence of art, dancing, bodily adornment, games, gift-giving, joking, and rules of hygiene (1991, p. 46).

We too easily and very dangerously demonize all hierarchical patterning and linear operationalizing, as postmodernism is wont to do, as the source of all our woes. For here, at the end of our world-historical day, they are also indispensable means to help us deal with those woes, which have been caused by a great multiplicity of factors. The difference is that we must now make "technical rationality" (Schon, 1987) our servant, not our God. We can do that by attending to some of the problems that we now see in historical perspective as being an inherent possibility in Hrc and IP models.

Another structural problem in the hierarchical mode. A large problem, one that we might call an "architectural problem" in hierarchical arrangements, is that they require a constant balancing of contradictory patterns of force to stay in one piece: Top-down against bottom up patterns of force. Here postmodernism must be credited with being on to something big in surfacing this problem. Then again, it but evidences a universal dialectical principle (as announced by Lao Tzu 2,600 years ago in the *Tao Te Ching*) that anything pushed to its extreme, begins to revert to its opposite. "Keep sharpening your knife and it will blunt," he warned (Yutang, 1949, p. 128).

The problem of excessive "pushing down" from a privileged, superordinate group to keep things in a present unjust order, is the tendency of extreme conservatism. The problem of excessive "pushing up" from an aggrieved subordinated group in such a reckless manner as to disrupt even essential cultural narratives and ethical codes that are salutary all round, is the tendency of extreme progressive instincts. The trick in avoiding that political equivalent of a psychotic break called "civil war" is to push down in a way that is *responsive* to the needs of the marginalized and push up in a way that *responsibly* acknowledges—indeed affirms—what is sound and to be revered (if such there be) in the present order.

In other words, there must be a commitment to *dialogue* on both parts, which requires a mature affirmation of the virtues of the other's worldview and a willingness to be *educated* by it. Dialectical processes effect change with a minimum of pain and a maximum of creativity if both sides enter into dialogue in a *generous* spirit of teaching the other and the *humble* spirit of being taught by that other (Buber, 1965).

Heraclitus reckoned this a cosmic law. It is implicit in Hegel's theory of history. And Jung, himself a Platonist in his own way, claimed it was at play in the innermost motions of psyche (where psyche becomes spirit)[1] in the reversion of psychic energy at the limit of its workings in any particular direction, to turn towards the opposite direction (Jung, 1970c, 1969b. See also Harding, 1963). Drawing from Heraclitus, Jung named this process *enantiodromia*.

For, although Hrc and IP preserve, value, and orient action, at their limits they create insupportable dichotomies—or "binaries." This is especially true of Hrc models. For, there is the inherent, possibly inevitable risk that, because its infrastructure is along a vertical, super-ordinate/sub-ordinate axis (and here again, we see the political tension that a mere prefix or suffix can prefigure, even incite): There is always the chance of top-down impositions to conserve a present order-of-things for the privileged and bottom-up insurrections in the service of an excessive unsettling a present order-of-things. This can lead to civil war.

However, even when such things don't result in civil war, they may result in warlike incivilities—vicious verbal attacks eating away at the possibility of constructive, mutually responsive public conversations, without which a democracy, predicated on mutually educative talk in "demilitarized" spaces, cannot survive (Dewey, 1916. See also Lasch, 1995). In short, hierarchies have always been seen as a threat to democracy, particularly by the Left.

The danger is extremist political bifurcation. On one hand are conservative patterns of force, which tend to form a top-down, imposed order in the service of preserving the privileges of the elites (Rawls, 1971; Steinbeck, 1986). On the other hand are liberal patterns of force, which tend to be bottom-up, in the service of disrupting established power in order to transfer fiscal and cultural capital to those at the base (Nozick, 1974; Rand, 1957). In their more pugnacious forms, they present opposite but equal risks—structurally present in any hierarchical system as a possibility.

In its most problematic manifestations, extreme conservatism freezes a system with "venerable" precedents of injustice that parade around under the guise of "tradition" but essentially exist in the paranoid service of order-as-such. Liberalism in its most problematic aspect promiscuously relativizes a system's time-honored, authenticated virtues to the point of disequilibrium, even anarchy. Both states-of-affairs *in extremis*, totalitarianism and anarchism, are variations of what Habermas (1975) called a "legitimation crisis." If not resolved, they can result in either totalitarian stasis or anarchic metastasis.

Calcifying into a rigid obsession with order (a depressive entrenchment) or catching fire in a reckless disregard for any time-honored virtues (a manic dissociation)—these are the unhappy prospects of an overly cautious conservatism, on one hand, or an over-reaching progressivism, on the other hand. They can prove to be a fatal structural flaw in hierarchical design. (See Klein, 1935, for the psychological basis of this political analysis.)

We are thus thrown onto the horns of a dilemma that can easily undo an individual in a system or the system itself. It is reminiscent of Bateson's famous double-bind (Bateson, 1972). There is a choice someone must make between polar opposites. They are antagonistic, equally toxic, and ultimately fatal. Yet the individual must choose between two death-dealing contrarieties. Such a paralyzing dichotomy is *schizogenic*—crazy-making.

Ladders and the Sociological Turn of the Mid-Nineteenth Century

This schizogenic double-bind also operates at the sociocultural level when the collective organism is split into warring "factions" and lines of communication break down.

When that happens, then a polarity that should be a creative tension becomes a threat to the system, for the polarity is not generating new ideas and perspectives in a useful "synthesis." Instead, the polarity is generating static and other "noise" foreclosing communication.

Each extreme has become so consumed by its diatribes against the other that there is little or no chance for those compromise solutions that fuel democratic processes. No one can hear the other voices because of all the static. Indeed, few people really *want* to hear other voices anyway. Each side of the bifurcated system is too caught up in its own polemics for that. Democracy cannot thrive in such conditions. It is becoming a serious question if it will even survive for much longer in such dire, anti-conversational straits.

Rather, as in the example above, there are two alternatives, equally dysfunctional and ultimately corrosive of democracy, which, if unresolved, can cast a society into that schizogenic state called "civil war," on one hand, or to either totalitarianism (inauthentic order/a depressive position) or anarchy (absence of order/a manic position), on the other hand.

The Sociological Project, which gets properly underway in the mid-nineteenth century in its attempt to become the "scientific" means of regulating such potentially fatal tensions as these in the new democratic "Nation-State," wound up reflecting it instead (Barzun, 2000; Giddens, 1986).

On one side of this new "science" was Herbert Spencer and his conservative application of Darwinism to the governance of a society. Believing that sociology should be deployed to study, steady, and sustain the ordered-ness in a system that had proven its ability to survive in the jumble and jungle of national and world contestations, Spencer argued in his (1851) *Social Statics* for a wisely conserving purpose for the social sciences.

Equally compelling, however, was Lester Frank Ward's (1883) ideal in his *Dynamic Sociology*, informed by a radically different, progressive reading of the implications of Darwin for the organization of the state. Ward asserted that sociology should dedicate itself to constant evolution in the ethical vision and political vibrancy of the state. The boldly liberating application of the social sciences to the critical scrutiny of the state and its problems and then its promulgation of programs of betterment would lead to an ever improving and therefore more evolutionarily "adapted" state.

The danger from the Spencerian Right, inherent in Rightist sociologies that descended from him, was that in the name of "law and order" it may freeze a state in speciously "legitimated," entrenched social injustices—a strangulation of democracy (Rawls, 1971). Conversely, the danger from the Wardian Left, also inherent in its sociologies, has been that in the name of "social justice" it is too willing to cast off necessary restraints, leading to disequilibrium and the breakdown of conversation—a disintegration of democracy (Nozick, 1974).

What is needed, especially when a system is in a state of critical disequilibrium, is an alternative that heeds the ethical imperative for sober judgment of new ideas, on one hand, while simultaneously recognizing the absolute equality of all its members to challenge that system with transformative ideas, on the other hand. For, without the capacity to make binding judgments, a system degenerates. But if it falls into judgmentalism, it asphyxiates. What is wanted is a model that honors the inherent rights of the individual but also recognizes the functional requirements of the collective.

Hrc and IP models are capable of this. The problem is that they are capable of *not* doing this as well. No model is foolproof, of course. The question is, "Is there a model that is less structurally prone to invidious distinctions that too easily play out in ultimately counterproductive and undemocratic scenarios—one that can be used in addition to Hrc and IP models—as a useful *third* approach in a methodological trinity.

Jung was fond of the medieval axiom *Tertium non datur*: the third is not given, the "third" representing a solution to a problem that seems to have only two solutions but each one less adequate than a third solution that yields the advantages of the first two but is less liable to fall into their disadvantages.

Is there a way, in other words, out of a "Hierarchy Pathology" that can cause an individual or group to wind up in the emergency room of history as either ethically starving to death by the lack of ethical nutrients in postmodernism's junk-food (too prone to "disestablish" what is good in a present order of things: a reckless Progressivism) or almost poisoned to death by being force-fed a fundamentalist ptomaine-morality that outlived its shelf-life long ago (too prone to cling to what is no longer useful, if it even ever was: excessive conservatism)?

We will approach this question from various angles in the next chapter on the integrative model of choice—the holarchy, which I believe to be the *third* we are looking for. Then in chapter 3 we will harvest this third for its many educational fruits.

Note

1. See Mayes (2017a). *An Introduction to the Collected Works of C.G. Jung: Psyche as Spirit*.

CHAPTER FOUR

The Integrative Option

It would seem that the most serviceable system and the one that would unite the apparently contradictory claims of the Right and Left in a dynamic balance. On one side is the necessity of certain generally accepted values to provide stability and "integrity," yet not only tolerating but celebrating the need for diversity among its parts and social change. These constitute that productive dialectical energy required to move any organism forward. What is called for, in other words, is *an order that sagaciously sponsors innovation as well as innovativeness that respectfully attends to order*.

Such a system would function well if it had two parties in mutually respectful dialogue: A *responsive* conservative party and a *responsible* liberal party. This would be a society that honored its founding narratives, upon which a society must rest and to which it must appeal in order to keep good order (1851; Tillich, 1959), on one hand, but a society that is also self-aware of its shortcomings and is ever on the move to seek a better order, on the other hand (Niebuhr, 1986; Ward, 1883).

Throughout this book, especially in chapter 3, we will examine these, as it were, "spatial" problems of extreme "Right" (excessive downward-pressing influences from the upper half of a hierarchy) versus extreme "Left" (excessive upward-pushing influences from the lower half of a hierarchy)—and we will do so with special reference to educational issues.

To make matters tougher, there is a "temporal" problem as well.

The Reign of the *Puer* and *Puella*: "The Case of the Runaway IP"

The temporal problem in standard taxonomical structures regarding human development is that most of them "max out" in describing the individual's psychological development at about twenty years old and leave it at that. They assume, it would seem, that the six or seven following decades of maturation are just an elaboration of what was developmentally achieved by the individual in the teenage years. Although highly counterintuitive, this is the case with traditional IP models of development. For the fact is that they come to an end at precisely the still-undeveloped stage they glorify: early young adulthood.

Since we are looking at social phenomena as being largely a function of the psychodynamic processes of its members at the same time as we are looking at how social dynamics shape the individual psyche—a positive feedback loop that Giddens calls a "double hermeneutic"—there will inevitably be problems, both individual and collective, if our group consciousness is overly determined by the archetype of the adolescent and is therefore susceptible to all the issues of adolescence.

These problems include: secondary narcissism issues, sexual obsessiveness, preoccupation with the opinions of primary reference groups, mythic-membership belief systems, playing to imaginary audiences, a disregard for the wisdom of the elders, being alternately stuck in unexamined myths and pushed precipitously forward by them, masturbatory self-gratification, and in general a possession by the archetype of the *puer* or *puella*, Latin for adolescent.

The Integrative Critique of "Adolescence-Fusion" in Education and Psychology

According to Gellert (2001) in his archetypal analysis of contemporary America, this is just what we see in surveying the contemporary scene: A culture that is stuck in a collective developmental arrestment because it is possessed by the archetype of the *puer* and *puella*—the *Eternal Youth*–with his or her insouciance regarding the stabilizing wisdom provided a culture by its ethically orienting, archetypal wise old men and women. Various transpersonal developmental psychologists have called our attention to this social archetypal pathology (Boorstein , 1996; Cortright, 1997; Ferrer, 2002; Scotton, Chinen & Battista, 1996; Walsh and Vaughan, 1980; Wilber, 1980).

Beginning with Carl Jung in the early years of the twentieth century, reaffirmed by Maslow in the late 1960s during the apogee of the "Youth Movement," and reasserted by the "transpersonal psychologies," and more recently by Chinen (1989), Ferrer (2002), and Wilber (who has since broken his ties with transpersonal psychology) (2000), it has been concluded that we live in a "teenager society"—a society, Gellert concludes, that operates under the banner of the adolescent. Little wonder, then, that our cultural landscape is pocked by a cynical relativism that is quick to deconstruct anything in its line of sight—an adolescent trait.

The transpersonal psychologies point out that much that happens developmentally—and increasingly so as an individual approaches the later and final phases of her life—represents a transcendence of the ego-centered issues of the first two decades of life in the direction of much broader truths. This lifespan process relativizes the *personal ego* and, if development proceeds well, establishes a vastly wiser, eternity-contemplating *trans-personal* "Self" (as Jung, drawing on the terminology of Hinduism, put it) at the center of the personality.

At least, that is the ideal although many people do not rise to it but cling to ego even as time and the tide are washing it away with one wave after another of life's assaults and indignities. One should no longer, therefore, refer merely to **psycho**-dynamics as an adequate descriptor of the whole of the person's inner life as she matures but rather her **psychospiritual** dynamics.

IP in Developmental Models in Holistic Theory . . . and Beyond

In both psychology and education, however, the standard models are still highly influential. Indeed, they still reign in education—privileged models at the most privileged domain in terms of public education—D4. And the most famous of those remains Freud's "Item-and-Process" paradigm of psychosexual development. Transpersonal educational theory resists that bias, wishing to include but transcend Freud's and other "ego-maximum" developmental models in framing the purposes of education and imagining how to bring them about, as we will discuss in more detail in the transpersonal education analyses (Brown et al., 1976; Harris, 1991; Kane, 1999; Mayes, 2017b, 2012, 2004; Murphy, 1975; Whitmore, 1986) in the next chapter regarding teaching and learning in Domains 6 and 7.

Freud's famous model of psychosexual maturation, relating to different areas of the growing infant's body, postulated an *oral stage* from birth to about one-year-old, an *anal stage* from one to three, a *phallic stage* from three to six, a *latency period* from seven to eleven, and the culminating *genital stage* beginning in adolescence and continuing throughout one's life.

Piaget (1969) believed that *cognitive* development unfolded in fairly universal and invariant steps: a *sensori-motor stage* from birth to two, a *preoperational stage* from two to six, a *concrete operational stage* from seven to eleven, and the culminating *formal operation stage*, starting around twelve-years-old and continuing throughout the adult's life as she continued to refine her ability to reason.

The Holarchic Plus for Holistic Theory: Developmental Psychology and Its Educational Uses

Of special interest here is the fact that *even holistic development models favor IP structures*. However, an integrative developmental model is much subtler and truer to life—much more "holistic," in a word.

An integrative development model sees maturation as proceeding in stages, of course, or else it would not be "development." However, it does not do it in the same way as both standard *and* holistic models do.

They would have the individual moving from A pure and simple, to B pure and simple to C pure and simple, and so on—in a "unitary" and "invariant" IP manner. But was ever anything human ever so pure and simple?

As Wilber brilliantly demonstrates (2000, 2999), Integrative developmental theory sees the individual as more typically moving from, say B to C in *some* aspects of its super-complexity, from B to D in *other* respects, and quite functionally back to A in yet other ways that might (at least for a certain period of time) be a good developmental strategy on the individual's part. Moreover, the highly developed individual might retain elements of Stages B, E, I, and W along the way and never give them up for reasons that serve that individual well.

The point here is simply that the Px2 Advantage allows these endless human developmental possibilities as instances of the illimitability of human identity, agency and creativity. To constrain development to an IP lockstep, as holistic developmental theory no less than standard theory does, is yet another example of how, to rise to its fully liberated stature, holistic education must turn increasingly to Integrative theorizing and holarchic modeling and look with a grain of salt on other taxonomical structures. The Integrative Alternative could effect a sea-change in holistic educational theory and practice, radically redefining what a "developmentally appropriate curriculum" might mean from its inception in early 20th American educational Progressivism (Cremin, 1988, 1964; Kliebard, 1986; Tyack, 1974; Watras, 2002).

We see similar conventional biases in other developmental theorists. For instance, Kohlberg (1987) hypothesized that one's ability to reach moral conclusions about problematic situations also unfolded in three stages: *preconventional, conventional,* and *postconventional.*

As useful as Jung generally found such models, he noted that they all tended to operate on the strange assumption that sometime during adolescence, the individual's growth came *substantially* to an end and that the rest of her life was more or less just an elaboration of what she had already become at that early age. To Jung, this seemed unnecessarily limiting, consigning the later years of one's life to the outer darkness of developmental oblivion—as if those years were simply a falling-away from the heyday of youth, and not a legitimate and important—indeed, crowning—element of one's experiences.

If genius resides, as some have said, in the ability to see and the courage to proclaim the obvious, then Jung's theory of development is certainly the product of genius, for what could be more obvious than the grossly overlooked fact that not only the first eleven or twelve years of life but also the remaining six or seven decades evolved towards ever higher syntheses and visions? Jung thus likened our lives to the course of the sun. In the first half of life, they rise to their zenith but sink toward sunset at the end. These two periods—roughly until midlife in the first period and from then on until death at the end of the second half—have two major parts, and these correspond to two aims:

> Man has two aims; the first is the natural aim, the begetting of children and the business of protecting the brood; to this belongs the acquisition of money and social position. When this aim has been reached a new phase begins: the cultural aim. (1967b, p, 74).

By the "cultural aim," Jung meant more than just an involvement in the arts and humanities, although that might be part of it. Rather, he wanted to signify that the aging individual, moving ever closer to death and what might lie beyond it, could make and share deep psychological, moral, and spiritual discoveries. These could then become part of the collective wisdom of the family, group, nation, and even species. Jung is certainly one of the cornerstones of adult education (Wacks, 1987; Wrightsman, 1994).

A society that disprized old people, therefore, culturally valorizing primarily sexual, social and financial desires (as he believed was true of American culture) was doomed to cultural catastrophe. For, it ignored the elders whose wisdom was alone capable of both maintaining and enhancing the valuable traditions of the people. In this way, a holarchic model largely resolves: 1) the temporal problem of incautiously privileging whatever is "newest" in item-and-process models and 2) the spatial problem of unfairly privileging whatever is socially "at the top of the heap" in hierarchical models. The holarchic model, with its integrative dynamics, retains within its coevolving, fluid, Px2 circumferences, the energy and the memory of the ancient stone and its primally creative, teleologically orienting purpose, and the evolutionary process that started when that ancient rock was let loose from a Divine Hand.

In sum, at both the micro-psychological level as well as at the macro-socio-religious level, the spatial as well as the temporal—the best system is one that harnesses the energy of the generative tension between the "conserving function" of the systolic contraction and the "progressive function" of the expanding diastolic as the heartbeat of a culture. Something that is both conservatively stable and progressively robust is best able to evolve in a safe but also vigorous fashion.

And that is precisely what a holarchy is, with its Gestalt balance between the "discrete-part" distinctiveness of domains (the conservative focus on the independence of small constituent parts) with the larger vision of global interdependence, or "field sensitivity" (the progressive striving towards ever-wider globality). The bifurcation of such an entity into two major ideological parties (one of time-enamored expansion and one of time-suspicious contraction) allows this dialectical process to proceed best, and why it is such a structurally attractive model in both evolutionary (diachronic) and epochal (synchronic) terms.

So, what is a holarchy and how does it accomplish this? To answer this question, we need a new image, for it is out of images that new worldviews are born before they become encoded and established as concepts (Bruner, 1996; Kuhn, 1970). Turning to depth psychology is a sensible move here, for it is *in* the depths of psyche that images are formed, *out of* the depths of psyche that they emerge, and *as* articulable concepts that they get framed as theory. In terms that the depth psychologies provide, it is out of the womb of primary, image-producing processes that secondary, concept-forming processes are born (Mayes, 2017b, 2016a, 2009).

The Pebble in the Pond: The Wisdom of Concentricity

In contrast to a ladder (structurally embedded power: its "spatiality" or "just how things *are*") and conveyor belt (procedurally directive power: its "temporality" or "just how things *get done*"), I will, drawing on Koestler (1969) and Wilber (2000), use the image of a holarchy as *simultaneously expanding concentric rings in a pond where a pebble has been dropped.*

Although each circle reaches out farther than the previous ones and thus has a greater scope (progression to ever-wider associations/unions: the collective/Progressivism), the holarchic "expanding-circles" model recognizes the equal importance, indeed the structural indispensability, of each constituent part in a fully synergistic system. This is emblemized in the fact that no circle is *higher* than any other ring, thereby honoring the *integrity*, in both the structural and ethical sense of that word, of each domain regardless of its range (local embeddedness/personal fiduciary commitments: the individual/Conservatism).

In other words, a holarchy is unlike a hierarchy insofar as a hierarchy implies a vertical/spatial/organizational privileging of each higher rung on a ladder. It is also unlike the horizontal/temporal/procedural privileging of each next stage on a conveyor belt as being just that much closer to the "finished product." No domain in the holarchic model of expanding circles in a pond has the right to dominate or denigrate the organic necessity of any smaller ring. Indeed, it would do so at its own peril; for, the survival and growth of the entire system resides precisely in synergistic interrelation, even interpenetration, of its parts.

This is a *forte* of the holarchic model, which is all about the complexity of each domain as: 1) *itself* a field of complex *intra*-action, along with 2) the Px2 Advantage of the vast permutability and ready penetrability of itself and other domains, in *inter*-action. This differs from many curricular taxonomies, including holistic ones, whose tendency, implicit in every rank-ordering, is to see each "aspect" of what is depicted as a hierarchy as being existentially unitary (and thus static) and functionally independent (and thus potentially inconsistent with the organic spirit of holism).

That said, each outer circle, embodying an evolutionary "emergence" out of its inner spheres/domains, is more "complex" or "articulated." Far from privileging outer circles, this extensiveness lays on them the responsibility of widening the scope of every domain through their own enlightened expansion. This makes of an outer ring not the ruler of all incorporate in it, but the servant of all that it embraces in the *caritas* of a Christ or the *karuna* of a Bodhisattva.

What is more, in a holarchy the system is open-ended. There is no prescribed spot where development culminates and the process ceases. On the other hand, Hrc and IP typically (although not always) have a vertical- or horizontal-limit, respectively.

Witness, for instance: 1) Piaget's upper-limit of "formal operations" in his (1966) Hrc psychological developmental model, which, for all its virtues, disregards existential development after about twenty-years-old, a counter-intuitive implication built into the model itself and 2) the horizontal-limit of the impersonal 100 percent mastery of the standardized curriculum as measured by standardized testing in human-capital, factory-line approaches to education, which reduce the student to striving to be nothing more than a perfect "object" but eviscerated "subject" whom schooling is seducing into living inauthentically, which is to say, neurotically (Moe and Chubb, 2009).

Spring (1976) has so aptly characterized this in IP imagery as a "Sorting-Machine." As evidenced in the *Bauhaus Movement*, structure is ideological, and as Michael Apple showed in the structuring of curriculum, there is no curriculum that does not at some level have inscribed in it certain ideological assumptions, whether or not the teacher and student are aware of this (Apple, 1979).

I have attempted so far to indicate how the structures of Hrc and IP, although not necessarily negative in their applications, carry within them the possibility of being misused. In an integrative structure, however, with its qualitatively and quantitatively much greater degree of interconnectedness of elements, it is less likely for that to happen.

For, each larger circle not only contains all the smaller circles it embraces; it is powered by them, and its present existence and future expansion depend on them. Similarly, those enclosed circles depend upon their outer circles to draw them towards increased articulation and heightened potency within themselves. For a larger domain to *oppress* a smaller one would be to chop off its own feet. For a smaller domain to *undermine* a larger one would be to chop off its own head.

And in both cases, the total organism would soon die since an Integrative System not only *evolves*, but it expires if it does not. The ripples in a pond cannot exist in a paralyzed state except as a postcard picture. They are either expanding or they expire almost on the spot. An Integrative System does not excel at evolution so much as it *is* evolution in its structural manifestation.

An item in a hierarchy, on the other hand, can shut down a level above or below it in an act of insurrection or oppression, respectively, and often be able to continue functioning in *its* element in a perhaps somewhat truncated but still relatively stable way. People do this all the time.

The intellectual who neglects his body and devotes himself entirely to his research may well suffer the consequences in the form of a shorter life, but this may be a trade-off he is willing to make to gain academic renown and awards. The athlete who neglects his mind and devotes himself entirely to perfecting his body may not live an "examined life" but it may be a satisfactory one physically and fiscally if he "makes it to the pros."

However, *the almost innumerable symbiotic inter-weavings between each element of an Integrative system with every other element is so complete and complex that one part cannot be violated without the entire system feeling the effect in a sizable way and shutting down very quickly.* Each element matters so greatly because every element depends on it. Integrative systems are thus, at their best, a dialectical balance between the rights of individual constituent elements (the classically conservative position) with the requirements of the collective whole (the classically liberal position).

An integrative organism is thereby constantly balancing in homeostatic process(es) the legitimate claims of conservativism's rigorous valuation of the individual with liberalism's constant and equally legitimate re-evaluation of that individual in terms of its duty to the whole. Spencer and Ward were both right. Valuation and re-evaluation both have their rightful claims in a political economy. The Buddha's "Middle Way" and Aristotle's "Golden Mean" remain in full force as part of "The Perennial Wisdom" (Huxley, 1996).

Stated differently, one may thus avoid saying: 1) "An organism is at Rung A, or L, or V of the ladder of its full and fixed maturation at Rung Z" or 2) "An organism is at Stage A, or L, or V on the conveyor belt towards a developmental terminus a static Stage Z." Instead, one may more correctly and generatively assert in a holarchic fashion that 3) "This particular organism is at a current coordinate in the ever-expandable Range of its unfolding, organically tied into the similarly unbounded unfolding of every other organism in the system of which it is a part, and all are joined in an open-ended evolution of the total Organism as Potential." As we will see in the next chapter, this different imagery/modeling underlies programs that are either liberatory or foreclosing. The image is all.

To shift from picturing the classification of curricula from a hierarchy or belt to ripples in a pond is more than just a stylistic matter. For if Kuhn is right in his explanation of scientific revolutions as first and foremost a shift in cosmological imagery, if Freud and Jung were right in the idea that conceptual thought is a secondary process that grows epiphenomenally out of the primary processes of psychically charged imagery, if Croce is right that poetry precedes prose, and if Heidegger is right that propositional language cannot approach the zones of ontological presence as closely or swiftly as poetry can—if all of these things are true, then the images that *depict* a system actually do more than just depict.

Rather, images *generate* systems. To change our imagery about a system is not to just prettify it with variety but rather to challenge it, to change the system fundamentally, and sometimes overthrow and replace it with a new image/system. That change can produce a more fertile imagistic starting point that will fructify in more nuanced and productive discourse.

A holarchic model produces questions, carves out routes of exploration, and suggests solutions that at a minimum adds a third arrow to the quiver of holistic theory and practice. Besides, Integrative Systems are synergistic in ways that hierarchies and conveyor belts could never be. They are therefore highly useful in the holistic categorization of curricula, and arguably even superior in many instances. I offer a first run at a holarchic taxonomy of the curriculum in this book—one that I hope interested educational scholars will build upon in their theoretical work and that educational practitioners will test and refine in their *praxis*.

And again, all of this has political implications, not just the pedagogical ones. (Indeed, there is no such thing as an educational system that can be divorced from its political implications [Apple, 1979]). For, consider the fact that *a Hrc and IP model serve either liberatory or constraining purposes equally well. In fact, the purpose of much totalitarian imposition is precisely* to establish a Hrc or IP order of things; *but a "hegemonic holarchy" is a contradiction in terms*. In its many articulations within and between categories, and therefore its overall tendency to more interaction and interdependence, integrative models may well emerge as inherently more democratic than other models.

The spirit of holism—from Lao Tzu (Yutang, 1949) to Schopenhauer (1819/2008)—and the radical independence of each part at the same time as each part is comprised of all the other parts—the paradox and perfection of this whole—is not "captured" (for what could capture such a whole except itself?) but is approximated, reflected, honored and invoked more faithfully in the Holarchic model with fewer possibilities of system-error than in the Hierarchic or Items-in-Process models, which, despite their fruitful uses and the good intentions of its users, are susceptible to structural-rationalization (as fixed ladders) and procedural-overdetermination (as conveyor-belt processes), which are inimical to the spirit of holism.

This is not exactly the latest-breaking news.

The ideological and spiritual roots of the holarchy stretch back at least two thousand years in the Western tradition. St. Paul used the image of a body and all its parts to convey what can only be called an integrative vision that is both practical and mystical, immediately functional and metaphysically meaningful. Wrote Paul around 55 CE:

> The body is a unit, though it is comprised of many parts. And although its parts are many, they all form one body. . . . If the whole body were an eye, where would the sense of hearing be? If the whole body were an ear, where would the sense of smell . . . ? But in fact, God has arranged the members of the body, every one of them, according to His design. If they were all one part, where would the body be? As it is, there are many parts, but one body. . . . The eye cannot say to the hand, "I do not need you." Nor can the head say to the feet, "I do not need you." . . . *[I]ts members should have mutual concern for one another. If one part suffers, every part suffers with it; if one part is honored, every part rejoices with it.* (1 Corinthians 12: 12–28. Emphasis added.)

Lao Tzu's *Tao Te Ching*, created about 600 BCE, proffers Taoism's exquisite view of the universe as an evolving organism, ensouled by the fruitful dialectical tension of Yin and Yang (the cosmic female and male principles), in which each component of the cosmos is tied into every other component. Lao Tzu expressed the ultimate integrativeness of the many and one, the infinitely complex multiplicity of things and their interactions, on one hand, and their primally simple Unity in origin and completion, on the other hand (both of which hands are, in the Eastern non-dual tradition, mystically considered just One Hand), as The Tao. "At its greatest," wrote Chuangtse, Lao Tzu's premier disciple, "Tao is infinite [yet] there is nothing so small but Tao is in it. That is how the myriad things come [into being]. It is so big that it encompasses everything. Deep like the sea," concluded Chuangtse, "it cannot be fathomed" (as cited in Yutang, 1949, p. 187).

In Praise of Holistic Education: Decades of Fighting the Good Fight and Keeping Faith

The Integrative Model is a strong addition to the armamentarium of Holistic Education as it fights the good fight of nurturing our children in the schools and of enriching educative processes in whatever sites they occur. The Integrative Model is also a way of even furthering refining the holistic vision so that it does not inadvertently trip into some structural mishap on occasion. But let it ever gratefully acknowledge the Holistic Education Movement. Its wise theorists and noble practitioners have been the sole (and soul) bulwark against what has been the devastating effects of political and financial interests that have compromised the critical mission of education in a democracy of helping to build up children intellectually and emotionally to be responsible citizens, enlightened family members, and compassionate human beings.

This historical mission is now the all but "forgotten dream of American public education," as Bullough (1988) has poignantly put it. It is the coopting of American education as now the third member of the "military-industrial-*educational* complex" as the greatest of all U.S. educational historians Lawrence Cremin (1988) so trenchantly put it. And it is holistic education which has nevertheless resisted this egregious worldhistorical tide with scant resources financially . . . but with moral resources in surplus.

I have maintained over three decades of teaching, researching, and writing, and continue to maintain, that the holistic approaches that we in the Holistic Education Movement have used and advocated for are more inclusive, flexible and productive than standard curricular approaches, which tend to be unifocal in their obsession with *either* cognition (Lipmann, 1982) *or* behavior (Taba, 1962) *or* cultural politics (Banks and Banks, 2001) *or* the canon (Adler, 1982) *or* expert-schemata (Bruner, 1960), *or* employability (Moe and Chubb, 2009), *or* citizenship (Goodlad, 1994), *or* economic justice (Torres & Morrow, 1995), or what have you.

Each of those pieces of the curricular puzzle is important, although some are more important than others, and a few, such as Moe's and Chubb's (2009) human capital view of students as "human capital" are simply reprehensible, and amount to what Block (1997) has exposed as "education as the practice of social violence against children."

However, in isolation they are futile, even dangerous, to try to implement in a totalizing way that excludes all the other legitimate and salutary functions of education. On the other hand, in addressing the multifaceted needs and capabilities of the *whole* student and, for that matter, the *whole* teacher, holistic education is philosophically rich, pedagogically engaging, and pragmatically efficacious.

And as for the focus of the whole enterprise, children, Dewey (1916) made clear just over a century ago (and his voice still goes largely unheard, and when heard, often unheeded) that interest is the prime motivator of robust and durable learning. It is a simple truth, yet (or perhaps, *therefore*) it is difficult for politicians, policy makers and even for gullible parents, whose judgment has been addled by the polemics of the politicians and policy makers, to grasp.

The point is just this. Children are delicate and complex beings. They respond best when they are treated with a healthy balance of deep care and high expectations in all aspects of their burgeoning existence. Do that, and you have the child's interest. Have the child's interest, and she will learn in each dimension of her being to the maximum degree that she is capable of in that dimension.

We are called *homo sapiens* for a good reason: We find our identity and energy, our focus and our delight, in *knowing*. We need to learn, we want to learn, indeed we crave to learn—not *primarily* as an instrumentality or strategy but as an emotional, ethical, and intellectual desire that comes straight from our core. We need to learn as flowers need water. It makes us human, and ever more human the more we learn. As Dewey quipped, "The only cure for education is more education."

Thus, the holistic cry to the nation has always been: Let teachers teach—*from* all the dimensions of their being that stirred them to become teachers in the first place, *to* all of the aspects of the child who is by her very nature instinctually primed to learn. These basic human facts about the existential centrality of education to our lives, indeed *as* our lives, needs no elaborate science to demonstrate.

Just look at any infant observing a new object, picking it up, feeling it, tasting it, putting it to some use, finding that it is better for some purposes than others, and then laughing out loud as she discovers its secrets. Encourage that and you will have discovered the desire to learn, the love of learning, indeed the instinct to learn, and the foundation of all sound pedagogy.

It needs no grand theory to establish that children love to learn, no statistical procedure to determine that they do it best when they are interested, and no political program or cost-benefit analysis to conclude they are most interested when they are being tended to in all of the many aspects of their whole being.

What teachers and children do *not* respond well to is being the objects of political and economic programs that insist (and usually with no great pedagogical or emotional sensitivity and even less historical knowledge) that education be standardized around politically and economically motivated purposes.

For, if a half-century of scholarship in American educational history has proven anything beyond a reasonable doubt, it is that the formation of educational policy and its implementation in the schools has had little to do—despite all its fine and fancy rhetoric—with the wellbeing of the teacher and student, but has had a very great deal to do with politicians getting elected and the *fakirs* of finance setting agendas that are designed above all to shape students into obedient "worker-citizens" in our increasingly inequitable society.

Dewey was right. The only cure for education is more education. And the only cure for bad education is holistic education.

However, having written some books in the field of holistic education, I know how, both in the work of others as well as my own, the problem nevertheless remains that holistic taxonomies, for all their many virtues and abundant good faith, sometimes tend in the direction of spatially reifying or temporally overdetermining, what should be a fluid and free process and therefore run the risk of unintentional elitism (vertical hierarchy), on an equally unintentional overdetermination/control (strictly linear item-and-process)—the very last things, of course, that they would want to do; but still an abiding, structurally embedded possibility.

The Integrative Curriculum is an addition to the virtues of traditional holistic education models and a corrective for some of its possible weaknesses at the theoretical level and therefore potentially in practice.

The last several decades of Holistic theory in Canada and the United States. None of this should blind us, however, to the great importance of what holistic curriculum theory and practice *has* been able to have both historically and currently (Forbes, 2003). It must be lauded for its noble intellectual pedigree, high purpose, and healing effects on those children fortunate enough to experience it not only in private schools but in certain public schools that have adopted holistic models, or at least incorporated some holistic practices (Forbes, 2003). It would be amiss not to mention the heroic efforts of Ron Miller and Charles Jakiela in growing *The Holistic Education Review*, now *Encounter: Education for Meaning and Social Justice* as the leading holistic education journal in the English-speaking world.

No survey, however brief, of holistic educational theory in the last several decades dare omit Miller's (1983) impressive seven-fold taxonomy in *The Educational Spectrum* of educational processes into behavioral, subject/disciplines, social, developmental, cognitive processes, humanistic and transpersonal curricula. Moffett's (1994) *The Universal Schoolhouse*, Miller and Seeler's (1988) *Curriculum: Perspectives and Practices*, Miller's (1983) *The Educational Spectrum* as well as his (1988) *The Holistic Curriculum* are also superb representatives of the holistic perspective in educational theory and practice.

Elliot Eisner (1985) answered the call to educational holism two years later. In his classic parsing, along with Elizabeth Vallance, of curricula in *The Educational Imagination: On the Design and Evaluation of School Programs*, he offered the terms: Developmental, technological, self-actualization, social relevance, and academic rationalism.

In all of these taxonomies, a social-relevance curriculum may, for example, be quite consonant with and adequate to one learning situation, inappropriate regarding another, and necessary but not sufficient for a third situation, which might also need admixtures of, say, developmentalist and academic-rationalist approaches to work best in a certain socioeconomic or ethnic climes—what Bourdieu and Passeron (1990) call a "habitus" and Nieto (2002) calls "positioning."

Such taxonomies do not do this just descriptively but rather with eyes fixed on social injustice when a group has been cast into a physical or symbolic zone of disadvantage. This is a goal my colleagues and I set out to reach in *Understanding the Whole Student: Holistic Multicultural Education* (Mayes et al., 2016), which, as far as I can determine, was the first and remains the only attempt at a holistic multicultural pedagogy, one of the topics I had explored throughout my earlier study (2005b), *Seven Curricular Landscapes: An Approach to the Holistic Curriculum*. Recently (Mayes et al., 2016), my colleagues and I updated our 2010 holistic approach to multicultural education: *Understanding the Whole Student: Holistic Multicultural Education*.

The problem in holistic curricula to date (my own included), as in Hrc and IP models generally, is that each domain is more or less unitary. Thus, even though it can be moved around to interact with another discrete domain as in a jigsaw puzzle, these domains do not interpenetrate in as many synergistic ways or as flexibly and even as playfully as they might. In fact, this kind of multivalence is still pretty much a *terra incognita* in holistic theory.

For instance, setting out to craft an organic taxonomy of the curriculum in 2005, I wrote *Seven Curricular Landscapes: An Approach to the Holistic Curriculum*, where I proposed four conflated holistic categories—sensori-motor, psycho-social, academic-procedural and ethico-spiritual. Not, I hope, without some merits, the book wound up being a jigsaw taxonomy as in the other "holistic" taxonomies. Later, a colleague and I presented another study (Mayes & Williams, 2012) using different rubrics in *Nurturing the Whole Student: Five Dimensions of Holistic Pedagogy*, with its five "dimensions" of a possible holistic pedagogy: Organic, psychodynamic, affiliative, procedural, and existential.

In an integrative approach to the curriculum, however, cross-fertilization, spontaneity, emergence, permeability and permutability, and, finally, as the watery image of a holarchy suggests, fluidity are defining characteristics, and they offer holistic theory and practice a treasure chest of images to explore, an endlessly intriguing possibility to ponder, and a gold standard to gauge our holistic theory and practice by. The more integrative an approach is, the truer it is to the holistic spirit.

Perhaps the most theoretically elegant example of holistic curricular categories is still Phenix's study—he is a largely unrecognized contributor to holistic education from over a half-century ago—*Realms of Meaning* (1964), with his classic subdivision into domains that he called: Symbolics, empirics, esthetics, synnoetics, ethics, and synoptics. Yet, even in those curricular taxonomies such as Phenix's that allow the greatest degree of interaction among categories, they are far from being as permeable or permutable as they are in the integrative model. The Px2 Advantage is key to expanding the horizons of holistic educational theory and practice.

A Brief Review of the Essentials of Holarchic Developmental Theory

To review: the idea of a holarchy may be *imaged* and *imagined* as an expanding system of developmental circles or rings (what in this book are called "domains" to emphasize the sovereignty of each epistemological division) as when a pebble is dropped into water. Each outermost domain is, at that moment, the system's most expansive developmental range—with each domain, in its optimal state, containing all of the less expansive but equally necessary developmental domains that are inside it and which it is both functionally wise and ethically obliged to honor and nurture.

As a dynamic evolutionary system, it is always expanding. Crucially, although a larger domain contains the smaller domains of development, it may not in any way diminish or dishonor them. A holarchy is not a hierarchy, in which each ascending level can dominate and in some cases even obliterate lower levels and continue to exist—albeit often enough in a truncated form; or in which a subordinate level can drag a superordinate level down and continue to exist, albeit in a diminished state, because it lacks the verve and direction of the outer spheres.

In a holarchy, each organically subsumed and fully celebrated developmental circle maintains its *integrity*—in the sense of keeping its evolving and ever-permeable boundaries intact. At the same time, it is also synergistically relating to all of the other circles. All circles depend on all the other ones to not only survive but thrive. Thus, the elements of a holarchic system are vastly more permutable and permeable than in any other model—the Px2 Advantage of holarchic models.

From this it follows that to: 1) *disprize* a less evolutionarily developed domain "in the service" of a larger one, or 2) *disrupt* a more evolutionarily advanced and articulated domain "in the service" of a less articulated one—and hierarchies are capable of doing both 1 and 2, even with the best of intentions—breeds a local pathology in the violated domain that will metastasize throughout the entire system. This can be called "The Dx2 Disadvantage" of hierarchic models.

Note that a holarchic model, because it is a system of gradients, assumes in a non-postmodern fashion that there is such a thing as *increments of value* in terms of developmental range. However, in a manner that evokes postmodernism's "better angel," a holarchy advocates for a *radical pluralism*, which in Deweyan fashion (1916) proclaims that the unique contribution and system-wide potential of each domain of the polity be equally honored.

For, without the vital contributions of each domain, the entire system collapses to the circle just below the dishonored one, which, violated, now gives up the ghost and dissipates. When it does, all of the more far-reaching domains around it also collapse, for they have now completely lost contact with their own inner rings, upon which they each depended as their vital inner-self.

Inevitably, what remains of the system is the next narrower domain inside the initially violated one. It is now the farthest-reaching evolutionary sphere remaining in the system. In what can only be reckoned a catastrophe in the development of the entire concentric system, a *devolution* occurs, for the range of the system has shrunk to its much-diminished new circumference.

That domain now finds itself perilously exposed as the leading influence in a complex environment that it is not prepared to handle.

This it must find a way to do, however, lest the entire system collapse circle after circle in a cascading implosion, until nothing is left except a patch of troubled waters that soon die out. At best, it becomes a historical memory. In many cases, it will be lost from memory as if it had never existed at all, a historical tragedy of the first order that erases all that its members had done, been, or had striven to do and become. An entire culture, sometimes an entire world, goes extinct.

Integrative Dysfunctions

"When Holarchies Attack!" No system is perfect. And owing to their extreme delicacy, Integrative Systems are prone to various dysfunctions.

For instance, if an organism becomes so embedded in its current condition—the perennial problem of conservatism—that it cannot or—in the case of that organism with moral agency, the human being—*will* not make an advantageous evolutionary move of which it is capable, then that organism is said to have fused with that less developed evolutionary range. This can happen with an integrative system although it is less common, one assumes, than in other systems because of its greater articulation within and interdependence among domains.

This problem is a variation of the Freudian (1923/1960) notion of fixation, which is a temptation for any system. In Eriksonian (1997) terms, it is the failure to resolve a particular developmental tension in order to acquire the "virtue" (e.g., power) of that stage. In Heideggerian (1964) speech, it is a refusal to engage in *Dasein's* ultimate existential burden and blessing of Being-Toward-Death. In Jung's *Lexicon* (Mayes, 2017a), it is the paralysis of the soul that, either timorously or exhaustedly, will not attend to the final teleological trumpet call of the transcendent function to be ever evolving. Whenever we are dealing with human beings, there is the possibility of bad choices derailing any system, even the best.

The moral drama of the human being lies in whether, in the exercise of his agency, he, or that group of people with and in whom he exists called a culture, elect to evolve; or whether, in the grips of a primal fear, he or they misinterpret the call to transform as something sinister, something fatal. Transformation requires relinquishing the familiar-but-moribund in favor the new-but-still-unknown. Understandably, but fatally, this invitation to transcendence may be misread by the organism as the issuance of a death warrant, and thus fought off in the throes of existential terror.

For wherever there is creativity, there is anxiety; and wherever there is anxiety, there is ultimately the fear of death. When violated, a disordered holarchic system may even become violent as the disrupted and dwindling system, now desperate for order (any order!) for the perturbed system to restore equilibrium, quickly morphs from a holarchy back to a hierarchy in an attempt to attain a new homeostasis.

For by now in the system, panic has supplanted peace, symmetry has skidded off into chaos, and "things fall apart, the center cannot hold, and mere anarchy is loosed upon the world" as W. B. Yeats wrote in 1919 of his internally embattled Ireland in "The Second Coming." This sets the stage for occupation by some hegemonic force or other to at least stabilize this now-radically disoriented thing, "where ignorant armies clash by night" (Arnold, 1867).

The fist of total force (wielded either by the Right or Left hand—does it matter?) will now not only be required; it will be frantically summoned from outside the system or covertly concocted from within it, to martially impose a sense of systematicity—however specious and sinister. This it generally gets done by deploying what Locke in 1682 in his *Second Treatise of Civil Government* called the state's "instruments of terror." This structural change, however odious or frightening, nevertheless restores at least a semblance of balance, without which no organism can long survive. Such are the inevitably hierarchic origins of totalitarianism (Arendt, 1951). Every totalitarianism begins in the wreckage of a failed ideal.

Naturally, any potential for the evolution of the organism is now foreclosed, and it will remain that way so long as that totalizing order reigns. For, the goal of totalitarianism, indeed its *raison d'etre*, is narcissistic. Its purposes go no further than its own installation, maintenance and expansion until a condition of cringing peace has been bought at the price of a bound-and-gagged servitude to a state that is ruled by agents who rule for no other purpose than to be the rulers. It is an evolutionarily primary exercise of sheer power-for-its-own-sake (Hayek, 1944). Fascism is not so much an extreme ideology as it is the death of ideology (Arendt, 1951). That's the bad news.

The good news is that this state-of-affairs has a certain rate of "atomic decay." For the entire cosmos is expansive in its every domain, microcosmically as well as macrocosmically evolving toward ever greater horizons—an insuperable law that is operative throughout the cosmos. This is the *Credo* of all Process Philosophy and Theology, found, for instance, in Bergson (1902), Whitehead (1964), Chardin (1975), and Hartshorne (1984). There is a cosmic optimism in the holarchic view of things.

True, the new total state-of-affairs on the fascistically frozen hierarchical plane cannot tolerate, and therefore is constantly searching out and destroying, any evidence of creative development—that is, evolution. Nothing is quite as dangerous to fascism as evolution. It does this in order to perpetuate its death hold—the imposition of censorship and the constant insinuation of punishment its primary tools.

True as well: A paranoid *animus* against art prevails, except in the sterile productions of art in the service of the state (Golomstock, 2011). Paranoia is a hallmark of totalitarianism, its police attempting to root out a corruption that it is to varying degrees projecting onto "profiled" groups. Thus, it is, finally, also true that that fantasized corruption in the "Other" may exist largely in that policing force itself (Chomsky, 2006; Jung, 1969).

But truer yet, more powerful still, and both timely and timeless, is the cosmic imperative to evolve, which an individual or body of them must either positively respond to in turning towards a new program of self-realization and teleological unfoldment, or else, in the fullness of time, it will simply die. Either way, the totalitarian condition cannot go on indefinitely, for it is in breach of a cosmic contract, a universal imperative issued by an eternally Creative Law. For Process philosophers, this Law is the transcendent, even the eternal Principle of Grace, which finally trumps the law.

This happens as what Jung (1967a) called the "Transcendent Function" is called into service. It is the reconciliation of dialectical tension in a new solution that embraces the poles of the dialect but, in a redemptive paradox, reaches an epistemological plane on which consciousness may now live, move and have its evolved, enhanced being. On this plane, too, the restored state, its purposes not only resuscitated but expanded, makes a quantum leap forward as an enhanced holarchic unity. It *evolves*.

Structurally and infrastructurally, in the realm of *praxis* and theory, holarchies are best suited to meet the cosmic call to evolve.

The educational implications of this are enormous and are the subject of the next chapters. In them, we look in depth at the seven developmental domains in the integrative model and their educational implications and applications : 1) organismic, 2) emotional, 3) empirical-procedural, 4) legal-procedural, 5) phenomenological, 6) immanent, and 7) ontological (consisting of 7_m/monistic spirituality and 7_d/dialogical spirituality)

In these chapters, we will be shuttling back and forth quite a bit between describing a developmental domain and discussing its relationship to other domains. This transitivity among domains is not only permissible but advisable in a discussion of a *hol*-archy, in which *all* elements are uniquely reflected in *each* element. This engenders an egalitarian energy that other models either do not have or do not have to such a degree due to those models' tendencies to structurally rank (Hrc's spatial privileging) or to dynamically prioritize (IP's temporal privileging).

PART B

THE INTEGRATIVE CURRICULUM: THEORY, PRACTICE, AND ISSUES

CHAPTER FIVE

~

The Growth and Consolidation of the Ego in Domains 1 to 4

Domain 1: The Organismic Domain

Although there is disagreement over how much the infant in its earliest perinatal development is able to differentiate between itself and its physical environment, it is obvious that the newborn has relatively little ability to do so (Crain, 2016; Wade, 1996; Washburne, 1994). Rather, it sees the world that surrounds it as more or less a literal extension of itself. Soon, however, the infant begins to register that the physical world that it perceives is not necessarily coextensive with itself. In short, the infant begins to feel a *difference* between self and world. If for some reason the infant does not "grasp" the true nature of its situatedness in the physical world, then the groundwork has been laid for later neurotic and psychotic disturbance.

This is because key to many psychological disturbances, ranging from the mildly neurotic to truly psychotic is what Gebser (1985) called "adualistic psychosis" in his classic *The Ever-Present Origin*.

In the syndrome of adualism, we see the failure of consciousness to fully recognize itself and then fully honor and care for itself as embedded in a discrete physical body in a teeming universe of other physical bodies. The pathology arises when consciousness misapprehends itself as either ecstatically or horrifically fused with the environment. The result of such adualism is the dis-embodiment and de-souling of an unanchored consciousness that may now easily spiral up into an amorphous sense of omnipresent potency (a manic position) or free fall into an engulfing sense of exposure (a depressive/anxious position) (Klein, 1935).

At any rate, it will not be until much later that even in health the infant completes the necessary developmental task of de-fusing from the primal maternal matrix, which of course is quite impossible at this point. But if this fusion is not finally broken, and the individual stays stuck in this or any other development zone, then that arrested element of the personality will fester and turn into a neurotic or even psychotic problem that will infect the whole system. In archetypal terms, the infant is ideally fed *by* the Primal Mother in appropriate portions and rhythms. But the good Primal Mother can flip into the form of the archetypal Terrible Mother if this process does not develop apace, lingers overmuch, and the child grows "fused" in this developmental zone.

What began as the Primal *Good Mother* now begins to morph into the Possessive *Devouring Mother*, who has taken on this awful aspect because she has persisted in the degree and duration of her all-consuming "nurturance" long past its developmental time. She has now grown shadowy in her Medea-like voraciousness, her lust to keep the infant trapped within her, and thus paralyzing her child the more easily to swallow it. Immersed in amniotic shades upon shades, a Miltonian "darkness visible," there is no light to guide the new soul forward on its now maternally engulfed, materially distorted, and archetypally stalled journey towards independence and identity (Campbell, 1947).

Kalsched (1997) in his groundbreaking work *The Inner World of Trauma: Archetypal Defenses of the Personal Spirit* probes the archetypal foundations of what have previously been seen in traditional psychoanalysis as merely *personal* issues. What the archetypal dimension of the psyche is, how it plays into human development, and what some of its educational implications and applications are, will be discussed as we move along in this study. For now, let it be enough to say that the archetypal dynamics of the psyche refer to the mythical realm of psyche, something that goes even deeper than the subconscious, and is not limited to personal experience but puts the individual in contact with humanity's most primal impulses and its most exalted hopes. This goes a long way in explaining why merely personal explanations and attempts to cure a neurosis often fail in normative psychotherapy. They are simply less interesting! Blinded by the cognitive-behavioral modalities that focus on reason and immediate conscious awareness, current approaches not only give but scant attention to subconscious dynamics; they do not at all consider even deeper archetypal dynamics.

In other words, given the cosmic, even proto-spiritual pull of the archetypal realm in both its dark and light manifestations, says Kalsched, the allure of neurosis and psychosis becomes very great and refuses to yield to less profound methods of "cure." It is simply more compelling at deep subconscious and unconscious levels to be mysteriously "ill" than boringly "healthy" at superficial levels by what the soul knows to be simplistic psychological perspectives and practices.

At any rate, in this first domain, D1, lie some of the somatic and affective roots of depression/anxiety in the agony of disembodiment and aperspectivalism.

Further, since in any integrative system every part reflects every other part, then even in this earliest domain potentially lie seeds of disruption and even disaster in the individual's development toward the farthest reaches of his future possibilities. If the specter of nihilism weaves itself around the neurological infrastructure of consciousness in this somatically and emotionally critical first period, it may affect all later development too.

It is in these early moments and movements of consciousness attempting to loosen itself from (in archetypal terms) the grip of the Devouring Mother—which Piaget calls the sensori-physical phase—that the complex construction of the ego commences upon somatic foundations and soon will continue doing so in the emotion-surfeited waters of Domain 2.

Deeply set in the somatic—and thus pre-verbal/pre-conceptual—core of psyche, many later psychological problems will not yield to mere talk-therapy and simple cognitive approaches but require pharmacological and/or alternative modalities like yoga, Rolfing, massage, and other means of accessing and addressing the somatic disaster in the center of the individual's psyche (Comer, 1998; Samuels, 1992).

This delicate process of "the hatching of the physical self," as Wilber calls it, is quite primary and primal (1996, p. 162). Subsequent development in consciousness rests upon it—as indeed in any integrative structure, where: 1) the nature and success of each developmental advance in the outer spheres/domains depends upon the healthy functioning of all the smaller developmental spheres/domains that comprise it, and 2) the nature and success of each developmental advance in the narrower spheres/domains depends upon the healthy functioning of all the larger rings that draw the smaller rings forward and help them become wider.

The sensori-motor domain is existential ground-zero.

The Body as Curriculum

The history of the body in American education through an Integrative lens. Even before the insights of psychodynamic developmental theory, some curricularists intuitively understood the crucial role of physicality in the curriculum. Each in his own way, Comenius, Pestalozzi, and Froebel made the student's engagement with the physical world an integrative part, indeed a baseline, of what and how the teacher should teach. Their recognition that education needed to include the physical domain was in no small measure what separated their theory and practice from many of the pedagogies which had preceded them (Broudy and Palmer, 1965). What Plato recognized in his vision of education—where the physical development of all children was a foundation of more advanced curricula—was again acknowledged and elaborated by Comenius, Pestalozzi, and Froebel (Broudy and Palmer, 1965). Comenius's held in his seventeenth-century classic, *Opera Didactica Omnia*, that the education of the child should unfold in a developmental fashion that paralleled general evolutionary patterns that one could readily observe in nature. This was the basis of his multisensory approach. Comenius proposed that:

> The sense of hearing should always be conjoined with that of sight, and the tongue should be trained in combination with the hand. The subjects that are taught should not merely be taught orally, and thus appeal to the ear alone, but should be pictorially illustrated and thus develop the imagination by the help of the eye. (Broudy and Palmer, 1965, p. 102)

Some three centuries before Piaget, we see evidence of sensori-motor considerations in curriculum theory. The focus on physicality grew even sharper 150 years later in the work of Pestallozi, one of whose pedagogical tenets was that the child learned best when involved in immediate sensory engagement with objects. These are what Pestallozi famously dubbed "object lessons." If the child was to learn in meaningful and lasting ways, he or she needed to begin with *realia*, which would then serve as the cornerstones of cognitive and affective elaboration in subsequent instruction.

Froebel significantly affected the theory and practice of Jean Piaget, who would begin to publish his first essays in child development a half-century later. The father of the kindergarten movement, Froebel "was enthusiastic about Pestalozzi but not uncritical." For all the spiritual power of the Pestalozzian presence, the instruction, according to Froebel, was in many ways "external, mechanical, and lacking in unity" (Broudy and Palmer, 1965, p. 118). It was, in short, holistic in its recognition of a crucial domain of consciousness but not yet holarchic in grasping its integrative nature, its synergistic potential with other domains. Froebel's main disagreement with Pestalozzi was that Pestalozzian pedagogy was not holarchic; it did not attend to the fact that the cosmos is an:

> organized unity, a unity in which any given thing is a whole in itself yet a part of a larger whole. The distinctive aspect of this relationship is not simply that of inclusiveness. It is rather that every individual thing exists only in its higher

unity; the finger exists only in the hand and in that higher unity has a special function. . . . Pedagogically, this sort of theory has the effect of leading the pupil on and on from one perch of significance to another more inclusive one. Furthermore, the individual pupil's significance swells as he is related to ever higher and more inclusive entities. (Broudy and Palmer, 1965, p. 120)

This integrative approach caused the physical to now be esteemed as rich with metaphysical import in Froebel's curriculum, just as the metaphysical could not be apprehended apart from its physical embodiments. To ignore it in education was to blind oneself and one's students to the divine dimensions of the physical as well as to the physical dimensions of the divine.

This was especially important to Froebel because of his belief, common at the time, that ontogeny recapitulated phylogeny. He claimed that very young children would see, think, and act from those primarily physical—even feral—domains of consciousness which characterized our earliest evolutionary inflection point. Froebel's argument provided not only the pedagogical tools but also the philosophical foundation of the kindergarten movement, which, after taking root in Britain, would finally make its American appearance in the early Progressive movement in the closing decades of the 1800s under the likes of William Torrey Harris and Colonel Francis W. Parker (Cremin, 1964). In later chapters, such connections between "pure" spirit and "pure" matter are discussed as the basis of American transcendentalism as well as in Mormon theology, both of which have been noted to be instances of D6, the Immanent Domain, which is the penultimate sphere of spirituality in the integrative taxonomy used in this book.

Here we have another instance of the inter-penetrability of two of the most apparently disparate of realms. This is a point that holistic philosophies have long recognized, and that has been put into practice in most holistic school sites in the world (Forbes, 2003). An integrative approach to this allows us to take that conversation deeper theoretically and to empirically explore it in action research in the classroom in greater depth owing to the rich articulation within each realm that creates more areas and avenues of practical research than we have previously expected.

That consequential statement of American educational progressivism, *The Cardinal Principles of Secondary Education*, produced by the National Education Association in 1918, declared that attention to the physical domain of successful educational and social functioning was necessary at all levels of public schooling, not just during the child's kindergarten years. Given the widespread consequences and thus historical significance of this document and its holistic spirit, it is worthwhile citing it at some length here:

> Health needs cannot be neglected during the period of secondary education without serious danger to the individual and the race. The secondary school should therefore provide healthy instruction, inculcate healthy habits, organize an effective program of physical activities, regard health needs in planning work and play, and cooperation with home and community in safe-guarding and promoting healthy interests. To carry out such a program it is necessary to arouse the public to recognize that the health needs of young people are of vital importance to society, to secure teachers competent to ascertain and meet the needs of individual pupils and able to inculcate in the entire student body a love for clean sport, to furnish adequate equipment for physical activities, and to make the school building, its rooms and surroundings, conform to the best standards of hygiene and sanitation. (Willis et al., 1994, p. 158)

This document insisted that theorists and teachers not overlook the bedrock significance of the sensori-motor realm in the total educational structure, which, according to Kelly's definition of the extra-curriculum, includes every educative (and miseducative) thing that happens at an educational site outside of the classroom.

It is in this all-embracing context of the extra curriculum, as well, that we can place the growth of the school-based delivery of health and social services in the United States throughout the twentieth century. This has been a process which, as Sedlak (1995) has shown, was, and continues to be, fraught with polemics from both the Right and the Left about the necessity or even moral appropriateness of including these sociobiological services in the public schools—with the Right typically looking skeptically at proposals for further inclusions of biologically focused elements at a very personal and graphically-explicit way in the curriculum and the Left typically promoting them.

This domain is also the region where behaviorist learning theory operates and is applied to the schools, such as in Skinner's *Technology of Teaching* (1968). Although behaviorism has fallen into disfavor among many educational theorists in the last several decades because of its undoubted patriarchal and corporate subtexts and agendas, it continues to serve important functions as established by such classic curriculum theorists as Taba (1962) and Tyler (1950). It is perhaps particularly important in special education, where the functional control of emotion and behavior is often a precondition for any further learning. Even in some richly socio-constructivist instructional approaches, certain behaviorist principles of reinforcement continue to play a salient role (Bandura, 1977; Brophy, 1994) just as they do in cognitive-behavioral therapy (Beck, 1995). The sensori-physical domain provides a valid and productive set of terms, issues, and practices for curriculum and instruction.

Indeed, if, as Merleau-Ponty (2012) averred, all our knowing and doing ultimately flows from our identity as "body-subjects," then it is impossible to examine curriculum in phenomenological terms without giving due attention to this fundamental realm. Furthermore, if, as Freire (2001) declared, our curricula and instruction must be liberatory in both psychodynamic and political respects, then we must teach from, about, and to realms that are much more than simply cognitive. By its very nature, an Integrative approach to the curriculum invites us to look at these various domains regarding this issue in more complex detail and richer articulation than holistic theory has tended to do up to this point. Holarchic theory offers the path forward in this regard.

Fay (1987) has claimed that critical social science needs to ground itself in an understanding of the somatic elements of political oppression and to offer not only ideological critique but also practical therapeutic modalities for dealing with such embodied psychosocial pathology. His observations apply equally well to any theory of curriculum and instruction that aims at the psychosocial liberation of students and that aims at an integrative analysis of political oppression that focuses on complex interactions of psyche, soma, society, and cognition:

> Critical social science assumes that people's activities can be understood in terms of the false consciousness which they possess about themselves and their society, and it furthermore assumes that it is by changing this false consciousness that a social scientific theory can be an instrument of social transformation. But what if oppression is much more physical than this? What if, that is, oppression leaves its traces not just in people's minds, but in their muscles and skeletons as well? If this were to be the case . . . then a quite different approach to understanding oppressive regimes, and a quite different conception of therapy to undermine these regimes, would be required. (p. 146)

The different "approaches" and "conceptions" can be found in education in such holistic therapists, educators, and theorists as Schutz (1976), in his essay on "Education and the Body," Sardello and Sanders (1999) in their phenomenologically oriented guide to "Care of the Senses: A Neglected Dimension of Education," and Hendrick's and Fadiman's (1976) "curriculum for feeling and being." More work needs to be done, however, in tying the physical domain to others since these studies focus on physicality, do not create networks between the physical domain and the other domains, and undertheorize why such networks exist and how they operate when they do mention them. An integrative approach, on the other hand, requires that such connections be made in both practical and theoretical ways—another instance of how holarchic theory may draw holistic theory and practice into the next stage of holistic theory's advancement.

These are examples of some steps in the direction of what needs to be a much more elaborated educational project exploring how there can ultimately be no such thing as disembodied liberation—whether that liberation is psychological (Mayes, 2009a, b); ideological (Freire, 1970), or (to use the Gnostic term) pneumatic (Harris, 1991; Hoeller, 1982; Pagels, 1992; Wexler, 1996). A truly liberatory pedagogy, therefore, must honor and cultivate the sensori-motor realm of curricular analysis and instructional practice, and it must integratively establish theoretical ties among these domains that can then be examined pragmatically in action-research and other types of qualitative inquiries into the integrative life of the daily classroom. Again, traditional holistic theory has certainly ventured out into these territories but could do so a great deal more and more effectively with solid Integrative theory as its model and map.

Domain 2: The Emotional Domain

As things proceed through this first circle of emergence, the infant is ideally learning to differentiate itself from its physical environment in its increasing interactions with it.

However, it has not yet learned to distinguish between its emotions and its environment—which it simply assumes is a sort of 3-D visual echo of its current emotional state. Consciousness is still incapable of seeing anything from any other than its own biochemically driven, affectively suffused perspective—now smooth sailing, now sleepily indifferent, now a maelstrom, depending on the current condition of these labile emotional waters that *are* the infant (Wade, 2001).

The infant, although beginning to literally and figuratively "grasp" that it is physically other than its environment, now globally projects the rapid, irregular sinewaves of its inner life into the shape of that oscillating mirage that is its outer world. The infant's environment is saturated by the infant with the spectral gradations of its own emotional condition at any particular moment—the environment but a mirror of its affective inner-scapes.

Hence, although the environment is no longer *perceived* by the infant as *physically* co-*extensive* with itself, it is nevertheless *felt* to be *emotionally* co-*intensive* with its own feelings, making of the world the infant's emotional *Doppelgänger*. The infant is on that account "narcissistic."

In psychoanalytic literature, the word "narcissism" does not mean to condemn, only describe. We all need to be legitimately seen as valuable and virtuous. That is a good desire—and a socially cohesive one too. It is called healthy "primary narcissism" (Kohut, 1978). It is only when an individual has not received the kind of nurturing in his life that affirms him in authentic ways that he then turns to inauthentic and therefore neurotic ways of getting "seen and heard." They range from flashing a crowd in a stadium to possibly becoming a president of the United States whose outrageous statements are always calling attention to himself. That is called an unhealthy "secondary narcissism."

In most cases, a person wishes to appear as if he "knows the rules and more or less agrees with them," is "playing by them," and is "one of the group" (Linde, 1993; Watson and Watson-Franke, 1985). Indeed, our life-narratives, however much they may appear to be self-critical (and they tend to become increasingly so beginning around adolescence [Dusek, 1994]), the crux of our narratives is: "I am a good person. I have tried to do the right thing. And if this is not true in general of my life, it is because of things that have happened to me. I hurt myself. I bear those scars. Maybe I hurt others. But at my core, I am good and where I am not, it is because I have been dealt a rotten hand."

This is part of the well-documented "ingroup"/"outgroup" phenomenon (Devine, 1996), leading to what is called "the ultimate attribution error"—one of the best documented facts in social psychology, where establishing "facts" is rare. The ultimate attribution error is easy to understand, and we have all been perpetrators and victims of it. It goes like this.

Simply by virtue of "*who* we are" and "*what* others are," if something good happens to one or all of us, it is because we deserve it; but if something bad happens, it is because some unfair outside influence stacked the cards against us. Conversely, if something good happens to someone from another group, especially one that "we" do not like, then the reverse is true in our minds: The event that redounds to their good is just an unfair advantage they were given; whereas if something bad happens to them, it is because it is "just what *those people* deserve and they probably brought it upon themselves."

Again, we crave affirmation from our primary caregivers and then our primary reference groups. We need to be narcissistically affirmed. If we are not, then we suffer a "narcissistic wound" (Kohut, 1998) that may fester throughout our lives. Not surprisingly, many of the personality disorders, especially the narcissistic ones, stem from what will become selfobject problems that launch from this second developmental domain but whose missiles will penetrate all the other domains.

Selfobject psychology, beginning with Melanie Klein (1935), and extending most notably through Heinz Kohut, also produced brilliant theorists in D. W. Winnicott (1992) and W. R. D. Fairbairn (1992). In the education sections of this study, more will be said about selfobjects and primary and secondary narcissism in educational processes. For now, suffice it to say that the seeds sown in Domain 2 (and whether they were spread in care, indifference, or contempt will make all the difference) send out their tendrils to every other domain, where they can either further beautify the other landscapes or choke those vistas' vegetation with their incursive weeds.

In sum: The maximal interconnectedness of everything with everything, the functionally infinite articulation of a complex integrative system (complexity being its premier selling point) is what makes a holarchy so generative but also so delicate. And its profoundly egalitarian spirit, its commitment to the ethics (and one is tempted to say even the metaphysics) of democracy is finally what makes a holarchy something both powerful and fragile.

Selfobjects and the Second Domain
The system-wide shockwaves of the first five-or-so years of psychic development persist for the rest of a person's life. This is true for some individuals more than others, of course, depending upon the "good-enough" nature of mothering during this time (Winnicott, 1992). At any rate, the origin of those psychodynamic tsunamis in the relationship with the mother (and/or other primary caregivers) is traceable to these first two domains.

Freud saw this with courageous, even outrageous clarity, however much he may be mocked or just cavalierly dismissed in our current fixation with cognitive modalities and their statistical measurability—all of which he would probably find overly cerebral, too controlling, too tight—a flight from the Argentina-of-our-Passions to the Iceland-of-our-Denial.

The infrastructure of a person's sense of self can thus be traced back to his earliest relationships with primary caregivers—or *selfobjects*, so called in Selfobject psychology—one of the major forms of post-Freudian theory and therapy—because they are the *objects* of the infant's earliest attention and affection, through whom he finds *himself* in their reactions to him. Through them the infant learns, through what Kohut (1978) called "the mirroring" and "the idealizing" transference (more about these presently) about the world and self.

Because the idea of the Selfobject will run through the rest of this book, I will briefly lay out its essential features here. And again, I'll note how these examples of the interconnectedness of all to all in holarchic models is a possibility—indeed a necessity—but that this does not figure nearly as prominently in most holistic studies. I will illustrate this by reference to ways this all plays out in educational settings and dynamics as seen through an integrative lens.

The selfobject is another psychological concept whose roots are in the second domain but are intertwined with the roots in the first domain and ramify out to every other domain.

The selfobject is not, in the final analysis, *actually* the other person. Rather it is the *image* of that person that the infant—and later the adult—has internalized or, in psychoanalytic parlance, has *introjected* (Kohut, 1978). Typically, the infant's most influential introject/selfobject is its mother. The infant's psyche is so dramatically shaped by its interaction with its mother because it is symbiotically fused with her at the two earliest stages, the origin of most of the neuroses that may come to a perverse flowering in later life (Klein, 1935; Kohut, 1978).

Freud was right on the mark in looking at the mother as the object of the infant's earliest passions (see also Melanie Klein [1935]). But he was wrong in attributing it all to sexuality. The Oedipus Complex is, at its core, not nearly so much about sex, and arguably not very much about sex at all, as about the nature of thought itself—its origins not in the universally abhorred idea of *coitus* with the mother but much more complexly in the murky matrix and heavenly horizons of the very concept of a "concept" itself: The etiology and teleology of thought. This would account for the paradox and bivalence of the word "conceive" as having both a sexual and psycholinguistic meaning.

Primary/Secondary Processes and the Second Domain
Finally, in terms of very early cognitive development (getting properly underway in the next domain: Domain 3, The Empirical-Formal), early images and symbols are just beginning to form during this second unfolding, throwing into stark relief the fact that primary processes of emotion are the matrix out of which secondary processes of cognition form into those earliest flashes of conscious thought. However, this proto-semiotic system of the earliest ideations has a very limited scope because the rudimentary images and symbols that constitute it do not have an autonomous existence but are, instead, primitively confounded with the things that these proto-thoughts signify.

Stated differently: Thought is not (yet) able to *transcend* the specific situation that gives rise to it, but, to the contrary, concretizes itself, even becomes isomorphic to the situation. It fuses with it. The susceptible infant's proto-cognitions are *shaped*. Like a sculptor kneads clay into *Ur-Gestalten*, so is the infant's consciousness patterned by the environment. But so may the shaped also shape.

For, in the laws of primitive logic, she "reasons": "If A caused B, then what is to prevent B from causing A later? In fact, isn't it bound to be that this will happen since A and B are so close and the tunnel of bidirectional-causation between A and B is so open and inviting that it must be true that just as nature causes me to do things, I can cause her to do things, too. And because I can, I will!"

This is simultaneously empowering and horrifying to the child. "Events cause my thoughts, so my thoughts can cause events. I am a mental savior of my universe. I am also potentially its destroyer who could make any terrible thing happen and not even know that I was doing it until it was over. I am equally the saint and the sinner in all I survey. And in any case, whatever this universe into which I have fallen is about, it is about me as its master and also its slave."

Along these lines of primordial major and minor premises and the intuitive leap to lyrical, hypnagogic conclusions, the melding of external and internal, of wish and reality, this makes for the child a potential reality out of its every wish as a psychic fact. This is called the young child's "magical thinking," her "omnipotence of thought," as Freud called it—the child's hope but even more the fear that just *thinking* something makes it so.

"Daddy was mean to this morning and spanked me. I hate him. I wish he was dead. I hope he gets killed in a car crash going to work to pay him back for what he did to me. I hope he dies!"

That evening, father returns home for dinner. He is alive but it doesn't matter to the child because the child killed the father in her mind. The fact that dinner is happening *now* does not mean that daddy did not die on the highway *then*. Contradictions are not a problem for the subconscious. They are its meat and drink. Let things be however they may be at the moment with daddy sitting in his favorite chair watching TV. Still, he died on the highway too. I killed him. I am that powerful. I am that wicked."

Thus, when the child, on the cusp of Domain 3, the Empirical-Procedural Domain, begins to learn that physical reality is law-ordered, legally primary in the Court of Concrete Processes, we utterly miss the high drama of this dawning capacity if we fail to see that it represents for the child something far deeper. At one and the same time, it signals both her Fall from Grace (in her omnipotence of thought) and her being snatched from Condemnation (because of what she might do with that omnipotence).

It is here, at the door slowly opening onto D3 as the child learns her first lessons about the lawfulness of physical processes, that she is really resolving the earliest dialectical tension of her life, of everyone's lives, one that she will encounter in many forms and guises on her lifelong journey. It is emblemized, both celebrated and lamented, at the very outset of Western culture in the Greek Drama. It is the mask of divine comedy and the mask of the earthly tragedy: dialectical artefacts of the human experience, they both reveal and conceal.

Even more basically, we miss the bedrock phenomenological and psychodynamic reality that a "concept" (even one as simple as how the quantity of water does not change even if you pour it from a stout little teapot into a sleek tall glass) only makes its perpetual emergences from the Morass-Palace of the Unconscious, the Blakeian Heaven *and* Hell that "thinking" fundamentally and forever is—rooted in something fearful, reaching for something beautiful.

Jung was driving at the same point when he wrote of the symbol (about which much more will be said presently) that it is "the primitive exponent of the unconscious, but at the same time an idea that corresponds to the highest intuition of the conscious mind" (1978, p. 30). Paradox is all.

All this is contained in the "omnipotence of thought" at D2, which, if we see it in simplistic standard taxonomical terms, we miss the complexity of; and which, if we see it in the holistically elemental interaction of a couple of unproblematic categories, we miss the poignancy of. Rather, it is the multiplex vision that integrative lenses allow on almost every question of any moment on each domain, as that question comes to bear on the other domains and they on it, that leaves us standing in awe of a thought, not attempting to master that thought for instrumental purposes. There is a place for technical learning. It is secondary. It is "training." Let us put first things first: Education before training. For when education *becomes* merely training, as in the human-capital agendas that have their heel on the throat of the schools today, then it is never really training for the good of the child but for the purposes of Cremin's (1988) and Tyack's (1974) "military-industrial-educational complex." Complexes in a different sense are the subject of the next chapter.

Complexes and the Second Domain
All of this comes to bear regarding *complexes* as well, the idea of a complex having been so important to Jung, who coined the term, that he initially considered naming his approach to psyche "Complex Psychology" (Diekman, 1999).

A complex may thus be pictured as collages of ideas, hopes, fears, and other psychic fragments and accretions that swirl around a pre-thematic/pre-verbal, emotion-charged nucleus. Jung called a complex a *"feeling-toned"* psychic cluster (Jung, 1969a, p. 96), which places the seeds of complexes richly in the soil of second-domain emotions. Such galvanizing energy and imagery as this at the core of the complex represents a proto-poetic capability in this very early domain.

Melded, the somatics of the first domain and the affects of second domain shoot a complex through with both a physical immediacy and emotional rawness that can make a complex a supremely stubborn thing to deal with as either a therapist or a patient. For what can be *understood* cannot just because of that be *overcome*. It is one of the arrogances of rationalism to think it could ever be otherwise. For if it were simply a matter of intelligence to deal wisely with a complex, then anyone who can understand the Second Law of Thermodynamics, The Louisiana Purchase, or Double-Entry bookkeeping should be able to beat a pretty short path to psychological wellbeing.

A complex is not the *servant* of thought. To the contrary, it is the *origin* of thought as Jung went to considerable pains throughout the nineteen volumes of his *Collected Works* to show (Mayes, 2016). The popular phrase "I have a complex about such-and-such" would, to Jung, mean simply: "I am thinking a thought."

And since it is virtually impossible to imagine thought that does not involve at some level some degree of conflict, we feel the full burden of Jung's notion of complexes as tantamount to thought when he writes that a complex simply indicates that "something discordant, unassimilated, and antagonistic exists" but that this can be a good thing, and in any case is a dialectically necessary thing, as "an incentive to greater effort" and thus to "new possibilities of achievement" (1971, p. 529). Thought being dialectical according to Plato (Gadamer, 1977; Jung, 1970c; Kelly, 1955; Riegel, 1979) and therefore always standing face-to-face with the un-dismissible countenance of the "discordant [and] unassimilated" every thought is therefore a complex (like *doubt*, that cousin to a complex, not being the opposite of faith but faith's precondition). Complexes are not pathological. They are human. To live sensitively in complexes is to be fully human.

Any program—psychological, political, or religious—that proffers the poison of simple answers and calls it an elixir to save humanity, is also prone to control human beings to save the system. What is left when complexity is banned is the banal; and where banality reigns, there is the totalitarian state (Arendt, 1951). Perhaps it is not finally freedom that is the opposite of totalitarianism as it is complexity, which it requires freedom to live *in*.

A complex's base is primally and primarily—that is to say, *instinctually*—somatic and affective. And though the ideas, images, and themes that orbit around the core of a complex can be conceptualized, the core cannot. For, in psychoanalytic language, a concept is a *secondary* conscious process that inevitably stems from primary subconscious processes, and these are to be found in the first two domains. Concepts may make up the outer casing of a complex, but they do not make up a complex.

Concepts are contingent mental formations that emerge out of primary subconscious dynamics. Thought is never purely ratiocinative because it is unavoidably emotional. That every thought is a "feeling-toned" complex is a point that I have explored throughout my own work in educational psychology (2017a,b,c; 2015; 2009; 2005a,b; 1999; 1998).

As we will see in the following chapters, the contingent nature of cognition as an out-stemming of affect has tremendous educational implications regarding "the emotional experience of teaching and learning" (Salzberger-Wittenberg, 1989) and the limitations of strictly cognitive approaches to educational processes (Adler, 1982; Lipman, 1988). That fact starts here—in the fertile bed of consciousness' affective soil.

Kant's Mathetic/Poetic Dichotomy and the Second Domain
If it is true, as Wordsworth famously wrote in his *Preface to the Lyrical Ballads* (1802), that "Poetry is the spontaneous overflow of powerful feelings," that poetry takes its origin from "emotion recollected in tranquility," then it is in the second domain that we discover the seeds of poetry in what Kant called our "poetic function." Those seeds fructify in all the integrative ranges from this primary one out to the farthest-reaching, most articulated sites of human awareness. Those seeds will become those articulations themselves, for as Heidegger (1964) asserted, Language necessarily *becomes* poetry when it enters "the sacred precinct" of Presence (Spiegelman and Mansfeld, 1996). Nowhere is the interwoven *élan vital* of cosmic evolution, the sheer synergy and ordered energetics of all the domains in a holarchy clearer than in this: That which not only enables transcendence but is in a sense transcendence itself, poetry, starts in the humblest soil of one of the smallest domains. This is a fact that is mentioned in some holistic theory but is not examined in its multiplex consequentiality in the holistic educational literature. This would change were the integral approach a significant feature in that literature.

These two epistemological filters are what Kant (1781/1997) called our "mathetic" and "poetic" faculties in *The Critique of Pure Reason*—our dual modes of experience and expression and equally important according to Kant despite the lopsided preference for the mathetic over the poetic in our decidedly unpoetic times. The bedrock epistemological duality of the poetic and the mathetic is present in every domain as we note in the infant's emotions first coalescing in the second domain at the same time as the raw building blocks of cognition are being patted into shape. Again, intra-domain interactions are a salient feature of T-Hlc "intregrativeness" that one does not typically find, or find especially cultivated, in Hrc and IP models.

The second developmental zone is the site of high drama. It turns out to be the birthplace of what will become our two essential means of experiencing and expressing our world—the poetic and the mathetic. According to Kant, they are bicamerally situated in the congress of our dialectical soul, its constitution set in the District of Domain 2.

Education in Domain 2: "The Emotional Experience of Teaching and Learning"

The focus on this developmental area in curriculum and instruction reached its peak during the heyday of educational Progressivism (the opening several decades of the twentieth century) in the faction that formed around psychoanalysis. Taking their lead from the classical Freudian concept of the Oedipal conflict in the male child and the putative, parallel Electra complex in the female child, these scholars and practitioners argued that the classroom was a place where the child would inevitably display and project its psychosexual issues regarding its parent(s) (Mayes, 2009a).

This is clearly a second-domain dilemma because it involves emotional fusion with and psychosexual separation from the contra-sexual parent. Applying psychoanalytic terms to its pedagogy, the psychodynamic wing of Progressivism observed that the child would "transfer" its emotionally and sexually volatile parental "imago" onto the teacher. The teacher needed to help the child negotiate the primal "family romance" at home—the son desiring the mother but being blocked by the jealous father and the mother, whose body is the site of libidinal warfare between the father and son—by helping him negotiate it symbolically at school in his relationship with the teacher, with other students, and in the very act of learning itself. The daughter brings a whole other set of issues to the classroom that stem from her Electra relationship with her father.

Hence, Isador H. Coriat, an early president of the American Psycho-Analytic Association, proclaimed: "In school, the teacher becomes a substitute for the father or mother of the child and in the emotional tie which exists between teacher and pupil, the earlier parent-child relationship is re-lived and re-animated" (in Cremin, 1964, p. 210). Similarly, speaking of how teachers are transferential objects, the great Freudian psychiatrist of adolescence, August Aichhorn, wrote in the middle of the twentieth century:

> We know that with a normal child the transference takes place of itself through the kindly efforts of the responsible adult. The teacher in his attitude repeats the situations long familiar to the child, and thereby evokes a parental relationship. He does not maintain this relationship at the same level, but continually

deepens it as long as he is the parental substitute. [With a neurotic child] with symptoms of delinquency . . . , the tendency to transfer his attitude toward his parents to the person in authority is immediately noticeable. (1990, p. 97)

Because the teacher may be so instrumental in this domain in helping the child work through these delicate psychosexual dynamics of fusion and separation, Aichhorn thought it imperative that every teacher understand at least the basics of the transference (1990, pp. 98, 106). During the Progressive period, some experimental schools formed around this second-domain concern with appropriate nurturance of the child in the formation of psychosexual identity. Most notable of them was Margaret Naumburg's Children's School—later known as the Waldorf School.

"In searching for a curriculum that would really nurture independence of thought and spirit, the faculty—at least half of whom had undergone analysis at the urging of Miss Naumburg—tended to emphasize the arts, arguing that artistic creations serve to bring into conscious life the buried material of the child's emotional problems" (Cremin, 1964, p. 213). The primary mission of the teacher at the Children's School was to relate to him or her in a way that satisfied, in a developmentally appropriate fashion, the child's D2 needs for nurturance while fostering the student's maturation toward autonomy. This is very similar to Nel Noddings' idea of teaching as care, which, when seen in this light, emerges as largely an affective pedagogy (Noddings, 1995, 1992, 1990).

Stemming from feminist psychological theory in the Eighties (Belenky et al., 1986), Noddings' approach to teaching asserts a feminine way of knowing and being rooted in what she fashions as a female propensity for caring. For, "in almost all cultures, women seem to develop the capacity to care more often and more deeply than men. . . . [T]he hope of moral educators is that both sexes can learn to care" (p. 192). To be sure, Noddings elevates the affective impulse to a moral imperative for dialogue (which, as we will see, properly commences in D5). Nevertheless, her approach stems from the second domain, as well as the first, biophysical one.

> [B]oys should have caregiving experience. Boys, like girls, should attend to the needs of guests, care for smaller children, perform housekeeping chores, and the like. The supposition, from a care perspective, is that the closer we are to the intimate physical needs of life, the more likely we are to understand its fragility and to feel the pangs of the inner "I must"—that stirring of the heart that moves us to respond to one another. (Noddings, 1995, p. 143)

Teachers who ignore the somatic curriculum run the risk of teaching in ways that are dull or dysfunctional. For better or worse, the teacher is often the displaced object of the student's desires and antipathies regarding his or her own parents. If that child comes from a dysfunctional setting (as increasing numbers do), it is all too likely that those hopes and fears may play out in the classroom in ways that may be passionate and problematic for both the student and the teacher (Bullough, 2001).

The ten-year-old boy who has been psychologically and physically beaten into submission by an authoritarian father may be unresponsive to a male teacher. The same boy (let's call him "Tommy"), an only child, is Oedipally enmeshed with a needy mother who is ignored by his father, who is always in adulterous relationships and, rarely at home, ignores his mother. Hypersensitive subconsciously to his mother's unmet psychosexual needs for his father, Tommy, in the throes of the transference, is also finely attuned to every female teacher's slightest emotional shifts and may strive to respond to them with a diligence which, although initially pleasant to the teacher, increasingly disquiets and puzzles her.

Tommy's different attitudes toward male and female teachers, and to men and women in general, may have little, if anything, to do with the teacher *per se* but everything to do with his hatred of his father and his subconsciously-rooted impulse to meet women's needs (whether real of just perceived by him) that he *projects* onto them.

Both "good" and "bad" behavior at school is often the result of such family-of-origin malformations that the child brings to the classroom and acts out there. I have studied this topic in depth in other books over the last fifteen years (Mayes, 2017b, 2015, 2012, 2005a, 2004).

For this reason, teacher education programs should consider including discussion of such matters in their curricula, for it is a very rare prospective teacher in a college of education who ever hears a word about these or related issues, much less their centrality to questions of interpersonal and intrapersonal classroom processes (Mayes, 2010, 1999).

An integrative model would help us theorize and pragmatically research much more than we presently do how actual cases of psychosomatic factors in tandem with psychodynamic family of-origin issues influence student behavior. Until this happens, until, that is, we begin to see learning in an integrative light as factors from various developmental domains interacting in highly complex patterns among all the domains that manifest in the classroom, our "holistic" view of the student will not be nearly nuanced enough.

The case of Tommy is just one example of the need for the more complex modelings of "holism" that integrative theory excels at and that can lead holistic educational theory into greater subtlety in theorizing and greater efficacy in practice in understanding and helping children like Tommy in the classroom.

Domain 3: The Empirical-Legal Domain

Metacognition Awakens!
Domain 3 spans Piaget's pre-operational to early concrete operational stage, from about two to six or seven years old, at which point consciousness is not only encountering and learning how to manipulate the physical world but is realizing that that world works according to laws. This now is beginning to think *and* feel—thinking and feeling being quite inseparable, a fact that even holistic theory does not sufficiently attend to. It *does* deal with these two domains as necessary components in the student's overall makeup, but it does not tend to explore their manifold interactions within the student, or indeed the complexity of each of these domains within themselves. Integrative theory is built upon these intricacies and complexities within and among domains.

For instance, in one of Piaget's classic examples of what I am calling the "Empirical Procedural Domain" and he calls the "concrete-operational stage," if you transfer liquid from a short, squat bottle into a tall, thin cylindrical one, the pre-concrete-operational child will tell you that there is more liquid in the second bottle than the first because the second bottle is taller and therefore must have more liquid in it.

When one fine day it dawns on the child that the difference in volume is the same despite the different sizes of the bottles, then that child has learned "the law of conservation," one of several Piagetian laws that a child will discover through experience and an emerging intuitive ability, and also through explicit instruction in concrete operational tasks. For Piaget, this stage runs from about two- to seven-years old. Until concrete operations, consciousness is venturing out into the physical world more and more and learning specific means of dealing with specific situations, but one-by-one and on a more or less need-to-know basis.

Moving into and then through concrete-operations, however, the child literally "comes to grips" with physical reality not only by mapping courses of action in the physical environment but also (and much more importantly) knowing *why* she is mapping things the way she is. This is the first flicker of the flame of metacognition, thinking about thinking, in the child.

What are the principles and protocols that show her, in abstract and in advance, what she might encounter and what her strategies are for each imagined course of action? These are what now arise in consciousness.

"Given that I find myself in physical situation A, what are possible responses to B, C, and D, and which string of consequences will take me to the place where I will be best off?" The child, in other words, does not now just manipulate things with her hands. She also manages them with her mind and this requires being able to hold, examine, modify, and move an image around in her mind—in short, to *re*-member it.

The upper-limits of Domain 3 is where the waxing consciousness begins to gain real proficiency in image-making, image-consumption and image-use to assess or produce handy objects and establish amenable physical conditions. In short, the child mentally *operates* on the *concrete*ness of her world: She is fully into *concrete operations*; she is coming to see the procedural nature of things in general, not just their specific dynamics from situation to situation. But this is not just a cognitive task.

Mother—and Beyond

Crucially, the child is at the same time also busy defusing from its primordial physical matrix: Mother.

The conventional wisdom has been that this is generally truer of boys than girls, boys tending to distance themselves *from* maternal-flooding in the service of contra-sexual gender-identity formation, girls tending to merge *with* the mother in maternal-immersion towards same-sex gender-identity formation.

This was the consensus of leading feminist psychological theorists in the 1980s (Belenky et al, 1986; Chodorow, 1978; Gilligan, 1982). However, since that time, this has become a topic of heated debate with both sides weighing in with compelling experimental and demographic evidence (Hartung and Widiger, 1998; Hyde, 2005; Lippa, 2006).

It is unlikely that this dispute will be resolved any time soon, if at all. And even if it *were* decided in favor of innate differences between biological males and biological females regarding this issue, it would still have to be acknowledged as only a macro-tendency. For what *is* undeniable is that all sorts of other factors come into play at the micro-level of the all-important *individual* child's lifeworld, including: family of-origin dynamics, wide gender-identity variations in cultural norms, the political climate into which a child is born, family narratives about gender, socioeconomic status, parents' level of education, and so on. And above all is the individual child's innate sexual and/or gender dispositions, which must be honored lest psychological damage be done to the child.

Metacognition is handled, even in holistic theory and practice, as a matter of a discrete holistic rubric: Cognition. Its relationship with other categories is usually limited to "Affect" or "Emotion," and it is done in very general terms. A holarchic approach, however, requires that we further relate it to political, familial, gender, relational, psychodynamic, worldhistorical and even spiritual vectors of influence and domains of the child's *integrative* being.

More: The integral approach is both a tightening of focus as in a microscope and a widening of focus as in a telescope that in practical terms can move holistic theory beyond its tendency to engage in limited "finite/steady-state" ways of approaching metacognition as mostly just a cognitive affair. Integrative Theory open it up to "non-finite/open-ended" analyses—much more refined in their examination of particular factors, including *intra*-domain factors, and much more inclusive in their consideration of *inter*-domain factors and their interactions, including organismic, familial, cultural, and even historical and ethical ones.

The possibilities that this provides holistic theory are exciting and virtually endless.

The Sign versus The Symbol: An Introduction

At first, Domain 3 development kicks off the formation of internal images as literal representations of a concrete entity in the world. Even though a child may not be in the immediate physical presence of its mother, it can now conjure up a mental picture of her. This is why at Domain 3 separation anxiety begins to abate and then dwindles to almost an airy nothing for the child later on, who can now fill the terrifying void left by the mother's physical withdrawal with an image of her.

This general phenomenological task accomplished, consciousness moves on to the second substage of Domain 3, which involves the earliest use of symbols—i.e., linguistic abstractions such as the word "mama"—that do not physically resemble the entity that they signify but that adequately stand in its stead as liberating place-holders, or cyphers.

Note in passing how an integrative analysis looks within any given domain to interrogate its intra-domain workings. This is something that is quite conspicuous by its absence in most paleo-holistic models, which take the category as a given, traditionally defined, and thus overlook the web of significations within that category. In Integrative Theory, such "deconstruction to reconstruct" is a standard operating procedure and one of the lessons it has learned from the brighter side of some postmodern theory (Best and Kellner, 1991; Kristeva, 1989; Lacan, 1977)

Crucially, we must take note at this juncture that it is not strictly speaking a *symbol* that the child is making and using but a *sign*. Between the two lies a world of difference. We will look at this distinction between a sign and a symbol at various points throughout this study, for it has educational implications and consequences whose significance cannot be overstated as we have already begun to see in the very earliest developmental stages (Mayes, 2017d).

Despite its phenomenological advances in "symbolizing," however, the child sees the world as an extension of its representations—which, although a conceptually subtler ability than it has previously had, still does not allow the child to transcend itself and imagine that there is any other perspective on the world than its own. With the current fixation on standardized test scores and the pursuit of economic dominance in the world of transnational corporate capitalism (Friedman, 2000), these developmental concerns are being given ever shorter shrift.

Instead of being allowed to move through Domains 1–3 at a comfortable and natural pace, children are increasingly being forced to acquire information and cognitive skills at a breakneck speed that runs roughshod over the normal rhythms of early childhood development and that violate the child as a complex integrative being. Instead of engaging in those play-based activities that are the most fertile ground for the blossoming of the child's early physical, emotional, imaginal and verbal potentials, the child must devote growing numbers of hours, even in the earliest grades, to homework, memorization, and cognitive skills. This collective national obsession with high scores on norm-referenced testing is particularly grotesque and damaging when it comes to the very young. The result is what is called in public health circles "the new morbidity" among children, which has only grown since the following notice by a Waldorf educationist.

> Children in the technologically advanced countries are beginning to show signs of serious stress and nervousness, and, in part, this is related to the intense pressure being put on their nervous systems at a very young age. In the United States, for instance, the number of children with a diagnosis of attention deficit disorder (ADD) . . . combined with hyperactivity is growing rapidly. The drug Ritalin is often being prescribed for such children. Statistics vary but range from 1 million to 1.5 million children in the United States now receiving Ritalin. . . . Whereas some children genuinely need help because of constitutional problems in the nervous system, many others appear to need help primarily because they cannot accommodate to current educational practices. These include developmentally inappropriate demands on the nervous system, such as the requirement to concentrate on academic subjects in the preschool when the child's constitution is geared for learning through self-directed, creative play. (Almon, 1999, p. 254)

Almon's early skillful analysis integratively combined basic neurology, personal psychology, cultural analysis, disciplinary critique, and pedagogical commonsense in a single integrative package—thereby moving in the direction of an integrative appreciation of a multidimensional problem. This is a welcome relief from the unquestioning acceptance of that diehard shibboleth "ADHD."

The irresponsible use of psychotropic medication on children in our schools today is an artifact of a perverse political economy. Forced by the insatiable demands of corporate capitalism (and whether those demands are encoded in neo-Liberal educational "reform" documents or neo-Conservative "reform" hardly matters at all), schools are compelled to treat students as "human capital" that needs to be exploited. In such work as Moe and Chubb (2009), such malpractices are given academic legitimation.

The result is a tragic picture of our children in the classroom, exhausted and dispirited from learning skills and performing tasks that are physically constraining, psychologically irrelevant, and ethically vacuous. And when a child, for whatever reason, does not dance to this frenetic corporate tune, he or she is simply drugged into submission. This will only stop when we truly *care* for the needs of our child in the first three spheres of development, and generously support teachers and schools in what most teachers and schools most want to do: To nurture the complete child.

Alan Block's (1997) trenchant critique—informed by selfobject psychological theory—of the commodification of children in America puts the lie to our professed child-centeredness. The subtitle of his book *I'm Only Bleedin'*, says it all: *Education as the Practice of Social Violence against Children*.

Domain 4: The Legal-Procedural

Introduction (Being a Primer on the Persona)
The passage into D4 from D3 and then the passage out of D4 into D5 are arguably the two most important moves in lifespan development and they both involve D4. The first turn leads to the ultimate consolidation of the *personalistic*, egoic perspective in D4, while the second turn launches consciousness toward a *trans-egoic*, *transpersonal* perspective in D5. Most people navigate the transition from D3 to D4. Only a minority ever leave D4 and head off to D5 (Fowler, 1981; Kohlberg, 1989).

This is the case because it is in the fourth domain that most people fuse in ego dynamics and socio-centrism, never leaping beyond those influences. They do not, or simply cannot, venture into realms that take them past egoic perspectives or past those broader sociocultural extensions of ego in the form of familial, cultural, or national passions and loyalties (Kohlberg, 1987).

They evince a fundamental incapacity or unwillingness to "go transpersonal" (Wilber, 1980).

The outer reaches of Domain 4—on the cusp between the egoic, social, legalistic, and strictly rational self and something "more" than that; something that is now only vaguely intuited, not "known" in the ways one had previously known something—goes as far as it can go without having to begin to fundamentally question its lifeworld assumptions and begin to see them in a different light.

The fourth domain is the area in which the developing consciousness will (ideally) learn, first, to establish and then, later, to spiritually temper its own ego so that it can work in the service of others—ultimately in the spiritual climes of D6 and D7. For, D4 is the territory in which the individual encounters himself as *an ethical being*. How well that self-encounter will go is the story of whether or not that person's development will continue on to the most advanced spiritual perspectives and practices in D6 and D7 or stay in the epicenter of conventional consciousness in D4.

D4 also spans the territory from the upper regions of D3 in "concrete operations"—learning how things work physically, the laws of nature—to learning how to think deductively and inductively about life in general: Its axiological dimension. This entails learning how to construct an argument and how to assess another's; how to adhere to certain algorithms and protocols in diverse procedures and conversations, and thus, in general, to learning how to develop and deploy criteria that cover a variety of disparate fields of inquiry and action. The goal is for one to be able to "operate formally" on varied sorts of problems and thus be prepared to move on to developing as *an interpretive being*, one who not only interprets specific situations (the crowning D4 capability) but who can also *interpret the various ways we interpret, one who can interpret interpreting*. This is our *hermeneutic* capacity, the full realization of which is in D5. Getting one's passport stamped at the outer reaches of D4 in order to be able to enter D5—*that*, as Hamlet would say, is the great (developmental) question.

First, however, there are all the tasks of D4 to master. Hence, at D4, one is constantly taking in how people act all along the range of social contexts. One learns about the repertoire of personas they wear as they act. One figures out what one's own place is in all of that. It is the defining and refining of *oneself as a social being*.

To become an ethical being, a social being, and, possibly, when all of that has been accomplished, to begin to become an interpretive-hermeneutic being—this is a terrific amount of terrain for the developing individual.

Picture traversing all of Domain 4 as the developmental equivalent of driving across Texas.

Entering the state at, say, its southwestern border to exiting at its northeastern border, one sometimes feels that one will never get out of Texas! Nothing against Texas. It's just so big. So to the adolescent and very young adult who is on this concrete-to-formal rules-and-roles trek, it may seem that he will never get out of the mental Texas of Domain 4. It can seem in Domain 4 that formal reasoning and social positioning is what life is about. It may seem that one may never get out of the rules and roles of his private Texas. And he may be right.

Through all the existentially difficult weather that wracks this seemingly endless state with the strict climate of its various laws—the person goes amnesiac, gets dizzy, dull, forgets where he was headed, forgets even, as in an episode of *The Twilight Zone*, that he *was* headed anywhere at all. Hasn't he always been here and won't he always remain? In a word he *fuses* in this holarchic circle (Wilber, 1999). It ends up being the outer limit of his existential capacity. He aims for nothing else than to be a reasonably successful and successfully "reasonable" being.

Fused in Four, the traveler is now an entrenched resident. He even comes to look at being anything "other" as politically and ethically dubious—precisely the opposite of what happens in D5, where, as we will presently see, the relativizing of all systems *is* the way of things. But in D4, ego and its symbolic magnifications in cultural and national affiliations and commitments become all in all for the individual. He will defend them to the death. He is inclined to impose them on those who are not like him. His colors never run. He thrills at the fatherly voice that beckons him to "make the nation great again!"

Looked at from one angle, this is tragic for a creature who seemed capable of so much more than ego and its local embeddedness. But from another angle, the individual has found a natural space for him to occupy, a place where he can, at his best, be of greatest service to an (at *its* best) ever-evolving social body. In Domain 4, the individual is primarily a citizen of the state, and his goal is to be an empowered actor in a good society, which is a noble aim, assuming that that society is good.

So contended Alfred Adler (1930), one of Freud's earliest disciples who, like Jung, broke away from Freud and was similarly marginalized by Freud and continues to be so by Freudians to this day because Adler felt it was this *social* need, not the sexual one, that is the engine of psychic functioning. Not sexual potency, not the idyll of the first three domains, but social potency, the idyll of the fourth, was the great motivator at the core of psyche.

Learning the lessons of D3 through D4—mastering their tasks and integrating their educative aims within oneself—is no small feat, but most people seem to learn it. They are card-carrying members of "consensual reality" and they are fiercely loyal to its existential party with its ego-cultural and sociocultural platforms. This not true of the transition into D5, where "many are called but few are chosen" (*Matthew* 22: 14).

The process is one of self-selection, however, for, as Thoreau wrote, "Most men lead lives of quiet desperation." The novelist Saul Bellow echoed this sentiment a century later in his acerbic notice that "most people have a rage for normalcy." To move from D4 to D5 requires a relativizing of all psychosocial perspectives, even, indeed especially, one's own and one's culture. This is a hurdle that is simply too high for most people, who therefore ensconced and adamant in the consensual "realities" and "conventional moral reasoning, set up their existential residence in Domain 4, The Legal-Procedural.

The Social Ego (Or "Further Adventures of the Persona")

As we have already seen, it is during this developmental period that the capacity arises to frame rules about one's social and ethical world. In the opening milestones of this stage, too, young people begin to be able to see themselves and others in terms of various social roles. It becomes essential to the adolescent's self-definition that he is a student at a particular school and a member of a certain clique or club there; that he and his family belong to this or that religion; that he is incorporate within a given racial/ethnic group; and that his family occupies *this* socioeconomic stratum and not another. The 1960s rock group *The Beach Boys* capture the ethos of Level 4 in the title of one of their most famous songs: "Be True to Your School"—and, indeed, to all the institutions that you fit into, and that have been fitted into you, to make you the person you are—one who is defined by the social roles he plays.

It is true that consciousness at the farthest reaches of this range is also beginning to bestir itself with a vague awareness that these roles are, to a certain degree, permeable and mutable, but even there, consciousness is still colored by its assumption that this is "just the way things are" and that the world is either his oyster or his ouster—that he was born to privilege in a life of unbounded possibilities or that he is among "the truly disadvantaged" (Wilson, 1987) and there just "ain't no makin' it" (McLeod, 1987) in a grim, fixed, and sometimes physically perilous environment in which his consciousness finds itself not only inexplicably contained but, in the less-favored circumstances, inescapably constrained.

One does not have to be a social determinist to appreciate that a child's perception of how his performance in school will affect life-chances after school will figure considerably into how committed he is to his studies or if he even decides to stay in school at all. Even now, the adolescent in his own simple way is beginning to grasp the stern validity of Marx's wry announcement in his *Eighteenth Brumaire of Louis Napoleon* that "Men make their own history. But they do not do it as they please" (1978 [1852], p. 565).

In terms offered by the sociology of education, the young student's awareness of his *habitus* (Bordieu and Passeron, 1990) and its wide-ranging effects on his performance in schools is one of the most studied issues in educational sociology (Anyon, 2001) and has been since President Lyndon Baines Johnson made education the primary tool of his Great Society program's "War on Poverty" to end the socioeconomic stratification of classes in the United States (Ravitch, 2000, 1963), which has only gotten worse since then. It is a topic that I and my associates tried to address from a holistic perspective in *Understanding the Whole Student: Holistic Multicultural Education* (Mayes et al., 2016).

Not surprisingly, the child's ability to role-shift is more or less limited, typically until later adolescence when greater role-flexibility has been achieved, *assuming* that it *gets* achieved. For, according to classical developmental theorists such as Kohlberg (1987), it is simply the case that not many people will fully develop the socio-cognitive ability to venture out very far from the constricted radius of convention that *is* the fourth domain. This makes the transition from D4 to D5 one of the major cut-off points in transpersonal developmental theory. As the American novelist Saul Bellow put it, most people have "a rage for normalcy," which precludes them from "going transpersonal" (Wilber, 2000).

Indeed, the "in-group/out-group" phenomenon with its "ultimate attribution error" ("My group is inherently good, yours is inherently less good and maybe even bad"), which is by now an established fact of social psychology (Devine 1996), in full swing here. A truly massive body of research established about as definitely as social science research can "prove" anything that the person in the fourth evolutionary domain can decenter physically, biologically and emotionally, but it is more difficult for him to decenter socially.

In my study *Archetype, Culture and the individual in Education: The Three Narratives of Teaching and Learning* (2020, in press), I look into the deeper possibility than current sociologies and anthropologies seem willing to consider in their Structural-Functionalist Parsonian (1951) parsimony, that culture has ontological dimensions, even metaphysical ones. As against the positivist grain of our current "human sciences," this would be a way of approaching and, even more, *appreciating* the ineradicable force of culture—why it does not conveniently just "go away" with an individual's "development." The almost gravitational pull of the *mores* of "my group" is exceptionally strong and one that relatively few people are ever able to see relativistically as just another set of *mores* in the world's great variety of such social arrangements.

In short, the person situated here can take multiple perspectives on roles *within* his or her defining social structure but is hard-pressed to assume multiple perspectives *on* that structure. Such consciousness is sociocentric.

However, for those relatively few who do begin to attain something of a more "global" vision in this developmental unfoldment, there is broader understanding and richer role-transitivity. The nascent ability to see oneself, others within one's groups, others outside of one's groups, and, finally, even groups themselves from multiple perspectives—this is a momentous socio-phenomenological leap. It also seems to be a continuum, with some people able to socially decenter almost at will, others occasionally able to do so, and most seemingly unable to do so (Conger and Galambos, 1997). The narcissistic personality disorders are an extreme personal form of the inability to decenter, just as xenophobia is an extreme social form of the same pathology.

"Each of us is a crowd." We perforce play many different roles in the vast theater of our social lives with its quickly shifting scenes in the course of a day, an hour, and sometimes even minutes. It is not necessarily disingenuity to be putting on and taking off various masks all day, although of course it can be. Mostly, however, it is simply inevitable. Society could not function if we were all going about telling each other the raw truth about them (and ourselves!) as we see it on each encounter. We would be at each other's throats all day—sometimes literally—and every day would be a pageant of emotional and physical violence.

The social order would then unravel very quickly and we would devolve virtually on the spot into that state of nature that is man's primal lot as Thomas Hobbes (1651/2010) described in *Leviathan*: "Nasty, brutish, and short." Despite Rousseau's (1762) ontological optimism in his pedagogical treatise, *Emile*, it is this insuperable fact about the rugged and raw nature of the human condition that requires binding social structures and practices within which the individual must live if she is to survive and an array of masks she must wear to do so. True, they conceal what she *might* be or become at more articulated reaches of her personal evolution, but they also guarantee what she *must* be and remain as long as her primary residence is in Domain 4.

The transition into Domain 5 does not require that we throw away all our persona-masks. It will require, however, that we limit them and that they look more like the face underneath than our highly-stylized, *Commedia dell'arte* masks of D4 had done. At the most advanced reaches of spiritual development, what Jung called "individuation"—or the discovery in D7 of the

Eternal as being *within* and *as* one's self as a timeless *Self*, not a time-bound, time-harried ego—one will cast of all masks. Indeed, individuation is removing those "false wrappings of the persona" (Jung, 1967b, p 174). But this is a gradual process and only just beginning as one later moves into D5.

Sexually, too, our feral lusts would overtake us and the social contract within which we all exist and which is our primary evolutionary tool of survival would go up in a scorched-earth campaign of "rape, pillage, burn" if there were no personas to temper our appetites. With the social order violated and our masks ripped to shreds, the danger that is not only *in* nature but in many ways *is* nature would overwhelm us and we would be internally and externally gobbled up by a primitivism that we can neither control as perpetrators nor defend ourselves against as victims. Without the social order that both protects and imprisons us, we would not survive. And without our masks, the social order could not function for a day.

As Freud, who theorized our sheer state-of-nature lusts (1932/1960) knew better than anyone: Our animal nature must find *some* regulated gratification or else it will either implode in frustration and neurosis or explode in destructive acting out in sheer rapacity. There are strict limits to how far we may be gratified, however, lest we incinerate the very social structures that protect us from nature's inherent violence. True: This arrangement leaves us ungratified in many ways, meaning that we will all be neurotic to some extent. But that is the goal of therapy, said Freud: To attain a state of *functional* neurosis that enables us "to love and to work" instead of falling into psychopathologies or criminality. Freudian psychology thus emerges as the psychic technology of Domains 1 through 4 *par excellence*.

Compromises must be made. Lines must be drawn. And those lines are etched into those many masks we necessarily wear. We all know the meaning of *persona* as such a mask. What is less known is that it was Jung who first referred to them in this current sense. Jung borrowed the name of the mask that an actor in ancient Greek theater held up before his face to identify to the audience the role he was playing. It is our *personas* that make social life function. And function it *must*, Freud insisted, and we must each discover how to fit into that if we are to survive individually and as a specie. For, social cohesion is *homo sapiens*' prime evolutionary tool of survival.

All of this entails what the sociologist Ervin Goffman (1997) called "facework." Unless one is putting on faces for predatory purposes or to avoid psychodynamic issues that are clamoring for immediate attention, *personas* are not "false." When they *are* false, however, and when a person so identifies with them that all that is left of him after a while are the roles he plays in society and not anything essential that he any longer is, then he is *persona-*

possessed, living inauthentically, and bound for a life of either emptiness (if the *personas* hold) or a moment of cataclysmic psychic reckoning in the form of a neurotic or psychotic break (if they do not).

Ideally, however, *personas* are not mendacious but "functional"—especially since a well-designed *persona* should also reveal something of the nature of the person wearing it. It is a careful authenticity, a discrete concealment, and a progressive revelation of the person as his trust in another person waxes. Interacting with others from behind a legitimate mask is no more a false way of interacting with others than dancing is a false way of moving with them. It is a stylized interaction, both a prerequisite and a product of a civilized life.

For the adolescent, however, who is just beginning to grasp the fact that people wear *personas* and that he is being trained to do so as well, this reality is often not only psychologically challenging but also morally problematic and he responds to it in the black-and-white judgmentalism that moral reasoning, here in its earliest stages, is given to. Simplistic judgmentalism is generally an artifact of arrested development around adolescence somewhere along that impossibly long highway that cuts through D4, and we may lay it down as a general principle that when political programs veer too far to either the Right or Left, there is a stubborn adolescent polemically ranting from its psychodynamic core.

For, like Holden Caufield in J. D. Salinger's (1951) *Catcher in the Rye*, the novice in the adult world of rules and roles may initially see this whole business of masks as both cowardly and aggressive, ignorant and cunning—as "phony" to use Holden's term of condemnation for anyone who speaks from behind a mask, which is to say: Everyone. The greater part of becoming an efficacious, responsible adult is learning how to wear a mask as the situation requires but to do so in good faith, consistent with who you believe yourself most essentially to be and as the situation pragmatically allows.

The psychologist Paolo Ferrucci has suggested the emotional complexity but also the existential possibilities inherent in our many roles in declaring that "each of us is a crowd." (1982, p. 47). For, consider: In a mere sixteen-hour period, one might be, say, a student, a boss, a parent, a partner, a friend, a member of a political party, a member of a club made up of people with the same hobby, a fan of a particular genre of music who listens to it and hums along to it on the car stereo as he drives from work to play or from one business engagement to another, a devoted fan at a sporting event wearing his team's colors and accoutrements and shouting all the usual slogans, and at end of day a lover.

In other words, we are all many things, genius and fool, saint and sinner—and all housed in one body. But these are not by any means pathological "multiple personalities." Rather, they are potentially harmonious *"subpersonalities"* that comprise the socially adapted and personologically creative individual (Assagioli, 1965).

As long as we are *coordinating* our subpersonalities in order to do the social dance well and productively, and they are not *controlling* us in a life of confusion and disruption of core-self and others, then over a lifetime, we grow into ever-richer beings—more compassionate and efficacious—more multiplex. We *mature*. As Edgar puts it in *King Lear:* "The ripeness is all" (Act 5, Scene 2, line 11).

The ego and its secrets: The shadow and psychoanalysis. Nothing is free, however. And thus, it is also the case that in D4 we are starting to build up the tar-like deposits that the conscious self, the ego, is surreptitiously offloading in the city dump at midnight in the subconscious—that psychic zone of zombies that come into being in an exactly parallel fashion to the sunlight development of the ego.

It feels at this point as if the subconscious were a parallel universe to our conscious one. It is constantly beleaguering consciousness in the development of the ego but protecting it too from those shadows in which it exiles the secrets it keeps so well that that ego cannot remember after a while where they are—or even *that* they are. They are like an impossibly irksome guest you finally banish from your home and after a while you, in a perturbed forgetfulness called *repression*, try to never even consciously think anymore that you *had* that dark friend. The problem is: that banished thing is finally an inextricable part of oneself.

It is this shadowy side of the ego that feels itself to have triumphed so heroically that must be confronted by the ego before its psychic passport gets stamped with approval to enter into Domain 5. Not doing this "shadow work" on oneself will cause the ego to *project* one's darkness onto others and do them psychological and ethical harm. For, the leading theme of Domain 5 is that the universe is essentially a moral phenomenon from the point of view of the human being *sub specie aeternitatis*. Hence, the individual must, in existential integrity and sobriety, face the fact of her own darkness head on if she hopes to evolve to Domain 5, the Phenomenological Domain. St. Paul knew something of this, expressing it in the terms that in first-century Judaism made sense of things to him. Exasperated at himself, he declared:

> I do not understand what I do. For what I want to do I do not do, but what I hate I do. And if I do what I do not want to do, I agree that the law is good.

> As it is, it is no longer I myself who do it, but it is sin living in me. . . . For I have the desire to do what is good, but I cannot carry it out. For I do not do the good I want to do, but the evil I do not want to do—this I keep on doing. (*Romans* 7: 15–20)

As Jung wrote of working therapeutically with the shadow, a term that he applied to the murky personal realms of (un)consciousness, it is "a suffering and a passion that implicate the whole man" (1969a, p. 208). Entrance into the fifth domain of phenomenological acuity exacts a cost. The price of admission is high. It requires not only the honing of the ego in its positive aspects but a severe interrogation of one's ego as a knotty moral problem—and, in a sense, the nailing of one's own ego to a cross, oneself both the ignorant Roman soldier at D4 but a phenomenologically resurrected being in D5.

Excursus on Teacher Education.
Conceptual change theory deals with how and why a person either will or will not change his ideas about something under analysis in a classroom. There is the notion that if the teacher provides enough "objective" evidence, then the student, like the totally unbiased hero-scientist in "the myth of sheer cognition," will change his mind and unproblematically embrace the new concept. That has come to be known as the theory of "cold conceptual change" (Posner, 1992).

More realistic, however, is the understanding that an individual will change or not change his opinions on a curricular item for reasons that involve not only his cognition but all levels of his being: his physical reaction to the new conception, how it serves or does not serve the integrity of his autobiographical narratives, his politico-cultural perspectives and positioning in a society, his family's narratives and commitments, and his ethico-spiritual views—his fears and hopes. Cognition is not "cold." It is hot—heated with the super-focused light of these existential beams that not only *shed* light on his life but *are* his life.

To change his conception A so that it becomes conception B may not be all that hard if it requires only a slight adjustment of the student's total being. To change it to E may call for some real existential work by the student. For A to become L may make the student begin to feel threatened. S may cause him to deploy serious forces of resistance. Z may stimulate open rebellion on the student's part and may cause other students to join forces with him in a classroom civil war if the new conception of something imperils their lifeworld. The teacher must respond sensitively to this array of allegiances and attitudes in her students lest she lose them not only on this topic but *en masse* throughout the rest of the semester. And at the heart of the matter is not so much a student's cognitions as her commitments.

We have already discussed how images are epistemologically generative—that is to say: how our primary processes, seeped in emotion, express themselves in images, and how these images are the predecessors of thought. These images come before our thoughts, and they color and shape them at every turn. That being so, it is not generally useful for a teacher to picture her students (or herself either, for that matter) as a scientist in a lab coat. But this is precisely what current technist teacher education curricula programs implicitly do.

In sum, in D4, the issue is: "The Emergence and Consolidation of the Ego." The individual strives mightily throughout the first two decades of his life to consolidate an identity that is solid, respectable, seen as competent—a "me" who will go off to conquer the world, or who will at least plant the flag of his identity on some slice of that world, however big or small, often with a partner by his side, sometimes with a family, but always as the established "I" who knows the rules and can play the roles he has been allotted or has elected.

The Ego and Its Cognitive Therapies
The ego is not a bad thing. It's an essential thing, in fact. Only its excesses are to be deplored. The efficacious ego of one who is of value to society, responsible to those who depend on him, living by a standard of reasonable self-interest but also service to others, industrious and in some cases even innovative—this is to live according to Freud's sagacious standard of a healthy life: To carry on one's existence in such a way as "to love and to work," as Freud famously put it. Then, in a certain degree of sanity, only mildly neurotic—for we all are *at least* that in this world of contradictions we cannot resolve and compromises we cannot end-run—we keep on keeping on. We "go on being" (Winnicott, 1992).

The strength of the ego lies in its awareness of its fragility. And thus, it is that without some sort of morally compelling vision to guide it, the ego runs off in every which direction and can all too easily wind up like Johnny Cash singing "Hurt" in one of his last performances, lamenting his emptiness—the ethical purpose of his life lost in that extreme form of social approval in its most alluring form: fame and wealth.

The fourth domain is a good place to learn important lessons, to be shaped in some necessary ways, but it is not a good place to stall—although many do, said Thoreau (1854), living out "lives of quiet desperation."

That is why Domain 4 is home to a spectrum of therapies that cater to the (re)construction of the ego not only *in* but *in the service of* D4. Starting with

Domain 5, we will encounter therapies whose purpose is for the individual to grow beyond the limitations of the domain in which it is presently operating. These are the therapies of transcendence (Giddens, 1991, 1990; Wacks, 1987; Walsh and Vaughn, 1980; Wilber, 1983). For now, however, let's turn our eye to those therapies whose primary focus is the health of a robust ego and its maximal social functioning—not to transcend a social order but to affirm it, and in affirming it, be affirmed by it.

Notable among these is Cognitive Therapy (CT), which, in the fourth domain, to which it is admirably suited when it minds its proper business and does not overreach itself, has had much success (Beck, A., 1990; Beck & Weishaar, 1995; Beck, J. 1995). A quick look at script theory (Tomkins, 1978) and its related therapeutic modality in the work of Aaron Beck and Judith Beck shows how this works.

According to script theory, throughout our lives we internalize a plethora of "scripts" about who we and others "should" be. These scripts crystallize the criteria against which we evaluate ourselves and others: the "rules and roles"—the "terms of engagement" characerisic of certain typical social contexts. This is an especially crucial matter when we are in the zone where rules and roles are what matters the most (Wilber, 2000), and that is D4, which dedicates itself to the Gospel of Sociality.

When a person's scripts are realistic, productive, and appropriate to that zone and suitable for that person, then she is able to negotiate her psychosocial world in a fairly comfortable and generative way. However, if those scripts do not empower a person because those scripts or her glosses of them are unrealistic, impractical, or even destructive, the result is one of the host of psychosocial agonies that go by the title of "the neuroses." A therapeutically powerful way of understanding and treating neurosis, then, is to approach it as a "script pathology" (Wilber, 2000).

In this mode, then, therapy consists in updating the script so that it is plausible, doable and productive, and, at the same time, recalibrates the patient's thoughts to match the readjusted scripts. The person thereby becomes less problematic to herself, ideally even "happy" with herself, and more socially utile. Improving the "goodness of fit" between the person and the rules or roles she is expected to follow or play functions to assure patient that she is "alright" and that the political-economy in which she is embedded and which therapy serves is also "alright." CT is *ortho*-psychic in the sense that its purpose is to "realign" the patient, "straighten" her out with whom and what her sponsoring society and place of work need her to be.

This accords with the findings of narrative theory, a cousin-subdiscipline to script theory. According to many narrative theorists, the gist of most of the narratives we live by, no matter how self-effacing we may make them at a surface level, is: "I am a good person. I have tried to do the right thing. Where I have not, circumstances have been against me. Where I have done right, that is truly who I am. And even though I have done wrong, I am more sinned against than sinning."

Importantly, one notes that here "morality" is conventionally defined as that which accords with social standards of right attitude and right behaviors in any specific social situation. It is what what Kohlberg called "conventional moral reasoning" (1987). Therapy in the CT sense is a reconstruction of a narrative that has social origins and social purposes. Not the deep subconscious issues that roil within the individual or the even deeper archetypal potential the individual has at her core as a spiritual being, but the realignment of one's thought processes to societal norms is the basic agenda of CT, and this is why it is the therapy of choice at D4.

In most cases, holistic theorizing looks at "cognition" as one of the components that make up the totality of the individual. It points out that it is important for both the teacher and the theorist to see and treat it as such. So far so good. But where it often falls short is in 1) its non-critical acceptance of what cognition means, its traditional (and therefore limited) signification and, relatedly, 2) its lack of consideration of the many problematics that surround cognition—those political and discursive factors that are inscribed in and render philosophically and ethically "difficult" the idea of cognition-as-such in the first place. But as has hopefully just been made clear, an integrative analysis ups the *ante* by critically refining the analysis in a manner that makes it not just more politically astute but truly holistic.

This is apposite in the present instance if for no other reason than that, generally, the society in which the patient exists and the business in which she works pay for this therapy. They expect measurable and profitable results from therapy with their "worker-citizen" (Spring, 1976)—and (time being money) they want it *soon*: Usually within the six to eight weeks that is the typical timeframe of the "Solution-Focused Brief Therapy" (SFBT) that the therapist (as a therapeutic "worker" in Marxian terms) is contracted to deliver and to empirically demonstrate to his employers that he has accomplished.

There is—it must be admitted—no doubt that CT is *the* therapy of Domain 4 in that there is no other therapy that even comes close to CT in building up patients' ego structures, in promoting a rationalist epistemology, and in defining the origin and cure of human dysfunctions, and, above all, getting the patient back to work at optimal levels of productivity. But this very strength is riddled with problems. One of those problems is that its reach exceeds its grasp. What does this mean?

An example is Judith Beck (1995), a key figure in Cognitive psychology and psychotherapy, making the global assertion that the cognitive distortions that arise during especially sensitive D4 developmental periods are a significant component of *all* psychological problems:

> In a nutshell, the cognitive model proposes that distorted or dysfunctional thinking (which influences the patient's mood and behavior) is common to all psychological disturbances. Realistic evaluation and modification of thinking produce an improvement in mood and behavior. Enduring improvement results from modification of the patient's underlying dysfunctional beliefs. (p. 1)

There is a good measure of respect and thanks that we owe CT for its signal successes in Domain 4. Indeed, one is grateful for how Aaron Beck and Judith Beck have alleviated certain types of suffering there by the "modification of the patient's underlying dysfunctional beliefs." But for all that, Judith Beck's above statement is still dubious and more than a little seasoned with hubris in that it takes CT's relevance and reach way too far. She falls into the *category error* of thinking that a certain therapy in a certain developmental zone is universally applicable, even to zones that are more evolved and articulated than *it* is.

For, it is important to note that CT's successes have been so many and so widely celebrated in Domain 4 precisely because CT operates off of and assiduously serves all the basic egoic and rationalist assumptions that comprise the belief system of Domain 4 itself, and it does this like no other therapy does, or indeed *could*. For, CT not only *shares* the assumptions of Domain 4; it *is* those assumptions in psychological form.

That CT and the many related therapies that have grown out of it should fit and further Domain 4's core ontological assumptions, epistemological commitments, and pragmatic interests so well is about as surprising as the fact that fish swim best when in water. They will outstrip an eagle, say, any day when it comes to moving through a lake. This is good to know . . . as long as it is fish and their problems that we are talking about.

But if it is the problems of those eagles that are the issue, then fish-therapy will not do the trick. In fact, it will probably do harm to eagles, or to any other creature that is passing through Domain 4—on a developmental pilgrimage not *to* but *through* D4, D4 as a *waystation*, not a *terminus*. For, the eagle's super-sensitive eyes are religiously set (well beyond the horizons of D4) on a very different kind of Canterbury that has been architected in very different Domains for purposes beyond that which Domain 4 has to offer.

What looks like a "crisis" and "dysfunctional" in a "patient's" belief system from the point of view of D4 may be how a soul is expressing its *metamor-*

phosis as it is, in fact, casting off the shackles of D4's restricted ethical and epistemological repertoire and evolving into something more complex and rare than is within Domain 4's kenning. Clinicians would do well when "assessing" such an *emergency* to determine whether someone is "sane" or not to stop for a moment and attend to Emily Dickinson's notice that

> Much Madness is divinest Sense—
> To a discerning Eye—
> Much Sense—the starkest Madness—
> 'Tis the Majority
> In this, as all, prevail—
> Assent—and you are sane—
> Demur—you're straightway dangerous—
> And handled with a Chain. (Poem no. 620)

Grof and Grof (1989) have described the process of *emerging* into a transpersonal realm as an "emergency." Grof and Grof are making a pun to make a point. The person may seem to be in a psychiatric *emergency* from a Domain 4 medical perspective. But what may really be going on is that this all may be a person's "*emergence*-y" out of a less evolved zone of being into a greater one. It is a spiritual *emergence*. To "treat" it as an illness is worse than a procedural error. It is a violence against a sensitive soul in the process of evolution (Mayes, 2017a, pp. 104–105).

CT is the *de facto* and even the *de jure* official therapy of some of Domain 4 institutions. Hence, its bodies of literature now get to define in academic psychology and clinical practice what is "legitimate"—that is, what is "functional" (and therefore exclusively "true") as "psychotherapy" and what is not. And what is not must therefore be surveilled and controlled or even eliminated by institutional ideology-police that range around (more and more surreptitiously and in virtual vehicles) to protect Domain 4's territory against ideologically illegal immigrants-of-the-mind.

Indeed, CT is not just allowed but empowered as "the one best system" (Tyack, 1974) to extend itself beyond psychological questions as *the* answer to the individual's deepest questions about his life—his "beliefs," which are now *not* to be assessed by their ontological depth and ethical heft but by the easier criterion of whether a patient can be made "functional" and his behavior calculably profitable.

CT does not so much take a negative stance towards religion as it *is* the new religion. Its tomes are all emblazoned in primary-colors with the *nihil obstat* of the Secular See of the APA. Its Gospel of Salvation is its very own *Diagnostic and Statistical Manual*, which not only clarifies what is functional and what dysfunctional thought and behavior but prescribes it. Institutionally approved and in some sites like public schools well-nigh institutionally *mandated*, the reign of the APA, CBT, FSFBT, and the secular litany of other acronyms comes replete with a starter kit of techniques, technologies, and medicaments to bring a "deviant" around to the "right view" (Kesey, 1962; Laing, 1969).

Foucault's (1975) *The Birth of the Clinic* demolishes this view of medical "treatment" as functioning in the service of a present political order. Jung (1954a), perhaps the most culturally prescient of twentieth-century psychologists, especially about where psychotherapy *was* in the first half of the twentieth century and where it was *headed*, foreshadowed Foucault by twenty years when he imagined in a dystopian musing how, in the near future,

> The totalitarian state could not tolerate for one moment the right of psychotherapy to help man fill his natural destiny. On the contrary, IT would be bound to insist that psychotherapy should be nothing but a tool of production of manpower useful to the State [in the service of] social efficiency. (1954, p. 107)

Jung could be prophetic. Here he gazed on the fate of normative psychotherapy with a hard accuracy.

Moreover, in its more elaborate critiques of what might be called "The Myth of Sheer Cognition," holistic theory, amplified greatly by Integrative perspectives, is positioned to offer sensitive, finely articulate critiques of this myth and to suggest further lines of research to provide alternatives to it.

Note as well that, although Integrative Theory resists postmodernism's tendency to careen off into ethical relativism, it also draws upon postmodernism's many fine critiques of established discourses that it has offered in making us all more sensitive to a wide range of injustices against and abrogations of the individual, and to how they are camouflaged and carried on by means of language that subtly enslaves others. Holistic Theory, in a certain degree of ongoing innocence and faith in the holistic operation of things as not only holism's methodology and teleology but also its central article of faith, has not been disposed to engage enough in such hard-hitting critique. With Integrative Theory now central in its efforts and the default hermeneutic orientation, that would change, as change it must if it is not to be cavalierly dismissed by standard curriculum theory as unprepared to engage in those tough talks that set the tenor of academic discourse in the twenty-first century.

The dawning of metacognition: The "legal moves and gambits" of thought as the object of thought. The burgeoning ability for some individuals to decenter emotionally and socially also begins to extend to cognitive and axiological domains at the outer reaches of D4. The person within the liberating range of the most advanced reaches of D4 is here beginning to learn how to systematically approach a wide variety of rational and ethical issues from multiple perspectives. Yet, far from everyone in D4 attains this epistemological acuity.

According to standard developmental research and theory, this entails the growth of hypothetico-deductive reasoning and the corresponding search for syllogistically serviceable universals:

> [U]nlike the concrete operational child, the adolescent is able to approach a problem by trying to imagine all the possible relationships among items in a given body of data. Then, through a process that combines logical analysis and experimental verification, he or she can determine which of the possible relationships actually holds true. In short, the adolescent becomes more capable of hypothetico-deductive reasoning, which is much like the reasoning of the scientist. (Conger and Galambos, 1997, p. 103)

D4 is thus the birthplace of *oneself as an epistemological being*—one who is not only always *learning* but is now *learning how to learn*, "*learning how to mean*," in Michael Halliday's (1975) felicitous phrase.

This is the land of *inductive and deductive reasoning*. Here, Sherlock Holmes, the Savior of the Syllogism, our Hero of the Enlightenment in slightly disheveled Victorian garb, finally gets it straight and sets it all right—proves to us yet again (and in Domain 4 we must believe that he always will) that reality is really and truly stable. And if Sherlock demystifies every mystery so coolly and reveals reality to be so stable that it is also a little boring (and sometimes very boring), then he has an answer for that too—his elegiac violin, consoling-cocaine, and the edibles left by the Oedipal Mrs. Hudson.

For, what we can reason about is the only thing that counts. Reason is the cosmos and the cosmos is God. In the beginning was the Logos. We light candles for Euclid, and our rational rosaries are perfect circles of axiomatic beads. It is the mysticism of logic, the symmetry of its triangular Godhead, that compels, convinces, and, above all, calculates, here in the fourth domain.

Cathy Ortega's private Vietnam: From cognition to metacognition. Metacognition is not just about growing degrees of cognitive capacity in an individual. That is wonderful to see, of course, but it is not a qualitative difference. It is a quantitative difference: More of what already is. It is a concept-map a student draws of her understanding of something now that is more worked out than the one she drew last week. But metacognition is more than just this "more."

Metacognition is an evolutionary leap to a more capacious sphere of existence. It is cognition that retains what it was but that goes beyond that to become more than it could have previously imagined. It is not about drawing a concept map about something. It is about *observing yourself* drawing that map, observing the person who drew the map both last week and this. What is *mind* thinking? What rules is *it* following in looking at evidence? Analyzing, yes, but cognition analyzing its own processes of analysis. Metacognition is analyzing how one analyzes (Anderson, 1977). As the ability to think not just about a system but about systems in relationship to each other from the vantage point of a broader system that subsumes and goes qualitatively beyond them into a subtler realm of analysis, D4 is also the birthplace of holistic and Integrative thinking.

In other words, at Domain 4 the individual not only learns. It now becomes a question of her learning *about* learning—thinking *about* thinking—and how well she can internalize this disposition and perfect its radically new protocols in intellectual action. This is doing "symbolics" in Phenix (1964) epistemological sense in *Realms of Meaning* or being a "symbolic analyst" in Robert Reich's (1991) economic sense in *The Work of Nations*.

And it also is the story of how metacognition developed for Cathy Ortega, who recently finished her degree in history at Arizona State University.

Cathy's journey to metacognition all revolved around an event that happened in a small Southeast Asian country, then called South Vietnam, during a military action by the North Vietnamese Army and the Vietcong. It was called "The Tet Offensive." It happened on January 30, 1968. Cathy's process of metacognition was launched in a war-torn Southeast Asian country twenty-five years before she was born one sunny day in Irvine, California.

During the Tet Offensive of 1968, soldiers from the North Vietnamese Regular Army and the Vietcong overran and briefly held the American Embassy in Saigon. They were then expelled by U.S. Marines and the Embassy returned to American hands. The whole thing took place in a matter of hours.

Some historians (in camp A) see the brief occupation of the America Embassy that night as crucial, as the beginning of the end for any American hope of victory in Vietnam. Some say (camp B) that it dampened that hope but didn't eliminate it. Other historians say that the course of the War would have gone on pretty much the same whether or not Tet had occurred (camp C).

A history major and a junior, Cathy Ortega reads three essays that are on the syllabus for week 6 of "History 335: The War in Vietnam" taught by Professor John Gliessman, who had actually been there himself as a Marine.

First, she dives with enormous interest into Historian A's essay "Tet: The Turning Point from Empire to Embarrassment." She also reads Historian B's essay "The Four Factors Leading to Our Defeat in Vietnam," one of whose four major sections deals with Tet. She concludes with an essay by Historian C, "Our Defeat in Vietnam: Inevitable Before the First Shot Was Ever Fired by an American Soldier." Tet is mentioned in this essay but given no special emphasis.

She finds all three essays well written and factually compelling. Indeed, she notices that although they come to different conclusions, the three historians pretty much agree on the facts and nowhere overtly disagree about them. She then writes her term paper in History 335, calling her essay "The War in Vietnam: The Major Pieces in the Puzzle of Our Defeat," explaining why she basically favors position B.

This has been an exercise in the growth of her *cognition*. She feels she knows something now that she didn't know before the class. She can engage in more informed discussions about why we lost in Vietnam. She is *cognitively* richer.

This matters to her a lot not only because she is a junior with a history major but also because her father, Paco Ortega, was a captain in the Army Rangers in Vietnam from 1966 to 1969 and walks with a heavy limp from when he was hit by friendly fire in Da Nang, where he was stationed.

She never understood as a little girl why daddy never picked her up or played rough-and-tumble with her during her childhood years. Was it because she was a girl? Did he love her less because of that? Was it bad to be a girl? Is that why he was so emotionally unavailable to her not only in her childhood but throughout her life? These questions haunted and hurt her throughout her growing-up years and were things she dealt with in therapy as a teenager.

They affected her behavior in high school, when she was sexually promiscuous. Her devout Catholic parents told her she was sinning. But she never felt she was, although she disliked herself for it because she disliked sex without love. It conflicted her. She discovered years later in further therapy that her sexual "looseness" was not about sex at all but about her need to be held and physically affirmed by a father-figure who had never done either.

When her priest, Father McPherson, warned her during a confession when she was fifteen that God was displeased with her and that she was toying with going to hell, she decided on the spot that she would never go to confession again and, at sixteen, a year later, stopped going to church and has not returned since. If God was just a crabby old man (which he was if Father McPherson was his representative) who could do nothing better with his infinite power and wisdom than lay guilt-trips on His children, then she rejected him lock, stock and barrel . . . just like he had obviously rejected her. Reading the work of a Vietnamese Zen monk and poet Thich Nhat Hanh, she dedicated herself to meditation and now sits with her *sangha* every Friday night in a Zendo in downtown Phoenix.

Even a brief integrative analysis of Cathy's *concept*, "The war in Vietnam," reveals its complex networks and massive scope in her psychospiritual economy.

The concept "Tet" is comprised for her of components from the physicality of the first domain (sexuality); the second domain of affections and self-objects; the third domain, which includes the logics of military logistics; the fourth domain, specializing in scholarly activity; the fifth domain, its *forte* being the comparison of theories; and the seventh domain with its synthesis of Western and Eastern spirituality in Cathy's personal journey from Roman Catholicism to Zen Buddhism.

As if these six domains were not complex enough in getting a handle on Cathy's concept "The War in Vietnam," consider that anything approaching a serviceable picture of Cathy's personal Vietnam would have to look at each of the 240 possible combinations of those six factors. How do the physical factors in her concept relate to the spiritual ones in Cath's case? How do the physical and affective together relate to the spiritual? How do her affects interact with her phenomenological proclivities, or how does they relate to the phenomenological in tandem with the legal-procedural. The list goes on . . . to the tune of a couple of hundred dimensions of the concept of "War in Vietnam" for Cathy.

It would take a scholar a lifetime of what I will call *Integrative Diagnostics* to understand Cathy's idea of "Vietnam." How could we ever have ever believed that a concept was a cold, objective, unitary thing, or that Cathy's understanding of the War in Vietnam could be even remotely captured on a standardized test? And yet, so it was . . . and so it remains in standard understandings of a student's cognition, and even in holistic theory's understanding of it, the view of the dynamics of a concept is quite undeveloped. A fully integrative and highly multiplex approach to education is just what is needed, and it is what integrative theory can provide.

Integrative Diagnostics is an untapped scholarly and therapeutic resource that, fully appreciated and skillfully deployed, takes us beyond the standard approaches to education and therapy at the same time as they more delicately parse the taxonomical categories and greatly extend holistic theory as it presently exists.

And yet, one more side of Cathy's story must be told for the account to be complete.

Everything we have discussed about Cathy's journey *in* the concept "Vietnam" is about her growth in metacognition—let's call it "*subjective* metacognition," for it has to do with her private experience of the concept from largely affective zones. The other aspect of metacognition may be named "*objective* metacognition."

In the case of Tet, Cathy, taking in her senior year the capstone course "History 499: Historiography," chose to revisit her junior paper. However, she did not in this second paper deal with the historical and ideological issues that had been her purpose in the first paper.

In this new paper she closely analyzed such structural and more broadly ideological issues as: 1) Historian A's, B's, and C's assumptions about what constitutes evidence in a historical analysis; 2) whether each of the historians believed in the idea of patterns in worldhistorical events or whether he rejects the notion of such "patternicity" in history; 3) the historian's own political commitments affecting his analysis of what, if anything, we were to learn from the Tet-event; and 4) how each historian structured his essay rhetorically in a way that was designed to *affect* the reading audience and also *reflect* each historian's ultimate faith-commitments.

At the end of this paper, Cathy was pleased to find that she had produced a good exercise in structural metacognition: the analysis of ideological and structural factors in *how* historians "do" history. This new paper did not lead Cathy to any new conclusions about the role of Tet in the loss of the War. But that was not her intent. Her intent was not to explicate the analysis of a crucial historical event. Her intent was to analyze how historians analyze. Her paper was metacognitive, in a word.

Cathy's passport is hereby stamped with approval to move to Domain 5, which is all about *analyzing analysis*. Cathy has phenomenologically and psychospiritually *evolved*.

Excursus on Anxiety, Projection, Trust, and the Cult of Expertise
Before going on, it's a good idea to pause for a moment and recall the danger of hierarchies as discussed above. It lies in a sense of entitlement, even a belief that one is actually a superior being because of his excellence in a certain field of endeavor. This may all-too-easily lead to his disprizing others who do not have this particular gift, which he, having, feels that it gives him the existential edge over others. But talent is no warrant to work emotional, political and even spiritual harm on someone who does not have that same talent or who does not have it to the same degree. It is the perennial problem of what hierarchies can all too easily produce—holistic as well as standard. And it is precisely what an integrative model of the curriculum is designed to avoid.

Although it seems a truism that just because a person excels in one prestigious area does not make him better than another person who doesn't, we often don't live that way.

On the contrary, we live in the "Age of Credentialism." Every age seems to come up with some distinctions or other that divide people into classes that in general make John better than Victor but not as good as Rashid, Maria better than Marina but not as good as Wendy. Different criteria are used to establish these social pecking-orders. In our worldhistorical epoch, we have fallen into the invidious practice of valuing a person existentially in direct proportion to the number of letters after his name. The man in the lab coat on a TV infomercial is not only smarter than we are. He has a PhD *and* an MD! He is somehow *better*. He is more trustworthy. We feel not only more secure as consumers in his sedating presence. We feel—since our culture's ethos *is* one of consumerism—more morally safe. We are not only doing the economically advantageous thing in buying the product he holds in his hand. We are doing the *right* thing.

Why do we feel that way? Why have credentials become the new hierarchical standard? The sociologist Anthony Giddens explains (1991) in *The Consequences of Modernity*.

First, it is important to note that our mad rush toward ever bigger and "better" degrees is nowhere measured more impactfully than by that Bible of "Better"—*US News and World Report's* yearly *Rankings of Colleges and Universities*, which it does by institutions and fields. Department chairs, college deans, and university presidents await its issuance in the hushed cells of their offices with dread and hope.

For, a good rating is money in the bank and a poor one is a fiscally toxic needle filled with a deadly substance in a PR syringe. It contains a statistical compound of percentage of admissions accepted (the lower the better, for this shows how choosy it can be), grant monies (the more scientific and answerable to business needs, the more prestigious the dollars garnered), volumes in the library (universities will go on spending sprees just before *US/NWR* evaluations to boost their library's holdings), and low student-to-teacher ratios (also demonstrating how picky it can be in establishing that it is an elite student body that "deserves" the best instruction). Good ratings mean avalanches of student applications and federal dollars. A bad rating is death by dearth of numbers. This is the reality of the modern "corporate university" (Giroux and Myrsiades, 2001).

Of course, the typical human need to be socially lauded as superior is as old as the hills and certainly plays into the credentialism of our times. But credentialism has never been so frenzied or ubiquitous as it is now, according to Giddens. It is, he argues, all about the idea of *trust*. We live in such complex times that we do not know whom to trust on the high-stakes issues and decisions that confront us every day—life-and-death affairs that we perforce face more frequently, consequentially, or mystifyingly than ever in the twenty-first century.

Which car has the best crash-protection system? Which pill can either cure or kill us and possibly genetically wound us and deform our still-unborn infants? Which home has toxic foam insulating it, its chemicals invisibly, odorlessly infesting us until three years later the owner lies dying in a cancer ward because studies are just now informing us that the foam is carcinogenic? And then, which lawyer can we count on to get us the biggest settlement for our children after we perish? Which "expert" interpretation of the ups-and-downs of the NASDAQ is correct and should guide us to invest or not invest in this company and not that one—a decision that may leave us scraping by in a shabby one-bedroom apartment in our "golden years" looking for part-time work, or sunning in front of our beach house in the Caymans?

An expert's trustworthiness is generally known best by the degrees she has and the schools she went to. A degree has become less the token of *deep knowledge* we have gained and more the sign of a crucial type of *technical rationality* we can claim to have mastered (and the higher the paygrade we can command) in our radically uncertain *fin de siècle* world. Not only that, but experts don't always get it right and in any event can't possibly know what hasn't been discovered yet. So, even what we learn from experts is, says Giddens, "only true until further notice."

It has been many long and laborious transformations that have turned the university—from its first appearance in 1088 as The University of Bologna—from an intellectual handmaiden to monasteries where one was called a "professor" because he *professed* belief in the manifestation of God's intelligence in what he studied and taught (Lowe and Yasuhara, 2013) to the modern professor as an intellectual worker in those intellectual branch-offices of the corporate state known as "universities" (Brubacher and Rudy, 1997; Giroux and Myrsiades, 2001).

The more credentialed in important areas someone is, the more trustworthy he is felt to be. And the more trustworthy, then the more his presence confers on others a sense of peace and protection (however provisional) in a world where people feel increasingly exposed and vulnerable, less-and-less in-the-know about things. The expert is thus "set apart." The root of the idea of being "set apart" is the Latin word *sacrare* (sacred, set apart, made holy). At a deep psycholinguistic as well as at a more manifest social level, increasing levels of "set-apart"-ness confer in this context an increasing sacredness projected onto the "expert."

Archetypes start getting set into gear at the deep unconscious level—that is, they start getting "constellated" in Jungian terms—when one enters the realm of what a culture holds up and sets apart as sacred—the top off the pyramid! At this "point," the elevated one becomes, in Jungian terms, a "hook" for others to hang their projections onto because he has been invested with *mana*. One has become a "mana personality" (Odajnyk, 1976, pp. 24ff) in one's cultural setting, electric with *mana*, which is a primordial name for psychic energy (Jung, 1969a, p. 65).

Thus, after his theophany on Mt. Sinai, Moses has a covering over his face for the light that flows from it is so bright that the rest of Israel could not look on it and live. Hence, the mana-infused/mana-emanating expert easily becomes a hook for the archetype of The Hero, The Protector, indeed The Savior. "These doctors! They think they're gods," is a common complaint. And there is truth to it but only because we are all projecting that function and significance onto them in our Age of Radical Insecurity.

But who among us is without sin in falling to this fallacy's sway? And who among us has not coveted a credential to establish and exhibit his broader worth? The ever-present danger in hierarchical models is that the higher one is rated, especially in a prestigious field, the more likely it is that one will be finally seen as not just higher in that specific area but in life generally. This is another reason that valorizing cognitive prowess alone to the exclusion of other kinds of intelligence, competence, and goodness is dangerous psychologically, politically and spiritually (Gardner, 1999). Yet, this is precisely what we do in schools today (Glazer, 1999; Noddings, 1995, 1992). This is wrong. It is also ironic that we should attribute some special ethical status on the basis of credentials in light of the fact that there seems to be no direct relationship between cognitive ability or performance and ethical insight or behavior (Lickona, 1991). Highly accomplished people academically can be morally obtuse while uneducated people can evidence stunning moral wisdom.

The most accomplished scientists in Germany performed advanced research on human subjects in death camps that were models of efficiency. On the other hand, when a poor rural rabbi who has made ends meet through carpentry is said to heal lepers, raise the dead, and answer life's most vexing conundrums with a few sentences and a story so simple that an eight-year-old could grasp it, does anyone care what this rabbi's IQ was or what degrees he held? And stories of the Buddha's life illustrate that it is only *after* he gave up a life of princely luxury and the choicest private tutoring that he gained an intelligence in the world of suffering where everyone's tenure ends with death and one's final publication is an epitaph.

An integrative approach to intelligence compliments traditional holistic critiques by identifying in greater clarity, complexity, and combinations what an authentic and humane intelligence is comprised of.

The Marvel of Metacognition

To return to the idea of metacognition, an example of a student engaged in a metacognitive activity would be, for example, one studying a concept-map of how a physicist would solve a certain type of problem in physics, learning the procedures that the physicist used, comparing it against how she had been solving the problem in physics (Chi et al., 1981). She would then have not just *factual knowledge* but also *procedural insight*, giving her an enhanced understanding of how physics in general is done, then how science is done, and finally even about mathetic knowledge in general (Kuhn, 1970).

In short, the student is now not just thinking about a stated problem in physics.

She is thinking about thinking about physics, and finally thinking about mathetic consciousness in general. This is a higher-order level of cognition, and it gets underway here in the farthest reaches of D4, just on the border with D5. How fully an individual can master metacognition will be key in determining if she will move on to D5 in her psychospiritual evolution or remain here in the procedurally fixed "consensual reality" of D4 as a social being but not as a hermeneutic one and thus never receiving in the mailbox an epistemological passport for entrance into D5.

Metacognition is introspective, a quantum leap in self-reflective cognition. In Jungian typological terms, it may be the individual's first *volitional and strategic*, not just instinctual, movement inward as a self-observer. For the student cultivating introspection on his internal processes in doing physics, Domain 4 may ultimately prove to tie in to the meditative traditions in Domain 7. Holistic theory has yet to seriously note or explore this connection between D4 and D6–7, but Integrative Theory demands it.

The Myth of the Cold Concept (and the Holistic Politics of Metacognition)

In *Understanding the Whole Student: Holistic Multicultural Education* (2016), my colleagues and I explored from the position of an epistemologically multi-perspectival multiculturalism how cognition is reduced in the models of mind that now prevail in education to merely cognitivist terms and behavioral indicators. The mystery and miracle of human consciousness being pared down to merely binary protocols, consciousness is turned into an an emotionless, binary/yes-no mechanism, a sterile android.

However, as we have seen, the psychodynamic and psychospiritual fact of the matter is that a concept is shot through with very complex streams of positive and negative energies, quite varied imagery, and differential intentions from other domains that integratively *embed* that concept. Together, those other domains, from the biophysical to the ethico-spiritual, add up to a clustered-meta-perspective on the formal-legal consciousness of D4. This is why metacognition is inherently integrative. That cluster is comprised of factors drawn from every domain of the integrative system. In the case of Cathy, the cluster featured factors from:

1. The organismic domain, the protocols of child-rearing, including (indeed especially) something as primary as breast-feeding schedules (Field, Cohler, and Wood, 1989);
2. The emotional domain, with the teacher as a "pedagogical selfobject" (Mayes, 2009a);
3. The cultural domain, with the teacher as either a friendly ambassador-of-the heart or inhospitable agent-of-the-state depending on how the school is "positioned" and how that teacher positions herself in the cultural economy of the sponsoring society (Nieto, 2002, 2000);
4. The social-roles domain, where our child's school experiences are the realization of "our best hopes" or confirmation of "our worst fears" in the sometimes century-old family narratives about what education means to *our* family—whether it has lifted us up or held us down (Heath, 1983);
5. The ontological domain regarding the congruency or malalignment of the curriculum with "our family's religion" or negative feelings about religion (Kniker, 1990; Nord, 1995);
6. The cultural domain again, regarding what constitutes "success" in education from a cultural perspective, mindful of the fact that it is precisely in *resisting* formal education that a child may be evidencing "success" in the eyes of her peers and even her parents and grandparents. McLaren's (1997) "Resistance Theory" holds that showing even the appearance of interest in the curriculum or emotional intimacy with a white teacher can cause a student to be excluded from his most important reference-groups, for it is seen as "selling out" to the culture of the oppressor: Being black on the outside but "really" white inside (an "Oreo"), red on the outside but "really" white inside (an "Apple"), yellow on the outside but "really" white inside (a "Banana").

These cultural resistances to cognitive patterns, manners of speech, various clubs and sports, and all the rest that makes up a school culture of privilege comprise the strategy of resistance to habits of the mind that are metacognitively evaluated and associated with the oppressor—and thus resisted in an act that is both epistemological, political, historical and cultural. A simple factual statement such as "Abraham Lincoln led our country through the Civil War" in a history class may have a very different emotional charge in one student as opposed to another—a point my colleague Neil Goslin made well in our *Understanding the Whole Student* (2016).

And this is to name only some of the factors that supercharge a "concept." There simply is no such animal as a hermetically sealed concept, an idea-in-isolation—unless there were such a fantastical creature in an epistemological bestiary. The idea of a value-free, context-free concept is a traditionalist myth—an idyll of conservative programs that aim at "Teaching the Great Ideas"—ironically, one of the most politically biased notions ever floated on the academic stock-exchange but forwarded by conservatives whose "righteous" intent is to depoliticize education (about as sensible a project as de-mathematizing physics)—but by replacing it with *their* agendas.

The spell of simplistic views of education will only be really dispelled by an integrative vision of a "concept" as nested within circles, within circles of organically interwoven factors—not one of them separable from the influence of every other existential domain in the curriculum and not one of *those* unaffected by *it*.

There are other considerations as well in addition to those just listed in getting an adequate hold on the integrative totality of factors that come into (inter-)play in something even as apparently unproblematic as a teacher asking her student during a third-grade show-and-tell session as: "Tell us about the tiara you're wearing today, although, you know, dear, that I don't allow jewelry in class." *Hamlet* would not be harder to analyze than that!

The Domain-4 Curriculum: The Legal-Procedural Curriculum

Quite a disproportionately large amount of attention given to pedagogy and curriculum in the United States is trained upon the fourth domain. Why should this be? There are many reasons, several of special importance.

Dollars and scholars. First, and above all, is that teaching students the "rules and roles" (Wilber, 2000) of how things work in a culture typically happens, second only to the family, in a culture's educational system—whether that system is under a Banyan tree with twigs for etching in the soil and rocks for reckoning or in the high-tech $500,000 classroom in the suburbs of Monterey, California, where the professional elite and their children live in gated communities (Riordan, 1997; McLaren, 1997). The United States is no exception to this. Indeed, it is a prime example of it.

In perhaps no other country has a nation so consciously tied its fate to its schools (Cremin, 1988, 1980). From its earliest public schools under the aegis of such social reformers as Horace Mann and Catherine Beecher in the middle of the nineteenth century, the hope was that schools would teach Americans what America means and it would teach its citizens what it means to be an American (Messerli, 1976; Sklar, 1974).

Furthermore, in solemn decisions and *dicta,* the U.S. Supreme Court has made it clear beyond any possibility of controversy that the state has a "compelling interest" in education. A quick glance at a list of perhaps the ten most important decisions of the high court regarding public schooling from various angles can only evoke an awed sense that, indeed, the Court, while protecting the rights of parents and students, has equally guarded the rights of the state, which *will* have its say about how education is *done* in the United States and toward what goals it will function. The interested reader might wish to refer to the following cases over the last sixty-five years that have proven definitive in establishing that this is so, regardless of the court's shifting ideological inclinations over the last sixty-five years. When it comes to the majesty of the state on the question of state's "compelling interest" in education, the following decisions exemplify the principle that "Roma dixit. Causa finita est.": *Brown v. Topeka Board of Education* (1954); *Abington School District v. Schempp* (1963); *Engel v. Vitale* (1963); *Lemon v. Kurtzman* (1971); *Wisconsin v. Yoder* (1972); *San Antonio Independent School District v. Rodriguez* (1973); *Tinker v. Des Moines* (1969); *New Jersey v. TLO* (1985); *United States v. Lopez* (1995); and *Parents Involved in Community Schools v. Seattle School District No. 1* (2007).

The second reason has to do with the extreme, indeed excessive, valorizing of adolescence in standard developmental models. "If 18–20 years-old is the height of human development," so this view of human development goes, "then the junior-high and high-school years are the most important ones and we had better get it right in the schools or the nation will find itself in a fine fix economically and militarily and it will all be the schools' fault!"—an opinion that usually gains its most vocal and least informed critics of public education in conservative politics (Tyack, 1974).

Third, President Coolidge announced his dispiriting vision of not only education but the purpose of the American experiment in 1932 (just sixteen years after Dewey's inspiring vision of education not only in but *as* a democracy) by duly and dully noting "the business of America is business." However, in 1961, departing President Eisenhower warned that the growth of a "military-industrial complex" was beginning to get a stranglehold on American democracy. In 1988, Lawrence Cremin, the dean of American educational history, predicted that the greatest threat to American democracy in the twenty-first century would be the military-industrial-*educational* complex as each member of this awful trinity would feed into the economic interests of the other two until American policy and processes would be devoted not to the good of the people but for the good of this governing triumvirate itself.

And it does not end there. There are other groups that monetize education, knowing which side their bread is buttered on: colleges of education, publishing houses, construction firms, specialists in goods and services to keep the physical and symbolic systems of the vast network of schools, districts, state-agencies and federal departments up and running; legal teams to either protect or litigate against school staff and administrators in the face of exponentially increasing bodies of laws and statutes regarding education; teachers unions, which once concerned themselves with pedagogical issues regarding the wellbeing of children and the future of democracy, now forced to focus almost entirely on financial and legal advocacy for disprized, beleaguered teachers; educational "scientists" looking tirelessly for ever-bigger grants to research ever-more efficient means of training teachers to train children to become obedient and efficient "worker-citizens" (Spring, 1976)—the dystopian assault on democracy promoted by Moe and Chubb (2009).

And above and beneath it all, politicians use education as a means to gain office by either terrifying parents with dire and uninformed warnings about what will happen to our children "if things keep going the way they are" or seducing them with impossible promises and panaceas of "how things *can* be . . . if only you elect me."

Yet at the center of it all, a teacher and a student, face to face, try to teach and learn. It is astonishing that they get *anything* of educational consequence done in the classroom, but they do. And that is the miracle of it. The Holistic Education Movement cherishes that miracle. The Integrative Curriculum offers new terms and tools, indeed it suggests a more elaborated ethic, an augmented evolutionary teleology, to move that Movement forward in new and generative theories and practices.

Teaching and Learning in the Formal Procedural Realm
Cognition and curriculum. In general, curricula that aim at fostering self-esteem in the student are quasi-therapeutic in that they are attempting to help the student rewrite and internalize a new script or set of scripts about himself as a learner because the old ones no longer serve—if, indeed, they ever did. This matters greatly since one's narrative of oneself as an *educational* being is inseparable from and determinative of one's narrative of oneself as a *existential* being. This is a theme that I take up in considerable depth in

my upcoming (2020, in press) study, *Archetype, Culture, and the Individual in Education: The Three Pedagogical Narratives*.

Brophy's (1994) theoretical and pragmatic little masterpiece, *Motivating Students to Learn*, for instance, provides a brilliant example of the best of curriculum and instruction in Domain 4.

Particularly addressing students who come to the classroom with a low sense of self-efficacy and a high degree of learned-helplessness, Brophy shows the teacher how to help the student reframe her vision of herself and her abilities in ways that are more realistic, productive, and satisfying for the student.

Imagine a student who is not particularly good at spatial reasoning. After learning that he had failed a difficult geometry test, he might conclude the following: "I'm no good at this stuff at all. I'm a dummy. I always fail and I always will fail at geometry. All the really smart kids are always getting good grades in geometry and I never do. The teacher must think I'm a total jerk. But I do study. It's just that it's hopeless! *I'm* hopeless. . . . So why should I even keep trying?"

According to the Cognitive Therapies (A. Beck, 1990; J. Beck, 1995), this student is operating off a script that reflects various cognitive distortions about himself as a learner—a fourth-domain script pathology, which Cognitive Therapy is at its best in addressing.

For instance, there is the problem of what cognitive therapy calls "selective filtering." This is when a person only allows himself to register evidence that supports his negative views of himself and discounts or even fails to see evidence of positive characteristics. In the present case, the student is forgetting or discounting the fact that his average score for the first half of the term was C+ and that during the much more difficult second half he was, until this last test, maintaining that C+—albeit with a great deal of hard work. The recent test has brought his average down to C–.

Clearly, he is no geometry whiz, and he should not plan on becoming an architect or engineer. However, he seems to have approximately average ability with geometry, a fact that he is now ignoring because he has selectively filtered out his modest successes, which to him were triumphs then that he is discounting now.

This has led to another script pathology—namely, what cognitive therapy calls "catastrophizing." On the basis of this single failure, the student has rushed to the conclusion that he will now always fail in the future. Not only that, but he is certain that the teacher will think that he is stupid—thus evidencing the distinctly fourth-range script pathology of "mind reading," or with no justification just assuming that you know what a person is thinking. This, and other script pathologies discussed above will haunt and can even undo a person in a given domain for the rest of his life.

The cognitive therapeutic armamentarium offers various ways to help the student to see his "F" in a different light, and the phenomenological benefits of this will prove to be innumerable through the rest of that person's life. This involves "re-scripting."

In our present case, the teacher can help the student see that although it is true that he is not bound to become the school's great geometry genius, it is not true that he is a total failure at geometry. In fact, all his grades, except for the most recent one, point to average ability. She has heard that at music and athletics he is exceptional and that he is pretty good in his history classes, too. "Different people have different skills," she says.

Furthermore, it is not true that all the "really smart" kids do well in geometry. The teacher has had many students who have been average or even below average in geometry but have gone on to do great things in other fields. She just had lunch last week with Hilda Morales, who wound up, just barely, with a B– in geometry but was a superlative student in civics and history, and is now a state representative in their legislature. And how about Mike Running Bear? He is the school's quarterback and is the best saxophonist in the orchestra. She asks: Might he be visiting her in ten years on a break from a pro-football team's schedule or when the professional orchestra for which he is first-chair saxophonist is visiting town?

In this example, the teacher is helping the student to update and rewrite his script so that his self-talk might now go something like this: "It's true that I got an F on that really tough test, but who doesn't fail sometimes? There are other things I'm really good at that some of the geometry geniuses don't have a clue about! And at least I'm average at geometry." Such re-scripting occurs within the fourth domain.

Integrative historiography. Moving from pedagogics to historiography with special reference to U.S. educational history, the fourth circle also provides an interpretive lens on curriculum history—the diachronic dimension of curriculum studies mentioned at the outset of this study. Here, standard holistic theory has shone in Scott Forbes's masterpiece, *Holistic Education: An Analysis of Its Ideas and Nature*. Yet, much more work needs to be done in charting and interpreting the history of holistic education. Integrative Theory, with its close attention to hermeneutic issues, could prove crucial in making such studies not only historically interesting but historiographically sophisticated as well, thus quieting criticism about standard holistic theory's political naivety and historical decontextualization.

As Cremin (1964), Tyack (1974), Kliebard (1986), and Ravitch (1983) have shown, the "administrative camp" of Progressivism in the first half of the twentieth century aimed at adjusting the child to the world of work and to do so in a manner that would be most bureaucratically streamlined and therefore fairest across the board in providing high-efficiency learning to all students, not just the privileged few. These Progressives felt that in streamlining an educational system that was still either unformed or corrupted by the Tammany Hall local politics of payoffs and personal favors, they would be creating a level playing field of educational opportunity that was indispensable to democracy. In order to fill her slot in the new political economy of urban industrial capitalism, the child was to "learn to earn" in the schools (Kantor, 1988). The student would learn in this fourth domain the "rules" and "roles" that would "train" her to fill her destined slot and make her a productive "worker-citizen."

Dewey (1916), Counts (1932), and other Liberal Progressives, calling for curricula that interrogated social structures and encouraged students to challenge them, were advocating for a more critically oriented approach, one that caused students to ask *why* things were the way they were, not *how* to fit into them. One of the frequent breakdowns in communication between the Liberal Progressives and Conservative Progressives can be located at D4, stemming from the fact that they were both committing the category error of insisting upon the exclusive value of their socio-phenomenological perspective without acknowledging the important values and functions of the other in the realm of the D4, politically-centered curriculum.

The same may be said of the collective national response to the launching of Sputnik in 1957—and this in a double sense. For not only were curricula to focus on those basic hypothetico-deductive abilities and skills that are at the heart of the fourth developmental circle cognitively, but they were doing so in order to protect "our way of life" in a rule/role orientation.

Indeed, it is arguable that whenever a conservative Back-to-Basics or Excellence-in-Education movement arises in response to the putative deficiencies of an overly liberal approach to curriculum and instruction, what we are seeing is a conservative attempt to maintain a D4 status quo at loggerheads with a liberal attempt to relativize D4 virtues, push the domain's boundaries, and evolve to D5. It is a fourth-domain civil war.

Such a call to "return to educational fundamentals" may be appropriate at times and not at others. That is not the point here. The point is that in these political controversies, what we are witnessing is an intradomain tension between different visions of what the fourth domain is: whether it is a Homeland that deserves defending in its own right, or whether it is a springboard into the next evolutionary domain. This is the kind of insight that an *integrative* analysis of any taxonomical category, with its nuanced attention to *intra*-category dynamics, arrives as a matter of course, but which a traditional *holistic* presentation of each category, with an almost naïve "celebration" of each category as a unitary and unproblematic thing in itself, does not.

The Aristotelian Curriculum

It is in this developmental expansion at D4, with its search for Aristotelian universals and Kantian categorical imperatives, that we can place what Ornstein and Hunkins (1998) called the intellectual-academic curriculum and its standard academic and developmental assumption that rationality is the apex of human knowing. It is because both the Piagetian and Kohlbergian model (and the educational programs that rely on them) stop at this point that they have been challenged by feminist theorists, post-Freudian educationalists, and transpersonal developmentalists. For, as I shall discuss later, all of these theorists agree there is more to consciousness than just the ability to create overarching propositions which, despite their conditional importance, are far from the last word in our experiential and ethical potential.

Still, Aristotle was right that, whatever else we are, we are also the animals that reason. It matters deeply that in a time when sweet reason itself can be cavalierly dismissed as just another "power discourse," that certain curricula focus on what Noddings (1999) has called the "formal conversation" of rational academic discourse. We jettison such things at our educational and cultural peril.

Miller (1983) calls this kind of curriculum a "curriculum as transaction" because of its Socratic, dialogical nature. It is difficult to imagine an education that can claim completeness that has not skillfully guided students into the conventions and potentials of formal, transactional discourse. This is an important insight that paleo-conservative critics (Adler, 1982) of many current educational practices justly offer to a school system that can stress "feeling great about yourself!" to such a degree that the importance of seeing an issue clearly, "no matter how you feel about it," is lost in a torrent of narcissistic emotionalism.

Furthermore, those same critics warn that a curriculum that heedlessly judges all canonical education as a merely "patriarchal white male discourse" is—no matter how politically correct—also politically disempowering for precisely those students who need such knowledge in order to advance in a society that will always value such knowledge (Mayes, 2016; Ravitch, 2000). Examples of such fifth-domain "critical thinking" curricula are many, but most of them have arisen upon two classics in this domain that appeared in the 1980's: Adler's *Paideia Proposal* (1982) and Lipman's (1988) *Philosophy Goes to School*.

The problem arises when either the public and/or educational reformers "fuse" at this domain, insisting that the Socratic examination of canonical philosophical, literary and historical texts and ideas is the *summum bonum* of all educational processes (Adler, 1982). It is educationally perilous when one becomes so committed to *any* developmental domain that one grows blind to the legitimate curricular place and instructional possibilities of the other domains.

I have argued elsewhere (Mayes, 2017b, 2001) that, in Jungian terms, this excessive, unifocal emphasis on the archetype of the teacher as philosopher to the exclusion of other important archetypal images of the teacher as, for instance, a priest, poet, therapist, mother or father, revolutionary, trickster, and wise old woman or man, can be injurious. Limiting a teacher's role as Adler would have us do, is often psychologically and pedagogically contraindicated for teachers who have a wide range of psychological and ethical reasons for being teachers.

As noted above, it is also at this phenomenological reach that we can place such cognitively based approaches to teaching as Jerome Bruner's historically notable (1960) structure-of-the-disciplines approach, where the teacher shows students how to define and solve problems in a given field of study by learning how "experts" in that field do their work. The idea is that this will then enable students to generate their own questions and answers in any given field like the experts do.

Again in Noddings's terms, teachers are to engage their students in "formal conversations." The specific terms and academic histories of these conversations will vary from discipline to discipline, but in every case canonical texts and standard evidentiary criteria will inform the classroom inquiries. A necessary part of a complete education and empowering to the student in a variety of ways, this approach to curriculum is also potentially limiting if it is the sole focus. For there are realms of teaching and learning that go beyond the confines of standard Western developmental models and Western academic disciplines (Reagan, 2005).

Domain 4, then, contains some dramatic, even fraught, developmental leaps for the evolving consciousness—here in the tumult, the storm-and-stress of "adolescence," initially "identified" (some would argue "created") by America's first PhD in psychology, Professor G. Stanley Hall, at Clark University, in his 1904 classic, *Adolescence*, and studied from every possible angle since—both psychoanalytic (Blos, 1940; Zachry, 1940) and more eclectic (Conger and Galambos, 1997; Crain, 2016; Dusek, 1994).

Up till now, the student has been inundated by bio-centric, early sociocentric and proto-egoic developmental tasks in D1 through D3. In D4, consciousness, still enmeshed in many of its primal tasks, begins also to coalesce into its first fully recognizable form as a viable ego. The formation of the ego is, of course, the *sine qua non* of mature ethical-spiritual growth, and it is a developmental Texas of the mind.

Ego-founded and ego-oriented, ego-reality is not the last word in human experience. It is an instrumentality for something greater. For, the mature ego now has *agency*, free will, that renders it capable of moral choice. The teleology of ego is not its own realization, merely. It is in attaining a vision of itself in relation to the cosmos, transitionally. And then as both its culmination and self-transcendence, it is in the love of others in the Divine, ultimately. This is the message of all the great religions and the experience of its great mystics. It lies in the sixth and seventh domains.

But evolution is all, according to the Process Theologies that inform this study—especially those of Bergson (1902), Whitehead (1964), Chardin (1975), and Hartshorne (1984) and their cosmic optimism. It is inscribed in the very heart of the holarchic view of things and summed up in the the words of the medieval English mystic, Dame Juliana of Norwich, whose culminating vision of Divine Love—that which resides at the core of all existence and also that which beckons and guides all existence towards a divine culmination—was expressed in her observation-although more a beatific promise than merely an observation, that, "all shall be well, and all shall be well, and all manner of things shall be well."

The fifth domain is the instantiating turn (tentative, to be sure) in that direction. The young person's nascent ability to self-observe is also the first step towards self-transcendence. For, in order to transcend itself, the ego must be able to step outside of itself, and this it does in learning to *observe* itself. This is the action of the fifth domain—the breaking free of ego from its own originating contexts and perspectives in now examining and making conclusions about moral, social and epistemological questions. These questions do not exclude, indeed they specialize in problematizing, that ego's own situatedness. Consciousness comes to understand ego metaphorically—as, for instance, the vehicle we ride (and ultimately surrender at the farthest reaches of human spiritual potential) to a new land. It is not the new land itself.

But that new land does commence in the first lonely steps past the outermost border of the fifth domain. With all of that domain's phenomenological self-awareness; its relativizing of all monolithic systems—rational, political and ecclesiastical; its first fearful, solitary and risky midnight ventures beyond "the great and spacious building" of ego and the social matrix in which it housed, Domain 5 is the ego's experience of what will in Domains Six and Seven become its own renunciation—and its transformation, too, into the peregrine soul in search of the Eternal in the Self and the Self in the Eternal.

CHAPTER SIX

The Emergence and Fruition of the "Self" from Domains 5 to 7

Domain 5: The Phenomenological Domain
(The Post-Egoic Domain)

Overview

The expansion to the fifth developmental ring of consciousness is a momentous phenomenological passage, a quantum leap in structural complexity and experiential possibility. According to Wilber (1999), consciousness here begins to take a transpersonal meta-perspective on the antecedent realms it encircles, but which it now goes qualitatively beyond (Wilber, 2000). For, consciousness increasingly sees any sign, symbol, concept, system, or even personality as a linguistic-phenomenological event, existing only in some degree of relationship to others—never in and of itself. In this realm, there is no Kantian thing-in-itself.

This emancipatory phase, D5, contains all the evolutionary spheres within it, stretching from the primal and pre-personal staging ground in Domains 1 and 2, the sensory and emotional realms, through the personal and legalistic landscapes of Domains 3 through 4. The quantum shift in Domain 5 lies in the fact that the individual is now transiting out of the ordinary orbit of egoic, consensual reality into a wider one. This can happen largely because of the marvelous ability of metacognition to show the individual how to transcend her personal perspective in order to take in many perspectives. To transcend one's ordinary world in order to appreciate different visions is inherently a spiritual act. Unlike Wilber, I therefore mark the beginning of trans-egoic capability from this stage, not, as he does, from the next developmental ring.

Still, as we will see, D5 is a *potential* for spirituality, its *first* formations. For, the D5 landscape still has traps of egoic quicksand and brambles of ethical relativism to negotiate. This is its prime task in D5: Refine the ego so that it may move towards the "transpersonal" and thus morph into a total identity in which 1) the Self, one's timeless identity as an eternal being, is beginning to appear on the horizon and 2) one still maintains an ego but now begins to rid it of is egotistical dross. This is what Edinger (1985, 1973) called the ego-Self axis and what Jungian psychology generally believes to be the fullness of human development: Individuation. It will only begin to become established at the farthest reaches of D5 development as we shall presently see at the end of this discussion of the fifth domain.

Moving into D5

As Plato announced in *The Republic* and as developmental psychology has concurred since its inception in Freud's model of psychosexual development over a century ago, most people find their existential residence somewhere in the fourth domain, to use the terms employed in this study. Plato called it the caste of bronze between the iron individuals of the philosophically less-advanced and the golden philosopher-kings. Kohlberg (1989) in his hierarchical "levels of moral reasoning" has called this stratum "conventional moral reasoning" between "preconventional moral reasoning" at the base and "postconventional moral reasoning" at the apex (1989).

For, the socially-ensconced ego may well not be able or simply not be disposed to move itself beyond itself—may not "go transpersonal" (Wilber, 1980) in seeing itself more broadly than his culture's understanding of what is "normal, average, or expectable." The person sees himself and is seen as "one of us" and finds his dwelling place here.

The litmus-test is whether or not the ego will cross the borders of Domain 4 and get its passport stamped in Domain 5, where there is that subtle but definitive qualitative shift toward the *trans-egoic*. The transition of certain individuals from a comfortable resting in the rational, empirical, and particularistic to a dynamic venturing into the transrational, intuitive, universalistic —this is the crux of the matter.

If, as seems reasonable to conclude, democracy revolves around the *rational* rights of a *particular* individual in specific *empirical* contexts as interpreted in *legal-procedural* terms in this domain's courts, then it is not without cause that some of its citizens may sound some red alerts when it is suggested that there are farther reaches of human development than just its own—perspectives that might threaten nation and ideology.

The patriot of D4 may well be agitated by what seem to him to be non-democratic inflections in transpersonal argumentation. Hence, one of the tasks of the remainder of this study will be to suggest that the integrative position and holarchic mode are not only consistent with the democratic spirit but indeed advance it in many ways that ladders and conveyor belt models militate against by their very structure.

Jung captured the notion—politically hard to handle in a democracy but intuitively resonant nonetheless—that there is a natural "spiritual aristocracy" among human beings. Hence his psychospiritual exegesis of Christ's declaration that "Many are called but few are chosen" (*Matthew* 22: 14) to mean that some individuals are chosen to attain "a higher degree of consciousness" and that "in this matter men differ extremely," for "nature is aristocratic" but only in this intangible sense that, far from leading to pride, should, if it is spiritually authentic, lead to ever increasing humility (1967b, pp. 116–117).

Jung is going out on a limb here to hazard a very non-populist idea in a populist day-and-age that certain kinds of aristocracies may legitimately exist, although he is also going to some pains in this passage to make it clear that the psychospiritual aristocracy he is describing does not, and should not, correspond in any way to political or social privilege. But how successful is he at that?

Indeed, the larger question now appears in stark relief: How "democratic" can *any* system ultimately be that speaks of gradations of any sort—which, however piously postulated, will, according to a Marxian analysis and Ricoeur's (1991) "hermeneutics of suspicion," still invite invidious distinctions that sooner or later must lead to inequitable distribution of very tangible capital and intangible but still highly important cultural capital. For, isn't it true that, his pious intentions aside, Jung's "innocent" observations about some people being more spiritual than others unavoidably generates a hierarchy, which, if it were ever taken seriously by many, must spell the doom of democracy? It is a nuanced and enormous political challenge to any notion of "differential spiritual evolution."

What the critic (Carrier, 1976, was one of the first and certain the most cutting along these lines) declares is that Jung's use of the imagery of cultural privilege to exalt the psychospiritually more "advanced" betrays Jung's elitism. Besides, says the critic, whether Jung *is* elitist or not hardly matters, for his metaphorical identification of spiritual giftedness with the politically noxious idea of an aristocracy plays right into the hands of any politics of privilege, which can then take that metaphor, wave it in front of everyone's face, and say: "See? The great Herr Professor Doctor Jung says that we are a spiritual elite. We *deserve* to lord it over you! And 'We' are not amused by your noisy nonsense to the contrary. And 'We' have ways of quieting you down if you cannot muster the good manners to do so yourselves. We take our psychological warrant from the venerable Professor Jung!" And this is not all.

A Marxian critique would go on to point out that, spiritually sincere or not, those who see themselves and are seen by others as spiritually advanced may soon enough start getting tangible rewards for those intangible gifts. The ultimate danger would be a theocracy. Yet even where the implicit privileging is not made so manifest as in a theocracy, means *will* be found to privilege some and marginalize others.

This Marxian critique is an important one, and it extends to the very notion of a holarchy/integrativeness. It is one that must be faced head on, especially in a study extoling the supremacy of democracy to any other political ideology. It is in Domain 5 that consciousness "goes meta-." That is, it not only engages in a cognitive activity but at the same time stands beyond it to gain a more global and dispassionate sense of how reason operates. It thinks about its thinking. This is the *hermeneutic* turn; it is the interpretive act of "engaging engagement." Hermeneutics, suspicious or optimistic, is the necessary vocation in the fifth domain: Consciousness observing consciousness.

Jung and Alchemy: Excursus on "The Hermeneutics of Suspicion" and "the Hermeneutics of Hope" at the Fifth Domain. To review: Paul Ricoeur (1991) and Peter Homans (1995) have, respectively, identified two basic, radically different modes of the interpretation (hermeneutics) of persons, texts, events, programs, and so on. These are two contrary *hermeneutics*: "The hermeneutics of suspicion" and "the hermeneutics of hope." This is an issue that naturally first arises in D5, of course, the hermeneutic domain *par excellence*, and its importance cannot be overstated, especially since one's orientation in this domain will influence the curricula one makes and the way one conveys it to students.

For, it is in D5 that the possibility of trans-empirical, transrational vision takes on its earliest recognizable form. It becomes spiritual or at any rate is proto-spiritual. This is good news. Then again, every silver lining has its cloud.

Having a cosmic sweep in one's perspective and thus being inherently, if embryonically, "spiritual" is no guarantee that that spiritual vision will also be friendly to the human being.

The fifth domain, especially in, say, Sartre's (1956) *Being and Nothingness*, is both proto-spiritual in its sweeping survey of the individual human being's place in the cosmos yet grim in what it concludes: Man's place is to have no place. He is alien, strange, doomed. Where heaven is a possibility, so is hell. We must thus take this dialectical tension between the two hermeneutic modes seriously and all the more so since the motive of our labors as educational theorists and practitioners must always be the well-being of children.

If what we offer does not originate and end in an essentially constructive, not deconstructive, position, then the educational project as it presently stands would need to change, for cynicism might infiltrate our practices and damage the innocent—and if anything ever qualified as a Kantian categorical imperative, surely it would be that not injuring children not only qualifies but sits atop the list.

This is not to say that the hermeneutics of suspicion does not have its necessary role in the dialectic between the two hermeneutics in educational processes and practices. In fact, it must be present if education is to be realistic, informed at every turn by the lessons that doubt and pain contribute in the formation of humane individuals, and not a fantasy of a no-fault/no-discomfort happy-talk cosmos.

As the Jewish concentration camp survivor and psychological theorist Bruno Bettelheim (1976) argued in *The Uses of Enchantment: The Meaning and Purpose of Fairy Tales*, it was important that the child encounter darkness in the stories he read and was read. Doing so gave him a means of coming to grips with the conflicting emotions he experienced in himself and the evil he even then knew operated in the world. Maurice Sendak's (1963) *Where the Wild Things Are* exemplifies this with what became a classic of children's literature. It parades darkness but in such a way that it is harnessed in the service of the growth of the child's psyche in realism and empowerment.

In other words, even in this early dialectic of light and dark for the child, the hermeneutics of hope and faith prevail as the last word, as indeed they must in any educational product, process, or setting of educational goals. For to engage in the opposite project—the inculcation of suspicion and the triumph of darkness in the hearts of youth—would be perverse: Emotionally devastating to the child, politically catastrophic to a democracy, and ethically indefensible by any sane standard.

The "hermeneutics of suspicion" operates from a position of radical doubt, sometimes even despair, and sees the human being as sexually voracious (Freud), economically predatory (Marx), driven primarily by the brute compulsion to survive at any cost (Darwin), or duped by childish mythologies and simplistic moralities that rob the individual of his heroic existential status and turn him into an ideological serf (Nietzsche). In confronting any idea or scenario, the hermeneut of suspicion asks, "What is wrong with this picture?" From that awful alpha she proceeds to extract from the text its toxic omega, exposing it in either its tepid grays or hellish scarlets. The ability to do this is a *sine qua non* of the truly critical mind.

In stark contrast, the second hermeneutic mode operates from a position of hope that sees the human being, our primary text of reference always, as improvable—as living, moving, and having her being in the basically beneficent context of eternity: *Sub specie aeternitatis*. A hermeneutics of hope does not naively turn a blind eye to human depravity and distortion. However, even at a person's lowest, indeed especially there, the hermeneut of hope descends to the base to make the ultimately salvific point that the Light will prevail. Again, Dame Julian of Norwich's cosmically affirmative assertion that "all shall be well, and all manner of things shall be well."

Despair in Domain 5

Before touching upon the rich varieties of Existentialist pedagogies, however, let us first look at the dangers that fusing at D5 can run into. For, the more articulated an individual and the domain in which she primarily lives, the greater the chances for system-failure, owing to the increased delicacy of the system.

Despair. The first pit in this domain is existential despair. Because the individual from the D5 perspective sees all signs, systems, rules, and roles as psychosocially constructed—and thus, by extension, critically deconstructible—consciousness may fall into "aperspectivalism" (Gebser, 1985). This is the belief that since there are no longer any hypothetico-deductive universals, no world-view is preferable to any another. Its newly found power to relativize everything can lead consciousness to catastrophe, it seems. This is one of the most dangerous and pivotal moments in the entire sweep of holarchic development. Upon the way the individual handles it hangs the issue of whether she will truly begin to move beyond the egoic or finally stay stuck in it, albeit in more phenomenologically rarefied form here at D5.

Good Faith and Bad Faith. The only healthy response to this problem (in D5 terms) is authentic being-in-the-world (Sartre, 1956). One lives authentically in the world when, in full and frank awareness of her temporal and epistemological limitations in a possibly indifferent universe, she nevertheless defines and pursues those life-projects that are most meaningful to her in the innermost realms of her moral and psychological existence. This is living in good faith—which Maslow, in his Existentialist phase, popularized as the therapeutic notion of "self-actualization."

Living in "bad faith" is the neurotic attempt to escape the truth of one's inherent existential limitations and the necessity of making hard choices. One can sidestep the imperative to live in clarity and courage in this world by investing all of one's faith in a possibly fictitious promise of post-mortal felicity—of salvation and life in Heaven with God. But the fact is that, whether there be a God or not, death is the end of the question *here*. To not face one's intractable mortal condition here by entering on an uncertain immortality project dedicated to a *hereafter* is to live inauthentically *now*, whether or not one's hope in God turns out to be true *then*. The reality and strength of faith that the individual attains in D6 and D7 depend upon the sincerity of one's grappling with despair at D5. It is the difference between what Bonhoffer called "cheap grace" (using faith as a means of trying to sidestep the reality of one's death) versus "costly grace" (the willingness to die to the old self in order to be born into a new and spiritualized one).

The two hermeneutics at work in the psychology of C. G. Jung. The hermeneut of hope attempts to extract gold from what is base—the actual project of the medieval and renaissance Christian alchemists in attempting to coax spiritual gold out of the most corrupt material they could gather up on deserted midnight streets and literally *out-land*-ish places that lay outside the city in order to take it back to their sequestered laboratories.

Crossing themselves thrice in the name of Christ, whom they worshiped as the Ultimate Alchemist, the Redeemer of all that is wretched, they collected their disgusting harvest in impenetrable dark except for the lamp they held in their chemically stained fingers: menstrual rags, rotting carcasses of rats, moldy globs of cheese that even the leprous cast away, even the tossed gauze that had dressed pustules—all of these were the alchemists' horrible *desiderata*.

These they scooped up into their ghastly bags but emblazoned with the Savior's Cross that betokened their high purpose. They would pound it with their pestles back in their labs into the element they would put into their "retorts" (test-tubes) and call what would be the starting point of their sacred process by various names: *the prima materia, massa confusa, nigredo*: "the first material, the confused mass, the black stuff." *This* was where the process must begin.

For if the process were to conquer the elemental despair into which the Fall had cast not only humanity but the earth, it was this excrescence of nature at its lowest that they must transform into the *lapis philosophorum, medicina catholica, aurum nostrum*: "The Philosopher's Stone, the catholic (universal) medicine, and *our* gold." Their motto to announce their sacred aim was: *Nostra aurum non est aurum vulgi*. "Our gold is not the popular/vulgar gold." Their work was not about making money in the financial world but redeeming matter in the material world.

Getting rich was the unworthy business of the huckster alchemists, out to make a buck. For the gnostic alchemist even that gold was useless because it was also fated to decay. So was the body of man no less than the violated body of the earth. Let the Savior then return to redeem man and his *moral* mistakes as the Ethical Redeemer of the whole cosmos: *Veni, Salvator Macrocosmi!* "Come, thou redeemer of the Macrocosm!" They, his priests in primordial chemistry, would do his *material* work in advance, each spiritual alchemist a *Salvator Microcosmi*, a savior in miniature working under the aegis of Christ. They were servants of the Redeemer, only secondarily scientists. It was another Mass they celebrated, and the mass itself that they handled, in their lonely workshop-cathedrals of the gnostic cosmic One, they would translate into resurrected matter (Hoeller, 1982; Segal, 1995).

This was *their* gold. Their manuscripts and lab books were filled with archetypal imagery—sensual and sacred, bizarre and beatific—to symbolize each step of the process. The culminating image was a king and queen in one person, attired in their gendered roles of power, holding both a sword (image of mathetic knowledge), that divides and analyzes, and a rose (image of poetic knowledge). Here, triumphant, on full display is the resurrected, integrated god that each person potentially was if she or he would learn to balance all inner opposite and thereby *individuate*—the great goal of this life and the justification for all of their suffering

Thus, Jung did not see alchemy as proto-chemistry when practiced by the spiritual alchemists. He saw it as proto-psychology, an extended symbol of the collective unconscious, which was not simply the repository of the reprehensible as in Freud's hermeneutics of the gloom of the subconscious. Not at all. Jung felt that the gnostic Christian alchemical process was emblematic of the fact that, in the end, the wretchedness of human life and death were divinely aimed at the emergence of ultimate psychospiritual re-integration, at salvation. Jung brought to the surface what he believed was the alchemical hermeneutics of hope in the ultimate salvation of the *physical* universe.

Now he, Jung, would translate those alchemical terms and processes into their psychological correlatives. From that he would create an entire "psychospiritual lexicon" (Mayes, 2017a) that pointed the way to psychospiritual integration *in* the individual and ultimately *by* the individual who, one by one, would undergo his private apocalypse and, growing into a newly and uniquely *individuated* human being, would *be* the inner Apocalypse's resolution. At that point, the individual did not *enter* the New Jerusalem. Rather, he *became* a New Jerusalem, each in his own way, in a new community of the psychospiritually redeemed.

Jung's psychological approaches embody a hermeneutics of hope in that, even in the most painful neurotic or psychotic symptom, even in the most terrifying or despairing dream image, Jung believed that hints toward health were also being given. For, nature is finally curative not cruel, and so should our interpretations be ultimately constructive and not de(con)structive. Even in our inquiries into the darkest craters on desolate interior landscapes, it is the hermeneutics of hope that yields the most generous conclusions and the most generative plans for action.

The proof is in the pudding. "Es ist wirklich weil es wirkt," said Jung in an unrenderable pun in German, but the sentence essentially means, "It's real if it works." And which works better? He asked. A hermeneutics leading to despair and paralysis or one leading to hope and action? To Jung, and to all hermeneuts of hope, the answer is self-evident and gives the decision to a hermeneutics of hope but with due respect to the dialectic opposite-number, the hermeneutics of suspicion. This is the tension that the educational voyager in D5 must look at courageously and solve creatively if his alchemy is to bear the higher fruit of students who, in his class, see both the dark and the light in any text and learn to harness the former in the service of the latter.

The Two Hermeneutics as Foundations of Democracy

The questions of the superiority of one hermeneutics over the other is *always* open for discussion in a free society but *never* susceptible of being decided. Neither can we chalk the difference in attitudes on this matter down to mere temperament. There are plenty of happy atheists and as many morose believers. It is, finally, a radical matter of choice (though not necessarily a radical choice). As Kierkegaard said, the most spiritual of people may look quite ordinary, even bland, and you pass them by on the street without giving them a second thought.

All that is necessary is that the conclusion comes from the entire "man"—the breadth of his experiences, his intellectual seriousness (which has nothing to do with the degrees he holds but the profundity of his insights), and above all the inclinations of his heart, which, if they are compassionate and clear, must be honored in each person, for he has come to his conclusion in what Existentialism calls "good faith." We can ask no more of a partner in our discussions and we should settle for no less, understanding in advance that democracy does not mean universal agreement or that no one's feelings get hurt.

What democracy does assert is not only that the majority rules but equally that the rights of the minority be jealously protected . . . if only because one may find oneself in the minority the next go-round at the ballot box! But even more because the majority has been known historically to make bad choices and it is only the protected voice of the implacable minority that has finally brought the benighted majority back to its senses.

And finally, democracy means that *any* view and *any* practice is tolerated—not necessarily affirmed, loved, extoled or even particularly liked, but punctiliously and respectfully *tolerated*—unless it can be proven that *that* particular minority view unfairly puts someone else in danger or at risk. Proving that it *does* so is a very high bar to clear, and that's the way it ought to be, of course. It will require compelling and massive evidence from varied sources and disciplines, tightly woven arguments that avoid all the errors outlined in classical logic, especially arguments *ad hominem* and *ad verecundiam*, and a super-majority of adjudicators, to pass.

Democracy in commonsense terms means "learning to agree to disagree" and moving forward together in good humor, good faith, and a compromise-but *shared*-program, shaped by all to some degree, and with the understanding that there will always be further discussion as scheduled and possibly different action mandated at that next electoral meeting. When those ground rules break down, so does democracy.

The point in all of this is simply to assert that: *The democratic frame of mind is distinctly a D5 event and commitment.* It requires that one *relativize all positions, including one's own,* not so as to *not* believe what you believe (that would be cowardly, hypocritical and even crazy-making), but certainly enough to know that *what* you believe may not be right, or only partially right, or right in some circumstances but not in others.

Relativizing, de-ontologizing *all* positions is a hermeneutic act of suspicion about all totalizing claims. But believing that this process will ultimately, in a dialectical fashion, further the cause of democracy is an act of belief and hope in a corresponding hermeneutics of faith.

As part-and-parcel of its ability to relativize all "positions," democracy requires the fifth domain ability to *tolerate ambiguity*, for ambiguity is inevitable any time deconstructing systems and juxtaposing them in multi-perspectival acts of metacognition is the *modus operandi*. It is seeing the forest *meta-analytically* from above all its systematic trees. It is metacognition at work.

And all this in the hopes of ascertaining what is good or bad, useful or inutile, relevant or irrelevant in each of the systems being compared.

In short, both a hermeneutics of suspicion and a hermeneutics of faith apply here.

All of this revolves around the fifth-dimension ability to appreciate that life is a "complex condition." H. L. Mencken quipped: "For every complex question there is a simple answer. And it is wrong." Democracy requires living in complexity. Freedom is valuable not so much in itself. People can do the most awful or just plain stupidest things simply because they are "free" to do so. Freedom matters because only freedom provides the conditions, latitude, and perspectives that allow one to dwell intelligently and humanely in complexity.

All of this is to say that at the fifth dimension one develops the ability to appreciate *paradox*. This means sometimes transcending, though never ignoring, the hypothetico-deductive processes of D4, in order to see more finely nuanced and ultimately more generative truths than our simple systematicities can account for.

Then, it all comes down to action: Going ahead anyway in a collective act of the hermeneutics of faith, in spite of (even better: *because of*) the relativity, ambiguity, and contingency of things that a hermeneutics of suspicion usefully revealed. One moves forward in a democracy, with other beings who can tolerate ambiguity. And remember: They are undoubtedly tolerating *you* at least as much as you are tolerating *them*!

Suspicious in your optimism, but finally optimistic even in your suspicions, you all move forward on this great Ship of State, faithful to the larger world-historical purpose of protecting and even magnifying the cause of democracy. This does not require that we all agree. In fact, democracy prohibits programs that force agreement. And moreover, democracy insists that we recognize the complexity at the core of the human situation, that we negotiate it in transactional innovation and with unfeigned compassion, so that we may together "seek a newer world," in Lord Tennyson's (1842) words.

Democracy does not mean sporting willy-nilly in a no-holds-barred "freedom" that is ultimately an invitation to psychological, ethical, and political anarchy. Rather, it is the freedom to dwell responsibly in a complexity that cries out for the perennial virtues of humility and compassion. The integrative model, being more complex and radically more egalitarian than either hierarchical or item-and-process models, is well suited to these goals.

Indeed, the very notion of cosmic evolution upon which integrative models entirely rest, is dialectical. Integrative Theory is not *just* optimistic, although it does lean heavily in that direction. It honors and mines both hermeneutics for what each has to offer about the ultimate nature of things insofar as such epistemologically limited creatures as we are *can* make such conclusions. Each position must honor the other in order for intellectually robust, emotionally satisfying and mutually respectful conversation to take place. It is that those who have the ears to hear and take part in such conversations can jointly create new spaces of ontological presence and metaphysical promise *through* those conversations. In doing so, they move the whole organism forward in an act of Christian *caritas*, Judaic *hesed*, and Buddhistic *karuna*. Such individuals comprise a spiritual aristocracy.

But this does not mean they are superior in any way that involves wealth, intelligence, power or academic degrees. It has nothing to do with any external markers or concrete benefits, nor, given the goodness of the motives among the spiritually advanced, is their reward or advantage anywhere . . . *except* in the knowledge that "When ye are in the service of your fellow beings, ye are only in the service of your God" (*Mosiah* 2:17).

Indeed, such souls assiduously avoid riches and acclaim, refusing it when offered, counting themselves not the masters of their fellow beings but their servants. They carry on their barely visible lives according to the above scriptural maxim. The broader domains that they inhabit, especially in Domains 6 and 7 are not places of privilege but districts of duty to others and to the Divine as they understand it, commune with it, and become entirely identified with it.

Transiting from the Hypothetico-Deductive Territories of the Fourth Domain to the Transrational Territories of the Fifth Domain

For those who can make the crossing from D4 to D5, what they will find, both as a reward and challenge, is that the transition is, as it were, an expansion of the grammar of psyche from *the conscious indicative* into the subtler syntax of *the phenomenological subjunctive* (Lacan, 1977). This is to say that, instead of being delimited by physical, personological, and social determinants ("the conscious indicative"), the D5 consciousness now can begin to picture worlds that do not exist—or do not exist yet (*the phenomenological subjunctive*). Consciousness may now begin to think in terms of "What if" or "As if." This highly consequential change is basically the result of the newly acquired noetic power of *metacognition*. This ability to think about thinking, rooted in D4 as we saw in Cathy Ortega's experience, begins to fully flower in D5.

An important characteristic at D5 consciousness is that it must now increasingly turn a reflective eye upon its *own* motions and notions as well as upon the social and ontological axioms that it had uncritically accepted before. In semiotic terms, the metacognitive consciousness may now interrogate and manipulate the signs and symbols that have heretofore functionally but naively organized its *own* sensory, biological, emotional, cognitive, and social worlds. Now, the individual can relativize and manipulate those signs and symbols in order to understand how, in so many ways, his universe is linguistically constructed. This allows the individual to call into question the semiotic tokens and structures that he had simply taken for granted at the previous domain.

Thus, everything becomes fair game for critique and relativizing. Postmodernism's 'linguistic turn" is *quint*-essentially a *fifth*-domain affair, which is why it is sees any symbolic system as a "discourse." Through the rhetorical gambit of the alienating effect of irony, the person may even engage in iconoclasm to disembed from her own indigenous values and, through irony, even sarcasm, actually be seeking more visionary global standards.

Here arises the biggest challenge in D5. It is when Domain 5 takes it upon itself to critique things beyond its purview—that is to say, the spiritual Domains of 6 and 7. When that happens, it overreaches itself and actually devolves to a Domain 4, adolescent cynicism and a tragic dismissal of people, ideas and perennial wisdom that it is not yet equipped to grasp, much less authorized to assault. In the terms of this study, a developmentally less-articulated domain has, in a holarchic malfunction, encroached on territory it ill-comprehends to tear down complex ethical systems that have been millennia in the making.

There are two things that are death to a liberal democracy and its schools: A pious certainty about a *particular* tradition and the attempt to impose it on every student, on one hand, and an impious dismissal of *every* tradition, on the other hand. *Absolutism* ever threatens democracy on its Right flank, *Relativism* on its Left (Watras, 2002). A liberal democracy's only hope in its always worldhistorically embattled existence, is its commitment to its central truth: The rights of the individual—indeed the duty of the individual—to be engaged in an ongoing discussion with other individuals (Bell, 1976; Nozick, 1994).

For this ongoing conversation that *is* a democracy to work, these dialogical "others" (the Jewish Existentialist theologian Martin Buber called them one's "dialogical partners") must also be lovers of democracy and its perpetually vigilant defenders—each bringing his or her commitments to the table in full force but no less in a humble spirit of courtesy; each genuinely agreeing to carefully consider the perspectives and needs of the other; each showing good faith by staying open to the possibility of being changed by what the other has to say, what the other has had to live, and live through, and what the other therefore deserves in the common courtesy and mutual edification that is the air that democracy breathes and without which it dies a slow death by anti-dialogical asphyxiation (Buber, 1985, 1965).

This is a point that holistic theory sometimes misses in not attending to harsh inter-category politics because of a somewhat reductive view of each category as a unitary phenomenon that we must simply celebrate and integrate. *The integrative instinct to apply a hermeneutic of suspicion as well as a hermeneutics of hope* is necessary to redeem holistic theory from an excessive optimism—or at least the appearance of it. For, the caricature of holistic theory as a "Birkenstocks-and-Granola Pseudo-Science" is not without some justification (Cizek, 1995). There is a *Realpolitik* pragmatism in Integrative Theory that Holistic Theory could benefit from.

Reason and Its Limits

Science: The good, the bad, and the differential (equation). Another major difference from the vantage point of Domain 5 in assessing Domain 4, has to do with science. In D5, traditional Western science is not all in all. It is believed in D5 that although science has its magnificent uses, it also has its limits. Three come immediately to mind.

The first limits are those that have to do with both post-Einsteinian physics and its destruction of the sole claim to ultimacy of the Cartesian Black-Box Model of space, where everything is localizable in a pair of abstract but absolute x,y coordinates and its movement traceable, predictable even, by the asymptotic genius of the differential calculus. These work well when things are not approaching the speed of light but not so well when they do. And in any case, if accepted lock, stock and barrel, Newtonian physics leads to an inadequate cosmology. In Heidegger's (1964) terms, the Newtonian model works well at the *ontic*—or practical—level, but not at the *ontological* level.

The second limits are not new but they *have* gained reputable and increasing experimental and theoretical support—those that have to do with the existence of the paranormal, the existence of which is less and less questioned in research into the paranormal. The question in this research focuses much less than it used to do on whether or not paranormal phenomena exist and more on how to explain the fact that they *do* (Griffin, 1994).

And third is the multicultural caveat about 1) what counts as evidence of causation in nature and 2) what technologies are appropriate and ethical from the perspective of a given culture (Cobb, 1994).

At D5, Western science is both celebrated and problematized, as is any and every system; for, problematizing and taking apart *all* systems is what Domain Five does so well. It *deconstructs*. This is indispensable to any principled critique of anything.

However, even our culture's archetypal Saint of the Syllogism, Commander Spock—graduate *summa cum laude* of the Vulcan Institute of Science and Technology as well as of Star Fleet Academy, logician *extraordinaire*, and esteemed First Officer to Captain James Tiberius Kirk—knows that logic alone is not enough. Spock's doubts and agonies mirror our own, of course, and that is *no doubt* why his character has proven so durable and attractive over the last fifty years. Only *half-*human, Spock has emotions that he must always reckon with and not infrequently must stumble over into his humanity. A *fortiori*, what greater problems must *we* have—human, all-too-*completely* human—with our fond hope that we could ever think in pristinely-packaged logic!

Thought is not cold like a computer, a metaphor brought to a catastrophic conclusion in the tragicomic figure of *HAL*, the onboard computer-guidance system in Stanley Kubrick's *2001: A Space Odyssey*. Human thought is not a chilly circuitry of impartial algorithms (Skinner, 1968). It is as heated as the tragic but triumphant human heart (de Unamuno, 1954). Cognition is "hot" as Pintrich et al. (1993) insist, and as researchers in fields as varied as the following lend their supportive voices to: The history of science (Kuhn, 1970), hermeneutics (Gadamer, 1977), medicine (Shamdasani, 2003), cultural anthropology (Girard, 1977), sociolinguistics (Bernstein, 1996; Halliday, 2016); second-language acquisition (Krashen, 2003), public policy (San Roque, 2000), the sociology of religion (Berger, 1995), and pedagogy (Palmer, 1998).

The Kuhn revolution about revolutions. The physicist and historian of science Thomas Kuhn (1970) rocked the study of the history of science with *The Structure of Scientific Revolutions*. In it he argued that scientific revolutions occur *not* when a present scientific discipline finds good cause within its own parameters of what counts as "evidence" and how to interpret it, calmly and under the gentle sway of sweet reason, decides to simply shift its paradigms in orderly processions of cheery scientists to and from conference podiums, where they unanimously toast the new scientific models with a glass of mellow wine and expensive cheeses. It's never that polite.

The real story about a revolution in science, Kuhn declared, is that one takes place when the reigning paradigm is forced to yield, its adherents kicking and screaming as they are carried out. They can do their share of professional damage to the new paradigmists on that way out, too.

Only after this agony of transition is a new set of ontological assumptions installed as the official assumptions of the discipline—and a new set of images osmosed as its new foundation. The revolutionary scientist is a sort of "sensitive reed" who is reverberating with, as much as he is creating, a new set of assumptions in the culture and in this worldhistorical moment, to which the ousted order of things has failed to answer. This, in addition to weird findings that the present paradigm cannot adequately handle, require this revolution.

And here is the wonderful and shocking thing about it. These radically reorienting assumptions are, of all things, at their base and in their essence, *poetic images*.

These are now constellating into a new cosmological "sense," although they have already been fitfully stirring in the scientist's culture for some time. But now they find a scientific embodiment and voice in him. Out of the fullness of his own soul—his own Kantian "poetic" function at a bedrock epistemological level—he boldly proffers another view *of* reality to his academic community. In this sense, Shelley's proclamation in *The Defense of Poetry* still holds good: "The poet is the unacknowledged legislator of the world!" Only, now it is the poetic image, usually conveyed in a dazzling array of digital technologies, that are calling into question not only political laws but cosmological ones as well, and perhaps even primarily those.

The paradigm-changing scientist is not the Einstein of popular myth laboring over reams of equations streaming out of the old paradigm. Einstein said he was terrible at math and had to have proper mathematicians translate his insights into equations once he had had his poetic flashes.

Einstein characterized his first intimations of The Theory of Relativity in a very human and simple way. It was in him pondering as a teenage boy what it would be like to ride on the head of a beam of light. A poetic image. This is just what he used in his famous "thought experiments"—exercises in stick-figure characters and quirky narratives.

These thought experiments were as similar to bedtime tales to a child as they were to a conference paper being addressed to one's scientific peers.

For instance: *What if* an observer were standing at a train station? And *what if* there were two trains approaching each other from opposite directions? And *what if* they were both going the speed of light? And *what if* lightning struck at the very moment they both were crossing the spot where the observer was standing? *What would* a person on one of those trains see in looking at the lightning as compared to what the observer at the station *would* see?"

The poetic power of the image in intuitively responding to otherwise inexplicable data is what instantiates a paradigm shift in science, said Kuhn. Thus, Einstein is supposed to have once remarked: "If you want your children to be intelligent, read them fairy-tales. If you want to make them even more intelligent, read them more fairy-tales."

What the revolutionary scientist is offering is emphatically *not* just another more elaborate view from *within* the academically established paradigm of the nature of things. To the contrary, the revolutionary scientist comes bearing the message of something wholly new. Something poetic.

He is a John the Baptist of science, calling out for the way to be cleared for the messianic advent of a new vision, and a saving one. This vision is made articulate flesh in the likes of Poincaré and his initial apprehension of a new math theorem as swirling colors or Watson and his biochemical model of the double-helix beginning in a dream of intertwining snakes. In a sense, the revolutionary scientists are all Einstein dreaming of riding the head of a beam of light across a forever mysterious cosmos—one before which they stand in humility, wonder and openness to new ideas.

And this messenger, this prophet of science, makes his stand (there is no guarantee he will prevail, at least not in his lifetime) with great courage. For such messengers have been known to have their heads chopped off—or, only a little less painfully, to be called before popes, heads of state, and (most terrifying of all) chairmen of departments to renounce their scandalizing discoveries.

Finally, a scientist, being human, and despite our idealizing of him since the Enlightenment as a demigod, thinks fundamentally the way we all do—from the processes of the poetic-affective-intuitive realm *primarily* . . . and then *secondarily* in the conceptual terms of cognitive processes.

Of course, the scientist is trained to think "objectively" and no doubt thinks more often in that mode than the rest of us do. But no training trumps the primary epistemological forces within us as human beings—forces, indeed, that *are* us—and that filter and sort all our perceptions, conceptions and apperceptions before we are even aware of it or have one conscious word to say on the matter.

Scientific training is itself carried on within the inescapable corral of those biases. Hamlet cannot reason his way to clarity about this relentless exasperation called human existence. He must *feel* his way through the maze of his life, our life, this life. Not reason will master the maze. It must happen (if it is to happen at all, even to a prince—for it does not happen for Hamlet) through that ultimate sense of direction that resides in intuition and image. It's not a syllogism that shows things up for what they really are. No. "The play's the thing!"

Add to all of this the more quotidian but still important fact that taking such a stand in departments and disciplines is ideological bad manners and can cost the professor tenure, even his career. Then, too, there is the hard reality that one and one's colleagues (some of them dear friends with whom one has labored shoulder-to-shoulder for many years) are often highly invested, sometimes monetarily by grants and personal financial ventures, as well as ideologically and emotionally, in certain theories being stamped with the institutional imprimatur of being "true."

The Mathetic versus The Poetic

Kant's distinction between the mathetic faculty and the poetic faculty has been alluded to several times in earlier sections. Now is the time to go in more depth into this—one of the most crucial ideas from one of Western philosophy's most influential philosophers, and it comes into sharpest focus and with special relevance here in D5.

"Mathetic faculties"—the term "mathetic" pointing to *math*ematical-like reasoning—refers to our various kinds of analytical capacities, our "systematicities." Its purest form is the syllogism with its major premise (i.e., "All men are mortal"), its minor premise ("Socrates is a man"), and its incontrovertible conclusion ("Socrates is mortal").

Overall, mathetic "knowing" includes our ability to engage in deductive and inductive reasoning; our construction of disciplinary fields each with its own specialized, internally consistent rules of interpretation and expression; and our hardwired perception of things as existing in three-dimensional space-time. In mathetic reasoning, control, replicability, precise formulations, and economy of explanation are key. This is why the principle of Occam's Razor is the first commandment in the mathetic domain—the simplest, most "elegant" (as mathematicians put it) explanation of something is always the best. In some current brain science, these things are seen as left-brain functions (Jaynes, 2000) although that is still contested in brain science.

"Poetic faculties," on the other hand, refers to such putatively right-brain functions as intuition, feeling, impulse, art, and mysticism. The poetic impulse aims at transcending established paradigms, problematizing consensual reality. This threatens the procedures and boundaries that the mathetic faculty has labored so painstakingly to establish, and it is why the poetic faculty tends towards the radical and even the revolutionary (Abrams, 1973; McNiece, 1969). The poetic faculty is holistic, feeds off hunches, spontaneously combusts in symbolism, and is often opaque and indirect so as to point us in the general direction of something indeterminate but compelling, even absolute in its own way—something that the precision of the mathetic prevents us from seeing because of the delimitations that exactness requires. Still, the mathetic must always be honored, for it is also that which guards us against when the poetic faculty overreaches itself and becomes just dangerously seductive illusion.

The power of the symbol. It is the ability to both appreciate and even create the multivalence of a symbol that is, in one sense, what propels a person into Domain 5 or, lacking it, keeps him locked in Domain 4. It is an epistemological litmus-test. Let us therefore look at this critically defining issue regarding transitivity from D4 to D5.

Before we do, though, note again the efficacy and efficiency of the holarchic model in not only naming a major component, as holistic curricular charts and models do with a certain element or domain, but how the holarchic model goes well beyond that in exploring a domain's inner dimensions and reaching out to its external domains and tying this all together—with oneself as the "interpreter," woven *into* the center and *as* the center even as she is weaving her interpretation of what has woven her. She is both *constituted by* other domains and, as the interpreter who will act on the basis of those interpretations, she is also *constitutive of* those domains. This super-synergy of a holarchic model—*the totality* present in *each component*, and *each component* present in the *totality*, each diamond reflecting all other diamonds in a unitary structure of ultimately One Diamond—this is one of its greatest strengths of this model. Its possibilities first begin to present themselves to consciousness in its preliminary awakening D5.

What emerges from this is a "web" of creative possibilities in the present and more attractive scenarios for the future. In therapy, a holarchic approach could bring to someone whose life-narrative has been ruptured a new hope that her life can be narratively reconstructed as she discovers that there remain many galvanizing connections—which holistic analysis with its less articulated categories is less effective at revealing (White & Epston, 1990).

The Heart of Art
Its major product being the intensely compact symbol, Domain 5 is also the staging-ground of art, which can 1) manifest as sacred adornment to D6 or D7 beliefs or 2) present itself in popular culture as a little tune one whistles while strolling around the mall in acts of consumption in the consensus-reality at Domain 4. However, art to *be* art *primarily*—and not, on one hand, a pendent adornment to an ideology or theology, or, on the other hand, a comfortable companion to everyday life—it must emanate from Domain 5, with its epistemic fealty to the symbol-as-such. For, art is a way of knowing what one has not known and *could* not know any other way than through its incarnation as a symbol, and symbol-making lies in the purview of the

phenomenological capacity of D5 (Jung, 1969a, p. 75; see also Greene, 1975; Handy, 1963; Sugg, 1992).

For, by the Existentialist view of art that prevails in this domain, art should not be just a secondary way of confirming what one *thinks* one *knows*, but a way of *defamiliarizing* something one thinks one knows in order *to see it for the first time*. More: Art is a way of stepping into the complexity of our lives, not to evade our lives with the sedative of sitcom truisms (the danger at D4) or the stimulant of dogmas (the danger at D7).

If the sign is what is produced in Domain 3, and the symbol makes its first appearance as a phenomenological possibility at the farthest reaches of Domain 4, then it is in Domain 5 that the symbol assumes independent status and comes into its own as, in addition to our mathetic capacity, *the other of our two primary epistemological possibilities: The poetic* (Kant, 1781/1997).

The aesthetician Bendetto Croce (1953) captured the primacy of poetry to analysis, image to argument; the lyrical to the empirical; the symbol to sign—all of which what Heidegger (1964) called the ontological to the ontic. Croce declaimed, with a touch of the poetical himself, that:

> The relation between knowledge or expression and intellectual knowledge or concept, between art and science, poetry and prose, cannot be otherwise defined than by saying that it is one of *double degree*. The first degree is the expression, the second the concept: the first can stand without the second, but the second cannot stand without the first. There is poetry without prose, but not prose without poetry. Expression, indeed, is the first affirmation of human activity. Poetry is "the mother tongue of the human race"; the first men "were by nature sublime poets." (in Vivas & Krieger, 1953, p. 86).

Even a culture's laws grow out of its myths and are, in the last analysis, polished expressions in the most decontextualized legal language possible of its determining originary myths (Bruner, 1996).

What, then, is the difference between a sign and a symbol? It is a question that has many educational implications.

Sign versus symbol. A sign refers to a specific thing, person, process, event, and so on, and it refers *only* to that. If a sign is to really be a sign—efficient and effective, literal and not lyrical—it must be empirically *functional* and procedurally *unambiguous*. A sign is unsentimental, impersonal, no-nonsense its *work-ability*, and absolute in both its claims and demands.

Perhaps the best example of a sign is an *actual* sign—a stop sign. It means one thing and *that* only. "Bring your vehicle to a complete halt. Do so immediately. Look to the left, right, and in front of you to gauge the flow of traffic. Proceed as indicated by the rules of the road in the manual of facts, procedures, and laws that you studied to get your license."

A sign is context-free. It claims universal validity. It does not ask for your interpretation of it, much less your feelings about it. A stop sign has nothing to do with anything except driving—not macramé, the life of Mao Tse Tung, or the migratory patterns of salmons. It does not mean slowing down to 10 mph and then going forward (although this is apparently the alternate interpretation in California). It does not require you to see it in any larger contexts than the one that the very presence of the sign unequivocally establishes: a vehicle, a driver, an intersection, and the smooth flow of traffic here and now.

A sign is not concerned with subjectivity. In fact, as we will presently see in looking at educational processes in the schools today, there is a war raging to impose the dictatorship of the sign on teachers and students alike; to coopt education properly, humanely, and *democratically* understood and practiced, into mere *training*—the schools a "sorting machine" (Spring, 1976) to fit each student as a cog into the larger social apparatus (Mayes et al., 2019).

As the greatest of all educational historians, Lawrence Cremin, warned in 1988 in his last, magisterial tome, *American Education: The Metropolitan Experience*, the greatest threat to American democracy in the twenty-first century would be the morphing of education into the third person of the totalitarian trinity that Cremin called "the military-industrial-*educational* complex."

To the sign, everything is *object*-ive, meaning everything is an object—or can, at least, be profitably handled as such. It can be measured, manipulated and managed—an objective maxim stated nowhere more straightforwardly or with such sangfroid than in Thorndike's enervating announcement that "That which exists, must exist in some amount and can be measured." A symbol is the opposite of all that.

On becoming a symbol. A symbol is *subject*-ive. Its concern is with the *subject* as she *experiences* herself and others. The symbol expresses and evokes feelings and typically stirs up many of them at the same time, sometimes even contradictory ones, just as it evokes many meanings simultaneously and, again, even contradictorily.

The symbol does not aim at clarity. It aims at completeness. It aims at discovering, deepening, and exclaiming the *moral* mystery of *life*, not listing and systematizing the *mechanical* data of how objects move in *space*—a very important business in its own right to be sure, but existentially less meaningful than the emotional, political, cultural and ethical "spaces" in which we finally, fully live, move, and have our being *as* human beings.

The concrete "entities," *things* in all their *Dinglichkeit* or "Thinginess" (Kant, 1781/1997) that the individual needs to form signs have their solid being and lie all about the infant in Domain 1, and he learns more about them every day in Piaget's Sensori-Motor realm, or the organismic realm as named in this study. The Kleinian dichotomies of tension and passion in their more personal forms and imaginal, indeed fantastical, nature—that which powers poetry—begin to come forth in Domain 2: The Emotional Domain. However, the advent of a mental formation that can *stand for* something else—that can *re*-present it at a later time, with larger and larger lacunae between the original perception of something and a subsequent memory of it—this makes its appearance in the Empirical-Procedural mind of Domain 3.

Later down the roads of Domains 3 through 4, that *signifying* ability to link up an external object with an internal image has begun to crystalize at the outer limits of Domain 4 into a *symbolizing* capacity to generate multiplicities of internal meaning from the occasion of an external object. This ability will come to fruition in Domain 5.

From the perspective of Jungian literary criticism (Snider, 1991; Sugg, 1992), poetry operates under the archetypal aegis of the Feminine Principle in Domain 5, which, as the general headquarters of phenomenology, is the most natural place for poetry to reside (Jung, 1966a). A symbol is the mythically feminine night-bird that dwells in ambiguity and paradox, for it is about life in its greatest depths, where things perforce morph into the misty Incomprehensible. Unlike a sign, which directs and even commands action in a certain mode and in one pragmatic, programmatic direction, the symbol is *non*-programmatic and not infrequently *anti*-programmatic, even to the point of revolution, and on that account Shelley reckoned the poet "the unacknowledged legislator of the world."

The symbol represents a variety, sometimes even a profusion, of alternative images, narratives, motifs, and resolutions that rive us to confusion and despair but also to illumination and hope. A symbol shows us, *challenges us* with psychological, ethical, and spiritual paths to take—paths that it does not so much discover as create by virtue of the generative power of the imagination. The power of the symbol lies not in its power to identify and command but rather to suggest by indirection.

Thus, when Emily Dickinson writes of death (Poem no. 591),

> I heard a fly buzz when I died

she is not, like an ER physician, typing out a death certificate, noting to herself, for no particular rhyme or reason except perhaps a complaint to the janitorial staff about hospital hygiene—about how a fly made a noise at the moment a patient's life-functions ceased and all the monitors went flat. That is simply language as sign, *sign*-ifying an *object*-ive fact. Important, to be sure. Someone died! But as an objective fact, how important is it really?

Creatures die in droves every minute. The corrupting fly reminds us of that. It is a horrifying fact, but horror that is so ubiquitous, so latent in every moment, leaning so suggestively against the stone wall around every corner that we turn, that we *must* normalize it.

If the human being is only a complex organic structure in time-space, and if he will, no matter his longevity, die very soon after he is born, then stark science is right in its minimalism, and the human bring is clinically comprehensible as, in the last analysis, ultimately an object. But that makes him *abject* too, for the only conclusions we can come to about him, the only conclusions *he* can come to about himself, are necessarily *object*-ive, finally.

The poet must mean something more.

That "something more," that surplus of meaning, which branches out into many different emotions and interpretations—and all at once—is not non-factual. It is multidimensional. It does not tell lies. It tells truths that are *beyond fact*, just as one hopes for something *beyond* this life of flies, death, carriages and certificates.

And did she really die at that moment? How could she be writing this poem if she had? Clearly we are now in a *supra-factual world*. We are in that world inside us, or rather the inside-world that *is* us. The objective sign is as mute as a two-by-four about our plight as human beings, our *Geworfenheit*, as (Heidegger, 1965) put it—our "having-been-thrown-ness" without our knowing by whom, why, or (ultimately) where, and (most nagging of all) whereto.

No science in the world, now or in the future, will ever answer the basic ethical questions of our lives. As the old philosophical saw goes: "You can't get to *ought* from *is*." Bertrand Russell, that Parthenon-pillar of mathematical logic, author of "On Denoting" (1905), considered one of the most influential philosophical essays of the twentieth century, Nobel Laureate in literature, and a leading proponent of agnosticism in the twentieth century, cleverly put the point about the unfixable gap between the objective material world and the subjective mental world of ethical values: "What is mind? No matter. What is matter? Never mind."

D5 is the highest level of the evolution of consciousness in classical hierarchic developmental theory. In cultural terms, this psychosocially reflexive turn enables the person to slough off many ethnocentric views. This is thus the phenomenological foundation of much multicultural education, too, which explains its close tie with postmodernism.

The Domain-5 Curriculum: The Phenomenological/Existentialist Curriculum

Eisner (1985) characterizes Existentialist approaches to education as self-actualization curricula. Not surprisingly, it was Maslow himself in a seminal article entitled "Some Educational Implications of the Humanistic Psychologies" (1968) who helped define education as the quasi-therapeutic pursuit of one's unique Existential identity and project:

> If we want to be helpers, counselors, teachers, guides, or psychotherapists, what we must do is to accept the person and help him learn what kind of person he is already. What is his style, what are his aptitudes, what is the person good for, not good for, what can we build upon, what are his good raw materials, his potentialities . . .? Above all, we would care for the child, that is, enjoy him and his growth and his self-actualization. (p. 693)

Maxine Greene (1975), an eloquent American Existentialist educational philosopher of the last century, insisted over four decades ago that curriculum should offer the student the "possibility for him as an existing person, [to make] sense of his own life-world." It should also provide "occasions for ordering the materials of that world, for imposing 'configurations' by means of experiences and perspectives made available for personally conducted cognitive action" (p. 299).

This *phenomenological individualism* underlay a good deal of the Reconceptualist Movement in curriculum theory. *Reconceptualism* was a turning point in curriculum theory that changed it from being an often technical exercise in the nuts-and-bolts of putting a curriculum together to achieve specific ends, on one hand, to viewing the curriculum as something that was made under the pull of a vast array of psychological, cultural, political, philosophical, worldhistorical, and spiritual influences that needed to be surfaced, discussed, and refined, on the other hand (Pinar, 1975).

"I consult the phenomenologists," said Greene (1975) at the outset of Reconceptualism, "for an approach to curriculum in the present day. For one thing, they remind us of what it means for an individual to be present to himself. For another, they suggest to us the origins of significant quests for meaning, origins which ought to be held in mind by those willing to enable students to be themselves" (p. 314). For Greene, art is the best way of achieving self-awareness, in this case literature.

> There must be . . . continual reconstructions [by the student of the piece of literature] if a work of literature is to become meaningful. The structures involved are generated over a period of time, depending upon the

perceptiveness and attentiveness of the reader. The reader, however, does not simply regenerate what the artist intended. His imagination can move him beyond the artist's traces, "to project beyond the words a synthetic form," to constitute a new totality. The autonomy of the art object is sacrificed in this orientation; the reader, conscious of lending his own life to the book, discovers deeper and more complex levels than the level of "significant form." (p. 301)

Because of the Existentialist view of the independent ontological status of a work of art (Handy, 1963), Existentialist curricularists often see art as a means of not only exemplifying authenticity and freedom (i.e., the artist's) but also as a stimulus to help each student discover her own freedom in her unique encounter with that work. It is undoubtedly because of this typical synthesis of humanist psychology and Existentialist aesthetics in Existentialist curricula that Ornstein and Hunkins (1998) called them "Humanist-Aesthetic" curricula.

Postmodern curricula also focus on the radical deconstruction and reconstruction of the self in the ongoing project of freedom. This is Kelly's (2000) ideal of curriculum as a continual process of self and social redefinition. In "Teaching a Post-modern Curriculum," Doll claims that any postmodern curriculum must rest on the idea of the student's "development [as] a continual process of reconstruction, of submitting one's personal and private thoughts to public scrutiny" (1993, p. 42).

Note how in Kelly and Doll, self-definition as existential liberation is closely tied into the idea that authentic self-definition must occur in a social context, not solipsistically. We can only know ourselves as individuals insofar as we negotiate our being with others—just as they, in similar sociophenomenological acts, are negotiating their beings with us. By extension, we are also existentially free to democratically construct our social structures and goals in ways that are most individually and collectively liberatory. It is no surprise, then, that most Existentialist and postmodern curricula have the twin aims of fostering of individual identity, on one hand, and "radical democracy," on the other hand.

This was true of that most liberatory and democratic of pedagogues, Paolo Freire (2001), who in one of his final works, *Pedagogy of Freedom*, concluded that the moral curriculum is the one that most productively interrelates the individual, the dialogical other, and their cultural contexts into rich and freeing conversations:

> In truth, it would be incomprehensible if the awareness that I have of my presence in the world were not, simultaneously, a sign of the impossibility of my absence from the construction of that presence. Insofar as I am a conscious

presence in the world, I cannot hope to escape my responsibility for my action in the world. . . . Of course, this assumption of responsibility does not mean that we are not conditioned genetically, culturally, and socially. It means that we know ourselves to be conditioned but not determined. It means recognizing that History is time filled with possibility and not inexorably determined—that the future is problematic and not already decided, fatalistically. (p. 26)

The fifth domain's stress on self and social deconstruction and reconstruction was also the basis of the teacher reflectivity movement that began almost thirty years ago and continues to thrive (Bullough, 1989; Mayes et al., 2019). For, teacher reflectivity encourages both prospective and practicing teachers to introspect about the biographical and political forces at play in their decision to teach and in how they teach. The purpose of doing so is to "surface" these largely subconscious ideas and images regarding teaching so that, in ongoingly creative acts of revisioning and reconstructing themselves, teachers may now see and practice their craft in a fashion that is more personally, politically, and culturally empowering for themselves and their students (Clandinin and Connelly, 2002; Bullough and Gitlin, 1995; Mayes et al., 2019).

In short, Domain 5 provides rich ground for some of the best statements and practices in Existentialist and postmodern education. As this juncture, consciousness has made linguistic and epistemic leaps which allow it to slough off local perspectives and personal inclinations in favor of a politically and culturally integrative global vision—a *desideratum* of the curriculum in our "Age of Multiculturalism," to which education must attend to be world-historically relevant (Fay, 2000; Gadamer, 1977).

However, the individual can get stuck on any realm, and the fifth landscape is no exception. In this case, the challenge is to push past a potential morass of ethical and epistemological relativism—a potentially crippling consequence of a thoroughgoing deconstruction of all previous perspectives—that makes it difficult to decide on a *purpose* for one's freedom.

For, freedom, to be meaningful, must obviously be freedom in the service of a meaning. It must be freedom-*for* or freedom-*toward*. Otherwise, it becomes freedom in a vacuum. One is then "to freedom condemned" (Sartre, 1960), without either moorings or destination—freedom not for self-creation-in-meaning but self-alienation and even self-indulgence in an axiological vacuum. This would not be a worthy goal for education. It would be personally and socially static—anathema to the dynamism of a robust psyche and culture.

This disorientation is, ironically, also the result of the opposite of education for freedom—namely, colonialist education. By stripping a culture of itself—those sacred narratives that make of culture a collective experience of, responsibilities toward, and enactment of the Divine—colonialist education has precisely the same effect on the individual as a curriculum for freedom but without a larger vision: Disorientation, despair, desuetude of the individual *in* the culture leading to an inevitable falling into disrepair *of* the culture. In that domain whose strength is the relativizing of all perspectives, the threat is the evacuation of any sense of larger purpose to which the individual must connect and commit lest she sink into Gebser's (1985) aperspectival madness.

In other words, the curriculum in the fifth domain must always be transcending itself—pointing the student, by *means* of the curriculum, towards the realization of an "existential project," ontologically rooted and *sub specie aeternitatis*, that goes *beyond* the subject-matter of the curriculum and brings the student *to* herself by pointing her to something beyond herself.

Teaching for transcendence: Life in the Dead Sea. Martin Buber (1985) gives a beautiful example of this in his essay "On Teaching," In it, he speaks of a young substitute teacher entering a classroom full of boys at the beginning of a geography class. The boys are noisy. The teacher predicts they will be a handful. Like many novice substitute teachers, this one is defensive, inclined to let the students know who is boss from the get-go and, in general (the teacher's pedagogy being, for better or worse, inseparable from himself at any given moment in front of a class) to take on an authoritarian identity, to solidify his power in the negative, and

> to say No, to say No to everything rising against him from beneath. . . . And if one starts from beneath one perhaps never arrives above, but everything comes down. But then his eyes meet a face which strikes him. It is not a beautiful face nor particularly intelligent; but it is a real face, or rather, the chaos preceding the cosmos of a real face. On it he reads a question which is something different from the general curiosity. . . . And he, the young teacher, addresses this face. He says nothing very ponderous or important, he puts an ordinary introductory question: "What did you talk about last in geography? The Dead Sea? Well, what about the Dead Sea?" But there was obviously something not quite usual in the question, for the answer he gets is not the ordinary schoolboy answer; the boy begins to *tell a story*. Some months earlier he had stayed for a few hours on the shores of the Dead Sea and it is of this he tells. He adds: "And everything looked to me as if it had been created a day before the rest of creation." Quite unmistakably he had only in this moment made up his mind to talk about it. In the meantime his face has changed. It is no longer quite as chaotic as before. And the class has fallen silent. They all listen. The class, too, is no longer a chaos. Something has happened. The young teacher has started from above. (Buber, 1985, p. 112–113)

When "the relationship between the teacher and student is one of *pure dialogue*" (Buber, 1985, pp. 112–113), classroom discourse is aesthetically and ethically life-giving. It is phenomenological fullness in freedom, but not simply freedom-in-itself, not just liberty in ethical lassitude, unlinked to a purpose, a place holder for a sad or bad nullity. For this is the Domain 5 pathology that may set in after the first rush of deconstruction and relativization empties out onto lack of bearings and the awareness that freedom means choice and choices may be vicious or vacuous if one does not tend to one's freedom with care. Without freedom being *liberty-to* or *in-the-service-of* something substantial and salutary, it degenerates quickly.

Rather, the freedom in Domain 5, to be upbuilding and not ennervating, reveals itself as Presence in the present and a yearning-forward for significance. The curriculum, having now proven itself to have been the occasion for this fleshed-out freedom, the student has grounds to hope that it can do so again. In this manner is the love of learning born. The teacher and student are linked, their dialog enshrined, their relationship secured in this purpose that is mutually-experienced because it was mutually-generated. The curriculum led them to this. They are its creation. Even more profoundly, however, they have made all of this *of* the curriculum, which thus stands forth in *its* manifestation of purpose, as their joint creation.

Something very like this is what McMillan is driving at in her highly generative idea of "a pedagogy of liminality," which she develops in her analysis of the educational implications of Soren Kierkegaard's works. She begins by looking at two quotes from Kierkegaard's *Fear and Trembling*, which she finds particularly relevant educationally:

> What then is education? I had thought it was the curriculum the individual ran through in order to catch up with himself. And anyone who does not want to go through this curriculum will be little helped by being born into the most enlightened age. (Kierkegaard, 2003, p. 75)
>
> In the old days [of Abraham] it was different. For then faith was a task for a whole lifetime, not a skill thought to be acquired in days or even weeks. (Kierkegaard, 2003, p. 42)

McMillan explains:

> The word curriculum is defined as a group of related courses, often in a special field of study. It comes from the Latin word "*currere*, "which means "course" or "to run a course." Kierkegaard invites us to examine two possible meanings for curriculum and education. One view of education is objective,

scientific and instrumentalist. The other approach presented by Kierkegaard is subjective, internal and promoting transformative possibilities within oneself. [T]his does not mean that education cannot have objective means and purposes. It does mean, however, that its primary orientation is the subjective enrichment of the student on her personal journey. (McMillan, 2011)

McMillan's larger argument is that this dimension of consciousness must have a transcendent teleology, if only an embryonic one, for which she finds warrant in Kierkegaard's reliance upon the story of Abraham and Isaac as more than just a rhetorical trope but finally a religious orientation. She does not insist on the Judeo-Christian paradigm of spirituality. She does, however, remind us that education-for-freedom must finally also be education-for or education-toward that which answers to what Huebner has called "the lure of the transcendent." Undoubtedly it is for this reason that Gardner (1999) added "existential intelligence" as the spiritual element in his catalogue of intelligences.

For, insofar as consciousness fuses within Domain 5 and gets caught in the quicksand of aperspectival relativism, it lacks that trajectory toward transcendence that characterizes a holistically adequate purpose. Domain 5 is thus proto-spiritual, as are its educational manifestations, and they point us forward to the most advanced exercises in making and assessing curricula in Domains 6 and 7. In the classroom, discussion of the subject matter is not the culmination of an educative process. It is a wormhole into another universe dialog that goes *beyond* everything that presently *is*. Recalling that the purpose of art at D5 is to *defamiliarize* existence—certainly the existence that we lived in D4 but also that which was discovered now at D5. The student may now come to see herself as the archetypal pilgrim. She sees herself as suddenly standing (and, *Deo concedente*, will ever see herself thus) as standing on perpetual thresholds of unfolding ontological mysteries. She will not rest in the conventionally known, but, at the same time, she will resist any capricious deconstruction of time-honored value. McMillan's pedagogy of liminality is a potent antidote to relativism at the same time as it is the booster-shot to freedom.

"Get a grip on your *Self*." In the many existential territories of Domain 5, one is, to use Jung's terms, actualizing as a self-aware ego but not yet as a post-egoic Self. "Self" is capitalized in Jungian psychology to denote its status as an eternal Center of Being with which one may come into contact as the center of one's own being as well. When that happens, then there is an "axis" that is formed between one's ordinary egoic consciousness and a consecrated consciousness of one's eternal center: "An ego-Self axis" (Edinger, 1985, 1973). It is the establishment of this axis, which Jung calls "individuation," that enables us to be responsibly *in* the world but not finally *of* that world.

Without the mortal ego's subtler, "pneumatic" guidance by the timeless Self as the North Star of a person's pilgrimage—she is left bereft of a sense of and orientation toward that which, in the vast cosmos, goes beyond the insurmountable limitations of mere egoic consciousness. Without that, we find ourselves stuck in this domain, indeed fused to it, and discover to our dismay (particularly poignant as one approaches death) that, however potent and articulated we may be as egos, we have not fully unfolded, are still unfounded, as Selfs, timeless beings for whom death is not really the terminus of the journey but an opening passage to even-more compelling landscapes, ever expanding, on a journey that has no terminus, in dialogue with the Divine that has no end.

When one gets to that breadth, then, although it is not Religion with a big "R," it is nevertheless true enough that it is starting to feel a bit like religion (with a little "r") (Maslow, 1968) because one has: 1) worked one's way to "knowledge" that goes beyond situation-specific "knowledge" in just a particular field of inquiry; 2) probably detached from at least a few conceptual paradigms and groups of people forming around them that a certain slice of one's ego went away with those now dimmed-because-relativized paradigms as people only in an unrecoverable past; and 3) marveled at the sheer scope of what one is beholding now, as if from outer space (astronauts sometimes experience what they describe as religious experiences and even undergo religious conversions as they sit in their capsules at 20,000 miles-per-hour and gasp at the beauty of the planet they are circling) and they thus feel that *mysterium tremendum et fascinans* of which Otto (1958) wrote and which infuses one with "the sense of the holy."

Put these things together and what you have in Domain 5 is not the full trappings and systematic theology of a particular set of beliefs, but you do have (or rather, you do seem to find yourself in) a sort of psychospiritual antechamber of religion. No wonder the ego now gives up at least a bit of the formerly comforting but now mildly irritating force of its grip on you. Concomitantly with going "trans-rational," one is now beginning to go "trans-egoic" too (Wilber, 2000).

Domain 6: The Immanent Domain (Entering the Transpersonal)

A Transpersonal Primer

The movement into the transpersonal *properly* begins and *stably* establishes itself in D6, out of the range of much of the egoic "noise" or aperspectivalism that confounded consciousness at D5 from time to time. At D6 and D7, Immanent Spirituality and Ontological Spirituality, consciousness is less bothered by that noise, for it does not go away, not in this world. For, this world not only *has* this noise. It *is* this noise. Eliot characterized our realm of existence as one in which most of us are, most of the time, "distracted from distraction by distraction" (1945). Monasteries in various faith traditions are where the D6 and D7 consciousness repairs to *be* repaired. They are repair-shops of the soul where the spiritual technologies of prayer and meditation are employed under the signs of silence and service to bring sensitive machinery into line with an exceptionally fine tuning. These institutions usually operate under the sponsorship of a particular faith-tradition.

However, neither transpersonal psychology nor transpersonal curricula require commitment to a specific religious doctrine, yet neither do they exclude it, for they deal with "levels of functioning of human consciousness that are potentially available in all cultures, with widely varying content and context" (Scotton, 1996, p. 4). They are well-suited to our broadly and minutely interconnected twenty-first-century world.

How necessary transpersonal psychology and education is for all of us, really, and especially those whose consciousness is particularly called to these farther reaches of human spiritual potential was stated at the beginning of the transpersonal movement by Abraham Maslow, whose influence in founding the transpersonal psychology and transpersonal education movement was great.

Maslow: The little "r" that could! Abraham Maslow was one of the most important theorists of psychology and education in the 1960s who spoke about the need to frame our educational and psychological endeavors in ways that include but go beyond only personalistic perspectives. Nevertheless, he is still much less known for the impact he had in this transpersonal arena than in his "Hierarchy of Needs" model that is still important as a phenomenological and Existential model for therapy and education.

From the father of self-actualization psychology himself, Abraham Maslow, came the call to aim higher than even the actualized "self" (which is not to be confused with the Jungian Self). Something more than just "the personal" was needed; something "transpersonal" as he called it. Maslow had led the movement for the establishment of an existentially-sound ego—one that had "realized" in thought and action its central, self-defined purpose, its "Existential project," in the full recognition of its own mortality and mortality. Now, he recalibrated his lens to a more distant and more fascinating star.

For in a surprising about-face, what Maslow suddenly understood is that strictly *individual* concerns (let them even be the *post*-rational mind's highest existential goal in "self-actualization" at D5) do not satisfy the heart (which would require the *trans*-rationality of D6). Coming from one of the chief founders of the self-actualization movement of the early 1960s, this assertion of a center in psyche that goes beyond self-actualization was a game-changer. But Maslow now grasped it and lost no time in announcing the message: There is an inherent human need to transcend ego, to forge a link with "the naturalistically transcendent, spiritual, and axiological" (Maslow, 1968, pp. iii–iv).

He called this "religion with a little 'r.'" One experiences it in epiphanic moments. He called them "peak experiences." This would supersede his famous "Hierarchy of Needs" developmental model with "Self-Actualization" at the apex, for which he is still principally known.

Maslow now proclaimed that a complete picture of the human psyche must include not only issues from one's personal history but also acknowledge transpersonal realities that inform both cosmos and psyche (Tarnas, 2006). Maslow publicly speculated in his seminal *Towards a Psychology of Being* that such a new psychology would be "centred in the cosmos" and, without neglecting the personal realm, would go "beyond humanness, identity, self-actualization, and the like." The task of engaging in psychospiritual theorizing and creating psychospiritual therapies in this more advanced domain than the usual Domain 3 to Domain 5 span of other therapies was becoming clear to Maslow. For, "without the transpersonal, we get sick, violent, and nihilistic, or else hopeless and apathetic" (1968, p. iiif).

Maslow must be credited with having made important contributions to featuring the need for a D6 approach to therapy in his final vision of it. Surely he hoped that other therapists might follow suit and lay claim to a more evolved transpersonal narrative for themselves as healers—so that they, similarly sighted, could empower their clients to a more evolved vision, a better story, for themselves and finally to a New Story for the world.

To Seek a Newer World

Picturing our journey so far as a journey by sea, one notes that different passengers—souls with varied and good purposes and potentials—have found themselves at home within different domains. The passenger list has been thinning out at each port-of-call since it sailed, outward bound, from that first small central island, D1.

It started with the child's everyday sensori-motor reality (D1/D2), transitions into new physical procedures (D1/D2/D3), its conceptual transitions (D3/D4) and ideological translations (D4/D5), the building up cognitive grammars (D3/D4), and at D5 the valid but variable imperatives of the Existential (D5). In that domain we found the flowering of aesthetics, the humanities, multiperspectivalism, multiculturalism, and hermeneutics.

We've visited very different ports-of-call in each domain. Each one carries on its lawful business with a fair degree of independence, yet all the islands are finally and firmly united—through the politics of the spirit under a single banner in a vast eternal ocean surrounding a United States of Earth, whose motto is still: *E pluribus unum*.

Our journey so far has been on the great liner *Creative Evolution*, named after the Captain's favorite book by Henri Bergson. The design plans for our liner have been in the making over the course of about 2,500 years by history's great holistic maritime architects, ranging from Lao Tzu to Eliade, Father Chardin to the Buddha.

We now venture into very different waters leading to the sixth island. It is the first truly *oceanic* water we have sounded as we have moved in them so far, and it will be our first time onshore a transpersonal domain.

Here, in the blink of a third-eye, our trek becomes more than a journey and transforms into a pilgrimage because the search for the Divine is never final, *sub specie aeternitatis*, but is always toward the next unfolding horizon.

Here, we move from fascinating points of interest on our journey to something even more compelling—to that *mysterium tremendum et fascinans* which Otto (1958) wrote of—"a tremendous and fascinating mystery." It is the oceanic sweep of the archetypal. It will be found in ever-greater luminosity and meaning as we move through the next domains, D6 and D7.

Paranormal events increase in frequency in D6's waters and on its mystic islands. There is wildlife that we have not seen before. And we note that the citizens of D6 do not merely love nature. We have seen that among the people in every island we have visited. But in the sixth domain there is a *reverence* towards nature—one is tempted to say almost a *worship* of her—an organic mysticism that pervades the perfumed air of the place, where, in the background, we begin to hear a perpetual harmony filling the air everywhere—simple, undulant, transfiguring—sounds we have never heard before, played on incorruptible instruments we have never seen or touched.

The Transcendentalist Movement in America and the Immanentist cause. Such nature mysticism is extraordinarily rich. It found its apotheosis artistically in the American Transcendentalist Movement of the early to mid-19th century. It is exemplified in the Emersonian notion of the Oversoul, the "God Principle," or perhaps even better "the God Presence."

In Ralph Waldo Emerson's work, this Principle and Presence invests every particle of nature in *essence*, while every particle of nature comprises this pantheistic God in *substance*. This renders matter spiritual and spirit material, with no discernible line dividing them.

This matters specially in this present study because the American Holistic Education Movement and American Transcendentalism are linked historically (Cremin, 1980; Forbes, 2003) just as American Romantic literature and American Transcendentalism go hand-in-hand. American Transcendentalism and Unitarianism are also closely related (Ahlstrom, 1972; Marty, 1987, 1970). The Holistic Education Movement is thus integral to American history generally, although little recognized as such.

Sixth Domain Immanentism is also still alive and well in another thoroughly American religious phenomenon in its origin. It was in the first stages of forming in the U.S. Northeast at about the same time as Transcendentalism was, and it now thrives more than ever. It is Mormonism (Bloom, 1992).

Mormonism's "Immanentism," noted by scholars of immanent religiosity, most notably Yale's Sterling Professor of Literature Harold Bloom (1992), is clear in its core principle that spirit and matter exist as the two poles of a continuum and that "There is no such thing as immaterial matter. All spirit is matter, but it is more fine or pure, and can only be discerned by purer eyes; we cannot see it; but when our bodies are purified we shall see that it is all matter" (*The Doctrine and Covenants of the Church of Jesus Christ of Latter-day Saints* 135: 7–8).

Matter is thus spiritual by the Mormon view (which accounts for its strict dietary, hygiene and sexual codes) and all spirit is matter; only, it is supremely refined matter, which can become "unclean" in "immoral" living, a highly charged notion politically that besets the Mormon church from within and without.

In Mormon theology, the glory of divine intelligence is gauged by the degree to which it invests human consciousness in *this* noösphere that *we* inhabit, for "the glory of God is intelligence or, in other words, light and truth" as a key Mormon doctrine goes (*The Doctrine and Covenants* 93: 96).

This sets Mormonism's view of Divinity's intelligence in stark contrast with much of the rest of Christianity, where God's intelligence is seen as so far beyond humanity's feeble reach that it is hopeless for a person to even try to get a sense of it.

And finally, in its triumphally announced precept that "man is spirit, [t]he elements are eternal, and spirit and element, inseparably connected, receive a fullness of joy," the human being becomes the epicenter of God's creative acts (*The Doctrine and Covenants* 93:33). The Immanence of the Divine in the form of the human being. That fact is second in significance only to the Incarnation of Christ in Jesus, a fact, indeed, that is made significant only *by* that Incarnation.

Immanent poetry. Maybe we best honor the immanence of God, the immanence that *is* God in the sixth domain, by letting it speak (or rather, sing) its natural language to us: Poetry. It does it with a fluency that might be an idiom in heaven in talking of even the most ordinary things, perhaps *especially* the most ordinary thing, if heaven is that "condition of complete simplicity / Costing not less than everything" that Eliot (1945) sees in vision at the end of *Four Quartets*. It is a place beyond place (but still involved with our place *here*) and a time beyond time (but still involved with our time *now*), where we will find that

> The end of all our exploring
> Will be to arrive where we started
> And know the place for the first time.
> Through the unknown, unremembered gate
> When the last of earth left to discover
> Is that which was the beginning;
> At the source of the longest river
> The voice of the hidden waterfall
> And the children in the apple-tree
> Not known, because not looked for
> But heard, half-heard, in the stillness
> Between two waves of the sea.
> Quick now, here, now, always—
> A condition of complete simplicity
> (Costing not less than everything)
> And all shall be well and
> All manner of thing shall be well.

Not by any means a nature poet, indeed a self-styled Christian classical one, even Eliot cannot resist, will not resist the allure of the Immanent, the earthly manifestations yet also otherworldly spell of the sixth domain.

We sense this artistic ethos a century earlier, unalloyed, in Emerson's 1847 poem "Each and All," which concludes with the poet recounting how, having lost the sense of the holy spirit of nature for a while, and after a period of dismay at God and man, the Immanent Revelation came to him again, and

> As I spoke, beneath my feet
> The ground-pine curled its pretty wreath,
> Running over the club-moss burrs;
> I inhaled the violet's breath;
> Around me stood the oaks and firs;
> Pine-cones and acorns lay on the ground;
> Over me soared the eternal sky,
> Full of light and of deity;
> Again I saw, again I heard,
> The rolling river, the morning bird;—
> Beauty through my senses stole;
> I yielded myself to the perfect whole.

The poet, in an implicit pun, first notes the reinstated presence of the Immanent beneath his feet, in his soles (soul), indicating both the spiritual intensity of the experience as well as the fact that it begins, must always begin, in the earth itself, for that is where God is manifesting and, from the Immanentist point of view, must always manifest.

At the other extreme is "the eternal sky / Full of light and deity." Of course, we think of a brilliant sky as full of light and *sun*. Another pun may be at play: Sun/Son. There is the implicit connection between the sun in the sky and the Son of God—only, now the Son is not necessary, for the sun itself is all that is needed by way of worshiping, being the most literally brilliant of the instances of Immanence in all of creation from the human perspective: The sun itself as *a god*, not the Son of God as a *man*—that is the eminently Immanentist point of D7 Emerson is top-to-toe filled with the inspiration of Immanence.

And all this happens "as I spoke." The prophetic voice is poetic, and the poetic voice is prophetic; it is God-like, for it brings worlds into being. Nature literally springs into being before his eyes and he, breathing in the violet's breath, is literally *in*-spired. He falls into a religious ecstasy in this moment of realized eschatology, this full presence of God not only *in* nature but *as* nature: "Beauty through my senses stole. / I yielded myself to the perfect whole." We are reminded of Keats' (1819) lines in *Ode on a Grecian Urn*: "Beauty is truth, truth beauty, that is all / Ye know on earth, and all ye need to know."

Indeed, Transcendentalism is allied to Keats' pantheistic "soul-making," as he called what we, at our best, are doing, or could be doing, and really *should* be doing, in this, our interregnum half-existence between two eternities.

The first eternity is the one which, as Plato claimed, we came from to be born into this world, only to fall asleep in forgetfulness in this life, now ignorant of where we came from and who we truly are. And yet, from that sleep, we awake again at death, to be born back into our native eternity, never to go out again, never to be born again, but to live forever in a new simplicity, but a better one than we inhabited in our pre-mortal existence because of what we learned while here.

Blake called this the difference between "innocence," which we lose in this life of "experience," but, paradoxically, become prepared to gain again through the grim mor(t)al rigors of this life, in our second eternity (which is both yet to come yet always potentially here, in the offing now, to the poetic sensibility). And it will come, Blake declares, in the form of an eternally wiser "organized innocence," the omega of the odyssey.

Our sleepwalk-lives here on earth needn't be for naught. We *can* use it for what Keats called "Soul-making." This means to try to awaken here and now, and in those wakened moments of soul-making here, learn and become something better, more suitable for our eternal status as citizens of the Timeless hereafter, when we shall become transfigured beings of "organized innocence."

Keats admits in a famous letter to his brother and sister-in-law on April 21, 1819, that many people call this life "a vale of tears." However, he, in a greater act of poetic imagination and moral courage, chooses to call this life an opportunity to employ our time well (his would be cut outrageously short at twenty-five-years-old) as we moved through this "vale of soul-making." He wrote to George and Georgianna Keats:

> The common cognomen of this world among the misguided and superstitious is "a vale of tears." . . . What a little circumscribe[d] straightened notion! Call the world if you Please "The vale of Soul-making" Then you will find out the use of the world (I am speaking now in the highest terms for human nature admitting it to be immortal which I will here take granted for the purpose of showing a thought which has struck me concerning it). I say "Soul making" Soul as distinguished from an Intelligence.

Like Emerson, after having possibly surrendered to a sense that either there is no heaven or that it is irrelevant to us even if there is, Keats bethinks himself and now insists that we can call parts of heaven back into us while we are here. We can thereby craft our souls, through poetry, into *becoming* poems, and feeling the immanence of eternity, even here and now, in the redeeming paradox of the Immanent worldview. It is *that* Eternity in this moment, in the earth on which we stand, and in her purest manifestation in unsullied nature. And we must note that the soul of which Keats speaks, that *Elan Vital* that breathes eternal life into us, is more than just "an Intelligence." Mere intelligence, the ratiocinations of D3–D5, do not confer the destiny of becoming immortal on the human. However grand, they do not extend that far. It is only the energy and imagery of the transpersonal at D6 and D7 that both fill us with the sense of immortality and then carry us home.

Immanence flows even more directly out of Lord Tennyson's (1863) deceptively simple "Flower in the Crannied Wall," a poem which, although chock-full of questions, still offers the individual a possible answer to the status of his soul. This he finds in the immanence within a root—the organic truth, the holistic truth—truth that is simultaneously physical and metaphorical, truth that he literally holds in his hand.

> Flower in the crannied wall,
> I hold you there, root and all, in my hand,
> Little flower—but if I could understand
> What you are, root and all, and all in all,
> I should know what God and man is.

This is the same root that Dylan Thomas (1937) would both apostrophize and lament a century later in the outcries of a shadowy immanence. For, a cosmic optimism is not the same thing as comic naivety. Dante's Comedy, divine, is not attained until he has passed through that flipside of a holarchy —the rings of hell.

There is no denying the shadowy side of existence. We must frankly acknowledge it in the world and see it in ourselves. If we do not, said Jung from a depth-psychological perspective, we will *project* it on others (Jung, 1967b). There are darker dynamics in every domain. This is a human reality that no mere developmental model can eliminate philosophically or therapeutically. The question here, as in every domain, is: "What do we do with the surplus of darkness that is always with us . . . and even more importantly *within us?*" I address that question in the following discussion of Deep Ecology in its center of operations: the sixth domain.

From the poetical to the ethical: "Deep Ecology." Deep Ecology (Deval, 1985) is a distinctly D6 phenomenon. It justly insists upon its status as an ethical project, and it is quick to clarify that it is only secondarily political. This is its critique of mere "environmentalism," which, from the Deep-Ecological point-of-view, is focused on the social and economic benefits of ecologically sound practices. These are important but they are secondary points, according to Deep Ecology, which accuses "environmentalism" of really being most concerned with only *ancillary* economic benefits to them and society of being ecologically wise, not the deep ethical imperatives about and commitments to nature.

For, even if such benefits did not exist, says Deep Ecology, it would not make it any less pressing to be as ecologically attuned as possible according to Deep Ecology, which sees "environmentalism," despite its *seeming* similarity of commitment, as *actually* being motivated by the economics of ecologically sound practices, not by its ethics.

Even in Eden . . . : Corruption in paradise. The problem with a "merely Environmentalist" position from the Deep-Ecology point of view, is that Environmentalists are still seeing themselves *not* as part of a holarchic system, but, rather, as 1) sitting atop a presumed *hierarchic* natural-order, perfectly empowered, if they please, to subordinate the rungs beneath them (this is a hierarchy-pathology) and also 2) seeing themselves as the latest and therefore the best that evolution, which they see as a value-laden *item-and-process* dynamic, has to offer (an environmentalist process pathology).

Here, on what seems to be the endlessly green fields of the Elysium of Holarchism, there is trouble in paradise because (so the originary Judeo-Christian myth implies) there are ideological limits (the apple tree's "gift" was also fatally limited) to what merely human wisdom and goodness can build, just as clearly as there is the ethical duty to try to do so.

The internecine problem in this particular D6 political tussle boils down to two Integrative critiques of environmentalism, which more generally illustrate how T-Hlc models often outstrip T-Hlc and IP models, the traditional models on which holistic theory so heavily depends, especially in Domain 6. For here in D6, Holistic Theory has built its base of operations (Forbes, 2003). However, it has done so with a naivety that Holistic theory and practice are criticized for—namely, that its faith rests on a charming but overly optimistic hermeneutics of hope with insufficient mixtures of a hermeneutics of suspicion. On the other hand, *Integrative Theory feels equally at home in the hermeneutics of suspicion as well as the hermeneutics of hope. It thus brings not only epistemological benefits but political ones in the service of holistic theory and practice. Integrative Theory not only sees an intradomain conflict (Holistic Theory too often does not), but it has tools for theorizing and acting on these conflicts decisively and muscularly.*

To return to the present issue from an Integrative perspective.

First, an Integrative perspective on the conflict between Deep Ecology and environmentalism argues that Deep Ecology is taking environmentalism to task for Hrc and IP models to establish an ethical superiority over nature that man does not inherently have. As discussed at the outset of this study, the use of Hrc and IP models, even with the best intentions in the world, too easily allows, even subconsciously and psycho-linguistically seduces, the user to believe himself to possess an *ethical* or *existential* superiority that is not real.

In this case, this is, say the Deep Ecologists, what is happening with environmentalists: They find their justification to go on exploiting nature under the cover of caring for her. Nowhere is the danger of Hrc models clearer than here. Holistic Theory, with its 1) excessive reliance upon a hermeneutics of hope, 2) lack of *intra*-category analyses to understand political, cultural, disciplinary, historical, and even ontological tensions within a given taxonomical category (and not terribly finessed analyses at that), and 3) *inter*-category analyses of domains that are usually limited to two categories, miss the complexity and thus lay themselves open to justified critique of their naivety.

This is made all the clearer by the Integrative use of a hermeneutics of suspicion *as well as* a hermeneutic of hope to break down categories into complex systems, not just simple "units." This lends subtlety to the analysis of any situation that Integrative analysis provides in much greater measure than holistic analysis has so far tended to do. The use of an Integrative taxonomy as a third hermeneutic model in Holistic theory—perhaps even its interpretive model of choice—would go a long way in strengthening the Holistic Movement.

From the poetical to the ethical: "Deep Ecology" (continued). To the specific domain under analysis here, the environmental position is, from the deep-ecological vantage-point, corrupted by its 1) unsurfaced prejudice that human beings are superior to other animal life-forms (an idea which Deep Ecology finds abhorrent), and also that environmentalists essentially assume that 2) Capitalism is the best economic system and that environmentalism's *actual* agenda and rationale is that treating the environment well will, in a final financial reckoning, prove itself to be the most monetarily profitable for the individual and society. It's not the double-tablets of the Decalogue that really inspires environmentalists, the Deep Ecologists imply. It's double-entry bookkeeping.

The *secondary*-process outcome of that, according to Deep Ecology, is that the environmentalists offer a set of propositions which seem rational and deeply ecological at a *surface* level, but are, in their emotionally primary "deep-structures" (Chomsky, 1965), their *hot* cognition, their primary processes, heated with a passion and a bias that are not true to what should be the basic ethical commitments of a *truly deep* "deep-ecology." In short, Deep Ecology sees environmentalism as a step in the right direction that ultimately goes off on the wrong foot because, at it core, environmentalism is just the same-old capitalist song-and-dance that landed us in our present ecological crisis in the first place.

In Marxian terms, environmentalism is false consciousness whose *primary* processes are ethically corrupt, which undermines environmentalism's putative ideological purity at a superficial secondary level of discourse because of its *actual* corruption at the *primary* subconscious level.

We cannot psychoanalyze every concept. But we are unwise not to realize that that molten psychic core is always there, in the shape of emotion-and-value laden images and impulses. And we are foolish *not* to examine those and deal with them when it comes to high-stakes decisions, and we are equally foolish not to honor them when it comes to their preeminent status in the creation of art; our interwoven patterning in the tapestry of nature; our trans-rational roles, rights and responsibilities as self-conscious beings *sub specie aeternitatis* against the overwhelming background of the timeless cosmos; and the primacy of poetry in the form of our foundational images in that most primal and transcendent of human things: the commitments of our hearts.

The Domain 6 Curriculum: The Immanent Curriculum
The success of the Holistic Education Press and its journal, *Encounter: Education for Meaning and Social Justice*, along with the appearance of other books in holistic educational theory and practice over the last thirty-five years or so (Mayes, 2005b; Mayes et al., 2016; Miller, 1983; 1991; Moffett, 1994) and most notably Scott Forbes's (2003) definitive study of the theoretical and historical foundations of holistic education over the last four centuries, *Holistic Education: An Analysis of Its Ideas and Nature*—all of these bear witness to the durability of this approach to curriculum theory and practice, which has increasingly turned its attention to how to bring its spiritual yet non-dogmatic framework for education to public as well as private schools.

Moffett (1994), tracing the philosophical genealogy of holistic education from Rousseau, Pestalozzi, and Froebel, through the Transcendentalists, to Montessori, Steiner, and Dewey, and to the Walden, Waldorf, and Montessori schools today, says that the core of this educational philosophy and practice is "an insistence on the total growth of each person—physical, emotional, social, intellectual, and spiritual" (p. 9). Another holistic educational taxonomy these forty years ago called for a "confluent education" in the synthesis of what its author termed the interpersonal, intrapersonal, extra-personal and transpersonal domains (Brown, 1976). Miller and Seller (1985) spoke a decade later of the potential curricular interaction of the behavioral, disciplinary, social, developmental, cognitive, humanistic, and transpersonal domains. I and several others have tried to keep the tradition alive in the twenty-first century in our work.

Despite the differences in these holistic taxonomies of curricula, they are all conspicuously informed by a sixth-circle propensity to think meta-systemically, insisting that the complete consciousness—and, thus, the complete curriculum—must combine all the components of functioning and experience.

But the D6 curriculum takes that next transpersonal step even farther, insisting that such integrative education must be pointing to a spiritual apotheosis in communion with the Emersonian "All." This spiritual expansion from Domain 6 to 7 is absent from the standard curriculum taxonomies such as those offered by Eisner (1985), Posner (1992), Kelly (2000), or Ornstein and Hunkins (1998), all of which extended themselves to fullest at the fifth reach of the Existential/Aesthetic curriculum. Holistic educationists call for us as both theoreticians and practitioners to push beyond these traditional discursive boundaries; for, we live in a world that is interconnected in historically unprecedented ways, and this requires holistic geopolitical thought and action.

> A new educational system with other social services [that rest upon] a thoroughgoing holistic approach, which tends to be spiritual, whether one thinks of it that way or not, because identifying with other people and creatures, and ultimately with the All, really defines spirituality in a nonsectarian way. The more inclusive *the wholes* that individuals dwell in, the holier the society they create together. (Moffett, 1994, p. xix; emphasis added)

Or, as Clark (1991) put it:

> A systemic ecological worldview is now emerging. . . . This new worldview is global, holistic, and integrative. Its primary mode of thinking is whole-brain thought, incorporating both inductive and deductive strategies, while integrating both rational and intuitive modes of knowing. Although it acknowledges that for certain purposes the concept of objectivity is useful, this perspective affirms that, at its most fundamental level, all knowledge and experience is subjective and value-laden. . . . This emerging view acknowledges the importance of science and technology, but holds that these must be understood and applied within the context of a global, ecological perspective. This contextual shift reflects . . . a change in the basic assumptions that have shaped the

purposes, goals, and methodologies of education since the early part of this century. (p. 17)

What is called for, then, says Bajer (2010), is "Ecological Education," which is a lot more than teaching students about the environment (though that's part of it). Rather, ecological education at its core is about is creating systems that reflect the patterns and principals of ecology.

> Why apply ecology to schools? Ecology is the most resilient and stable system known to us. Ecosystems are self-replicating, self-propagating, and self-maintaining. Natural systems increase in complexity and resiliency over time and use resources effectively by cycling them through tens of thousands of interactions. As it turns out, the web of life is a net held together by connections. If I may draw a comparison, an ecological network is not unlike neural connections in the brain or—perhaps more abstractly links within the curriculum, or social networks of our schools and communities. (Bajer, 2010, p. 1)

Here, as we now move properly into the transpersonal domain, let us recall how we got here and just how far we have come; for, the battle for the holistic curriculum has been long and hard, and it is not only far from won but quite at risk in the obsessively technist times into which we have fallen. Perhaps that is why holistic curriculum theories have stuck with such fairly non-problematic, indeed even standard, and therefore, strategically advantageous rubrics as did Miller and Seeler in 1985, when they offered a holistic survey of the the physical, cognitive, psychological, social, emotional, and spiritual domains of teaching and learning. Miller and Seeler, who characterize holistic curricula, as education for transformation, contrast these approaches with the two other, less complete types of curriculum that dominated twentieth-century education and (let us be frank) continue to do so today.

    The first is curriculum as transmission—the conveying of facts and the institutionally imposed standardized assessment of how well the student can recall and reproduce those facts. The second, curriculum as transaction, although markedly better, being dialogically oriented, nevertheless maxes out in assuming and encouraging the relativization of knowledge. Potentially breeding cynicism, D5 curricula are thus a far cry from the ethically more positive spirit of the fully holistic D6 curriculum.

Fortunate indeed are students who have the choice experience of being in one of Rudolf Steiner's Waldorf Schools, which exemplifies the transformative approach to education.

Especially in the earliest years of Waldorf education, but throughout its entire K–12 cycle, it employs art, music, poetry, myths, and world religions as the vehicles through which children ultimately learn the material that children in the public schools do—in addition to a great deal more than the public-school child is ever fortunate enough to encounter. This creates "the imaginative basis for an intellectual understanding" (Trostli, 1991, p. 345).

Waldorf students learn in sequences and paces that are developmentally appropriate, aesthetically stimulating, emotionally supportive, and ecologically connected. A Waldorf site typically has animals in a mini-farm. The children attend to the animals throughout the day. In the farm, some of the classroom lessons are brought home tangibly. The child learns sensorially, affectively, interactively, and always under the pull of an ethical imperative, important ecological facts and practices. The inclusion of such household tasks as baking, sewing, cleaning and repairing also accomplish these purposes as they cultivate educationally unconventional aspects of the student and foster in him a sense of solidarity with people engaged in all sorts of work.

This was the rationale behind Dewey's (1916) advocacy for "vocational education." Deweyan vocational education did not imply—indeed, it was a resistance to—cordoning off some students into vocational education and the privileging of other children in AP classes as essentially a pedagogical means of scholastically legitimating patterns of prejudice and privilege in the larger culture.

Such stratification of students would finally be more for political purposes than pedagogical ones, with the schools reflecting and reproducing the systemic injustice in the larger culture within which the school existed and by which it was sponsored. It would emerge as an invidious and undemocratic scholastic hierarchy that could all too easily be an academic "legitimation" for a deeper political program of the conservative maintenance of an unjust state (Bowles and Gintis, 1976; Kantor, 1979; Willis, 1977).

Dewey's idea was very different. To him vocational education meant that every child should experience work in many professions and in many socioeconomic sites to create a healthy respect in every citizen for what other citizens were doing in helping to maintain a democracy. All students would learn how complex a democracy is and how vital each component of it also is in fulfilling its indispensable role. Dewey's vision of education and democracy was holarchic, not hierarchic.

This brief portrayal of Waldorf education hardly begins to do justice to this truly remarkable system. Hopefully, however, it suggests how, as the Waldorf educator Joan Almon (1999) has said, the Waldorf approach embodies the holistic goal of fostering "living thinking [which] arises when body, soul, and spirit are allowed to interpenetrate and fructify one another" (p. 259).

Finally, this vision of education as transcendence, even education for ecstasy, as Murphy (1975) and Nikola-Lisa (1991) characterized it, is not only for children of school-age years. It is also well suited—and in some current models of development in the second half of life, best suited—to adults in their forties and beyond (Chinen, 1989). For it is becoming increasingly clear that, as Jung often said, the second half of life should be a process of increasing spiritualization of the psyche, a deepening sense of connection to Something or Someone that transcends bodily death. Transpersonal adult-educational theorist V. Quinton Wacks (1987) is right in observing that "full ego- or self-transcendence becomes possible only during the adult and gerontological years.... [B]ecause of life stage or developmental tasks of living, most individuals do not become concerned with such growth needs until the second half of life or later" (p. 52).

Most holistic, later-life education is some variation on the Transcendentalist tenet "that we are all connected in a common humanity and are part of a larger whole" (Wacks, 1987, p. 52). Living in and acting from this sense of universal interconnectedness is the essence of consciousness in the embrace of Ring Six—and the cornerstone of its curricula, which eventuate in the experience of "ineffability, a noetically heightened sense of cosmic clarity, altered perception of space and time, an intuitive grasp of the interconnectedness of all things, and a joyful sense of the ultimate perfection of the universe" (Walsh and Vaughan, 1980, p. 2012).

Domain 7$^{m/d}$: The Ontological Domain

Domain 7 is a combination of two basic approaches to religion that are roughly but probably still accurately enough described in most history of religion texts as *Eastern* and *Western* religion. I will call them Monistic spirituality and Dialogical spirituality, respectively, for reasons that will become clear as we go on.

Not wanting to set one up over the other in this study, I have made them co-regnant in D7. Especially in such fractious times as ours, when what is most needed is more dialogue and less diatribe, more accommodation and less entrenchment, more speaking *to* and less inveighing *against* each other, it is especially important to put both venerable religious traditions on a par.

Besides, it seems reasonable to assume that the most natural place for that ethos of mutual respect to take hold and for those conversations to take place is in interactions involving faith, for faith is where kindness, tolerance, and civility should thrive. If not there, where? It is where seekers-of-Ultimacy in its many forms can embrace the wisdom captured in Ferrer's

(2002) exceedingly lovely image of salvation as an ocean that has many different shores.

And finally, since I believe that Eastern and Western religion are dual expressions of the same Eternal Field/Personal Divinity that one could call the Buddha-Christ, then I must believe we all have much to learn from each other in mutually edifying, mutually honoring discourse that will help us apperceive the Light and live in the Love of that Being-Beyond-Being, that God-Beyond-"God," who seems dual to us but is One.

Such conversations were evidenced in the correspondences between and co-sponsorship of East-West symposia and publications by the Trappist priest and poet Father Thomas Merton and the Zen priest and philosopher Dr. Daisetzu Suzuki (Merton, 1967; Suzuki, 1964). Let us emulate them!

For the Eastern religions, an encounter with Divinity-as-Other with Whom the individual human being is in eternal dialogue is a valuable but penultimate form of spirituality. It is a phenomenological experience but not yet a primary ontological reality, which is absolute yogic inclusion of consciousness in the nameless, formless ground of Being that defies any linguistic categories or mental formations and thus can only be affirmed through negation. I am calling it "monistic" spirituality to highlight its vision of primal unity. It is not absent in the Western tradition.

We find a monistic religiosity in Meister Eckhardt's Being-beyond-Being and St. John of the Cross' *Via Negativa*, where one finds God only through renouncing all previous or current knowledge or experience, for they must inevitably miss the ineffability that is the Divine. It is also the "object" of the Zen *koan*, which, teasing the spiritual student out of thought, opens up an intuitive door through which she has a primal experience of the indescribable ground of all being. Or rather, she does not have an experience at all: She discovers herself in and as the *Ur-Consciousness* that is in all things and in which all things are. This Consciousness is, ultimately, simply consciousness of Itself and is thus "consciousness without an object" (Merrell-Wolff, 1973).

In the *Vipassana* and Zen meditative traditions, this is the observation of one's mental processes and thereby a type of metacognition, which was focused on in Spheres 5 and 6. The purpose of doing so, however, is to observe such processes but let them go as mere mental formations. First, however, they have to have been recognized as mental formations *qua* mental formations in order then to be let go of, as such, from an even more detached position that is observing the observer of the baseline cognitive processes (Hanh, 1987).

From this perspective, *meditation might be reckoned a metacognition of metacognition* to the point of such asymptotic delicacy that it lets go of any claim upon itself and becomes sheer presence: "Consciousness without an object" (Merrell-Wolffe, 1976), a "thinker without a thought" (Epstein, 1995).

It is said that meditation "is good for slowing your thoughts down." That may be true but it begs the question of how this happens. Herein lies a clue.

The clue is that part of the super-lucent effects of meditation, indeed, consciousness *as* super-lucence, may be that consciousness keeps bootstrapping itself to ever-higher self-referential degrees of meta-metacognition, to such a degree that the ego finally grows too attenuated to hold on to—and thus sloughs off like a gossamer web that just landed on your shoulder but in the same moment glances off, almost, it seems, merely because you noted it.

The asymptotic limit is not just *reached*. It is crossed, completing the four-hundred-year project of the calculus and disappearing into an emptiness that is fullness itself. Here perhaps are glances into the *Diamond Sutra's* "Form is emptiness. Emptiness is form." An integrative analysis reveals this sort of interconnection *cum* interpenetration, like a tube within a tube, each growing so "effaced" at each phenomenological step that finally they merge to disappear. Here perhaps is Bion's "O" (1984).

Yet again appears an example of Integrative Theory's wide-ranging but very lightly knit ties that join widely separated domains and that make domains, no matter how far apart from each other, also as close as they could possibly be.

Noble-prize winning physicist David Bohm (1986) in physics and Rupert Sheldrake (1981) in biology have argued for an "implicate order" and "morphic fields," respectively, that, in a post-Newtonian and even post-Einsteinian cosmology, underlie physical reality in a spiritual dimension. Its existence would explain the idea of the immediate communication of subatomic particles at different ends if the universe in physics. It would also support the immediate communication between members of the same species separated by centuries. This would allow for the *epigenetic* evolution of species within the space of just one or two generations. Integrative theory is primed to grow proximate to these mysteries.

The highest spirituality in the monistic mode is identification of individual consciousness (ultimately an illusion) with the One Divine Consciousness (the ultimate reality), which, by definition, is beyond definition. The rising and falling of every element of created existence, from the tiniest mote to the remotest galaxy, presents itself to the liberated consciousness as what it always ways—an image and projection of the eternal Consciousness/Self manifesting itself in and as a cosmic game in which Absolute Consciousness is playing hide-and-seek with Itself in the illusory, or at most merely conditional fields of "existence."

The fundamental error of human consciousness in its pre-liberation mode, and the source of all our pain, is that we mistakenly believe that this cosmic play is real. In so doing, we delude ourselves into thinking that we are separate from the Source of all Being—whereas, in fact, as Hinduism joyfully proclaims in an exclamation of great comfort, "Tat tvam asi," "Thou art That": You *are* the divine, playfully "forgetting" that imperishable fact in your specific mortal individuality.

To awaken from the nightmare of separateness, to grasp that one never was or could be anything but indissolubly one with the Universal Consciousness, to discover that that Consciousness liberated of its noisy lifetime of clamorous contents, its affiliations and aversions, may now rest and find unchaining in it its own focused emptiness—this is the last word in spirituality in the Eastern tradition. All other roads lead up the mountain to this formless peak and empty-fullness.

Monistic spirituality is beautiful and one is wise to attend to it, celebrate it, and, as in the Buddhist vow, take comfort, even refuge from time to time, in this sublime expression of "Buddha-Nature." And to be sure, most current transpersonal education and psychology simply take it for granted that Monistic spirituality is superior to Dialogical spirituality (Boorstein, 1996; Miller, 1994; Reinsmith, 1992; Whitmore, 1986). Domain 7^d is only mentioned—if at all—through the lens of monistic assumptions.

But because it is the assumption of this study that we must see these two forms of religiosity as being on a par, not one above the other, that they are co-regnant in D7. Besides, to reduce dialogical spirituality to simply the step before the highest monistic rung on a phenomenological ladder is to: 1) Fall into the hierarchical and item-and-process power-dynamics that holarchies are meant to avoid and 2) to dismiss the religious convictions of about one-third of the world.

There simply doesn't need to be a conflict here. Monistic and dialogical spirituality can cross-fertilize and enrich each other. Besides, there is always the consideration that at a primary-process level, it is often the case that whether one lends one's allegiance to, say, Judaism over Hinduism, or Christianity over Zen, is ultimately a commitment of the heart and often enough a matter of cultural conditioning, not the result of theologically rigorous analysis.

The only way to negotiate these basic differences/tensions between monistic and dialogical spirituality is for them constantly to be in a dialogue in which both forms of religion are seen as dual inflections of the most evolved forms of psychospiritual development. One may exclusively choose one form of religion over the other, one may choose one but with admixtures of the other, or one may balance the two. The point is that there be dialogue between two equal parties in this matter.

In the dialogue proposed here, it is neither necessary nor desirable to sacrifice one's foundational religious commitments. However, we must genuinely honor those of others in the belief that this conversation will psychospiritually enrich all of the dialogists, no matter what their foundational commitments. Individuals can bring their personal truths "into encounter with one another for purposes of dialogue and debate, conflict and consensus. In this sort of education the individual is honored but so is community, and the two are seen not in opposition but in living paradox" (Palmer, 1990, p. 161).

We can help create the conditions for such a conversation by bifurcating in Domain 7 into one developmental strain that culminates in monistic spirituality and another that results in dialogical spirituality. This fully honors both forms of spiritual commitment without privileging one over the other and allows fruitful interaction between the two. In much of my work, for instance, I have drawn heavily on monistic spirituality as a psychospiritual tool in my research even though my basic commitments are dialogical (Mayes, 2016, 2001, 2000, 1999).

What now follows is an attempt to lay out in curricular terms the two different but harmonious interacting territories that have been terraformed by two different religious traditions—equally lovely and lush, but with different curricular flora and fauna in each.

And over both domains that comprise Domain 7 is the flag of The Buddha-Christ as Embodiment of the One Spirit of Truth.

The Combined Domain 7: The "East-Meets-West" Curriculum/ Curriculum $7^{m/d}$

I (2002) surveyed the literature on teacher reflectivity in order to see if some teachers and teacher educators were producing spiritually related images of themselves and their work and if those images could be categorized. I found that there were various aspects of what I have termed "the teacher as an archetype of spirit."

These aspects divided naturally into four overlapping but nevertheless separate classes: 1) "Discursive spirituality" (embodied in images of the teacher-as-philosopher), 2) "Civic spirituality" (embodied in images of the teacher-as-prophet-of-democracy), 3) "ontological spirituality" (embodied in images of the teacher-as-Zen master/counselor/therapist/mother), and 4) "incarnational spirituality" (embodied in images of the teacher-as-priest or even personal savior).

The teacher-as-Zen-master, on one hand, and the teacher-as-priest, on the other hand, parallel monistic and dialogical spirituality, respectively.

The 7ᵗʰ curriculum: Teacher as Zen Master/curriculum as Presence. Reinsmith (1992) says that the teacher as a monistic Witness/Abiding Presence is the culmination of great teaching. The Zen teacher—so poignantly portrayed in the majestic figure of the Zen archery master in Herrigel's (1971) classic, *Zen in the Art of Archery*—is an absolutely present still-point for the student in his turning world. He is a flawless mirror for the student, reflecting him to himself with such accuracy and authenticity that he can see himself for the first time. But, paradoxically, seeing oneself clearly is to see that one does not really have a self at all.

One discovers instead that one is just a kaleidoscope of shifting phenomenological responses to shifting existential conditions—and that, truth be told, there is ultimately no ontological space between the mental responses and the physical conditions, that they are finally the same thing in the merger of consciousness and its illusory objects. Looking into the mirror of the teacher, therefore, the student discovers that there is no one there: The mirror is empty. The teacher has drawn the novice out of his illusory mental formations into that absolute negation, that pregnant Void, which, paradoxically, is also self-existent Being (Suzuki, 1964). This is the goal of Reinsmith's teacher as witness/abiding presence. Curriculum is the teacher's medium, but the riches of the Great Emptiness are his message.

> Teaching in this sense becomes mysterious; the teacher's "non-doing" paradoxically brings a feeling of fulfillment unlike that in the previous forms. Her "influence" has markedly decreased, yet in another way it is more refined, subtle, unself-conscious. Becoming totally student-centered, the teacher is moving toward a certain egolessness. (Reinsmith, 1992, p. 140)

In "Zen and the Art of Teaching," Tremmel (1993, p. 447) also talks about how monistic pedagogy pays rich relational and reflective dividends. "I am beginning to see that paying attention, not only to what is going on around us but also within us, is not only a necessary step toward mindfulness and Zen, but it is also the better part of reflective practice. For both Zen students and education students, without their paying attention, no skillful action of any kind can occur." O'Reilley (1998, p. 9) has explored the parallels between the teacher as Zen master and the Christian monastic tradition:

> Hospitality calls me to consider the singularity of each person, the diversity of needs. The discipline of presence requires me to be there, with my senses focused on the group at hand, listening rather than thinking about what I'm

going to say—observing the students, the texts, and the sensory world of the classroom. This is harder than sitting zazen. In zazen, nobody talks back to you. Hospitality, by contrast, implies reception of the challenging and unfamiliar: that student with spiked hair who has written on her card, "I'm the one with tattoos all over my body."

The teacher as a counselor and mother—two other images that frequently appear in the teacher-reflectivity literature—are variations on the image of the teacher as Zen master, for their goal is also the student's psychospiritual nurturance and balance (Mayes, 2002, 2001, 1999, 1998).

In American educational history, the notion of the teacher-as-mother was salient in the mid-nineteenth century in the work of Catherine Beecher, Mother Mary Seton, and Emma Willard. The image of counselor/psychotherapist also shaped pedagogies in early twentieth-century Progressivism (Cremin, 1964, Sklar, 1974; Tyack, 1974) and continues to do so (Noddings, 1992, 1995).

Images of the teacher as counselor (Whitmore, 1986) and caretaker (Noddings, 1992) stem from a "relational approach," which is "rooted in the natural relation of mothering, subjective experience, and the uniqueness of human encounters" (Valli, 1990, p. 43). Most transpersonal pedagogy shares this nurturing view of the monistic teleology of teaching (Whitmore, 1986; Roberts, 1985; Roberts and Clark, 1975). This very simple (and very complex) idea of presence to oneself and one's students has, one hopes, led to much more reflective and compassionate practice in the classroom.

The 7^d curriculum: Teacher as priest/curriculum as dialogue. The essential distinction between monistic and dialogical spirituality is that the latter holds that God is ontologically separate from, independent of, and superior to the human being, who, uniquely, is Its child. This is not to say that there is an unbridgeable rift between the Creator and Its children. On the contrary, each dialogical religion has its unique means of reconciling the person to God so that that he may rise to his full stature as a divine individual who may now enjoy eternal relationship with It—the primal and primary and but also timeless and transcendent Other.

The curricular and instructional implications of this radically dialogical spirituality are nowhere more eloquently laid out than in the work of the twentieth-century Jewish ethicist Martin Buber in *I and Thou* (1964) and *Between Man and Man* (1985).

Buber (1985) saw the relationship between the teacher and the student as the essence of education. He insisted that the I-Thou relationship—with its ontological dialogue and psychological intimacy—was the foundation of all morality. It is impossible, Buber argued, to enter into an open relationship with God if, as one of His (Buber's choice of pronouns) children, you abuse His other children by making them objects of your lusts or ambitions in an I-It relationship. This is evil. Crucially and unavoidably, one's personal relationship with God is defined by one's relationship with others.

> The extended lines of relation meet in the eternal Thou: Every particular Thou is a glimpse through to the eternal Thou; by means of every particular Thou, the primary word [which is "I-Thou"] addresses the eternal Thou. Through the mediation of the Thou of all beings, fulfillment, and non-fulfillment, of relations comes to them: The inborn Thou is realized in each relation and consummated in none. (Buber, 1965, p. 129)

In Buber's pedagogy, metaphysically consequential dialogue (which, after all, can only occur between metaphysically distinct persons) ultimately leads to encounter with the Divine Person. It is true, of course, that in all spiritually oriented instruction, either monistic or dialogical, the teacher and student, entering into ever closer relationship, simultaneously move closer to the Timeless. In dialogical modes, however, the purpose of this proximity is ongoing, creative and personal relationship with God as the sovereign, eternal, dialogical Other.

In other words, it is not the dissolution of one's illusory self into an impersonal Whole that is at the heart of the matter. It is the discovery of one's transfigured, deathless self in the light and by the grace of the Divine Person. In what Jung so attractively called "the divine precinct" of authentic personal encounter that the teacher and student may—even in the darkness of temporality—each discover something of the lineaments of their own eternal individuality. This differs radically from the monistic pedagogical aim of helping the student discover his individuality as illusory so that he may merge with (and arguably emerge as) the Ontological Ground.

Monistic pedagogies aim to make the student aware of himself as an eternal and impersonal presence. Monotheistic pedagogies aim to make him aware of himself as an eternal and personal possibility. In the former, "[a] curriculum of transcendence provides a context for engendering, gestating, expecting, and celebrating the moments of singular awareness and of inner illumination when each person comes into the consciousness of his inimitable personal being" (Phenix, 1964, p. 128).

Dialogical spiritual pedagogies are rare in transpersonal educational discourse, but they are not absent. Roman Catholic educational theorist Maria Harris (1991), for example, has written that "[f]rom the attitude of contemplation we discover that the teacher is . . . someone called by, called with, and calling upon the Creator God to save, to perfect, and to manifest the divine image . . ." (p. 125). This echoes Buber's declaration that "the educator who helps to bring man back to his own unity will help to put him again face to face with God" (Buber, 1985, p. 117). By this view, the teacher's true vocation (no matter what the subject-matter) is to galvanize students to their ontological and metaphysical status as individual reflections of the Eternal Individual.

When this theistic project is relationally embodied in dialogical instruction and embedded in curricular choices that focus on subject matter as revelation, then education is religious no matter what the subject matter may be or how strictly secular it may appear.

In the modern liberal Protestant tradition, Yale Divinity School's Duane Huebner (1999), the founder of the Reconceptualist Movement in educational theory and curricularist *non pareil*, wrote about how any curricular content or educational relationship may house the divine. This by no means requires explicitly religious terms, themes or dogmas.

For it is the case, said Huebner, that in all the best teaching and learning, the Spirit is inevitably present: "Hovering always is the absolute 'other,' Spirit, that overwhelms us in moments of awe, terror, tragedy, beauty, and peace. Content is the 'other.' Knowing is the process of being in relationship with that 'other.' Knowledge is an abstraction from that process" (1999, p. 408).

To settle for anything less than this in how we define the goal of education—whatever the subject matter and whatever the site—is to commit a moral and pedagogical mistake, for "[t]he journey of the self is short circuited or derailed by those who define the ends of life and education in less than ultimate terms" (Huebner, 1999, p. 404). One is reminded here of Paul Tillich's famous definition of spirituality as "ultimate concern" (1956).

One is reminded as well of Whitehead's proclamation that "[w]e can be content with no less than the old summary of [the] educational ideal which has been current at any time from the dawn of our civilization. The essence of education is that it be religious" (1964, p. 25). "The lure of the transcendent," mused Huebner, "must be present for education to happen . . ." (1999, p. 363).

Another difference between monistic and dialogical spirituality—and the pedagogies that stem from them—emerges in looking at their teleological metaphors. While the monist ultimately views the cosmos as an illusory game from which we must awaken and detach, dialogical pedagogies see the cosmos as a divine drama and destiny with which we must fully and personally engage. In curriculum and instruction, then, the teacher's essential message, said Buber, must be that "the world is not divine sport, it is divine destiny. There is divine meaning in the life of the world, of man, of human persons, of you and of me" (1965, p. 82).

Envoi from Cliff
An Integrative Pedagogy is both rigorous and compassionate, grounded and transcendent, rational and transrational. It demands a lot of the student but it gives even more in return.

In this, it exemplifies a general fact about rich pedagogy—namely, that it is dialectical. It heeds the transcendental mechanics of Hegel's processes (thesis-antithesis-synthesis) and adopts Jung's transcendent function as its *modus operandi*: To synthesize polarities in a more efficacious and sagacious "Third" that transcends.

Politically, direction can be found the Buddha's Middle Path and Aristotle's Golden Mean. It draws from philosophical-conservatisms and principled progressivisms—a non-dogmatic traditionalism as well as a cautious experimentalism—in search, ever, of that balance that is crucial to a holarchy. It sees holarchies and the Integrative Approach as most consistent with liberal democracy, which it passionately promotes, in almost a mysticism of democracy—although it fears the end of liberal democracy in our time is just around the corner, that a historical *Walpurgisnacht* approaches and that it can be registered on any number of worldhistorical radars.

Yet, ultimately teleologically positive, Integrative Pedagogy will not succumb to quietism or cynicism. For, although it values what a deconstructive hermeneutics has to give and draws upon it, its basic interpretive *élan* and algorithm is a hermeneutics of hope.

Tirelessly introspective to know the *actual meaning* of its own motives, Integrative Educational Theory and Practice is always outward-bound to make that *meaning actual*. Hence, so that the Medieval Catholic alchemist's motto "as above, so below" not render alchemy only an exotic cosmology, Integrative Pedagogy joins in with a contrapuntal motto and *motif*: "As within so without"; thereby judiciously making the subjective objective but never by objectifying the subjective.

Integrative Pedagogy reveres something as simple as a Tennyson's flower in a country wall whose roots contain all in all; at the same, it attends as best it can to the Böhmain super-complexity of a series of integral signs betokening an archetypal field in a fifth dimension.

It honors the Eastern as well as the Western religious canons, although it does not insist on either. It also affirms that one person may prefer one orientation over the other with no harm done and, indeed, always with a great deal to gain from each other in mutually respectful dialogue that is not only pedagogically core but ethically incumbent. It also celebrates the individual who does not especially refer to either orientation but is forging something quite personal, even idiosyncratic.

Finally, Integrative Educational Theory is a vision of educational processes that insists on the sacredness of education in life, and of life as a sacred education. It is the spirit of holistic education given additional tools to carve out ever greater refinements and to carry out ever broader visions in its mission to resist whatever is inhumane and to promote whatever nurtures teachers and students joined in the service and under the sign of that which eternally *is*.

Introducing Professor Martin Kokol
Let us move on at this point to see how a master secondary-school teacher, Dr. Martin Kokol, has put his calling and commitment together in the integrative terms that have been deployed in this book to lay out an Integrative theory of the curriculum.

Marty heartfully shares with us here his exceptionally rich experiences of being a university professor and teacher educator who has returned to the high school classroom to bring to his students what he has learned over these last thirty-five years of his career, and to solidify his own understanding of four decades of commitment and calling in the classroom.

PART C

AN EXERCISE IN INTEGRATIVE TEACHER-REFLECTIVITY

CHAPTER SEVEN

The Commitment and Calling of a Teacher

An Integrative Reflection on His Life as a Teacher by Dr. Martin L. Kokol

Yes, I am aware of my initials. They have inspired me since I was an elementary school student, now at home, taking a breather from practicing the piano, before my father got home from the mill. You see, I was quite aware of the man who was on the TV set in the kitchen that late afternoon. And if there was something deep within me that lasted throughout the decades of my life, it was to offer something meaningful to others so that my life would not just be a happy one, but a purposeful one. As I began my journey into adolescence, teaching my much younger brother (with a blackboard and some chalk) anything he might be interested in that I was learning, playing street hockey with him down in the unfinished basement, and of helping to get things calm in the house via my creative juices flowing on the keyboard.

As an elementary school student, I don't really recall school or any homework—just wanting to help my friend Val learn how to read in second grade, as he lived on a boat in the nearby canal. But, what is apparent to me from this vantage of reflection, is that even at the beginning, even before adolescence, I was being inspired by Dr. King, and then allowing this MLK to teach, to explain, to motivate. The commitment was starting to form. It was my ticket to a healthy relationship. The gift was starting to appear. Twenty years later, the commitment became obvious, as I exploded past a two-year experience that I thought would "get it out of my system," as I found an exciting integration of head AND heart. Thirty years later, as I began my efforts at the university level, the calling became obvious, as I committed to a powerful integration of head, heart, AND spirit. It would be only fifty years later that my body would not be so willing, as I would find out that "the spirit was willing, but the flesh would start to get weak."

What I ask of you is to become comfortable with the developmental stages of a teaching career (Ryan and Kokol, 1990), in which the desire leads to gaining preparation which leads to a core fulfillment leading to commitment —followed to the experiences of hauntingly difficult work, frustration due to many factors, deep questioning that this work should be a life's work (rather than simply a fascinating chapter of one's adult life), and perhaps a U-turn after leaving, resulting in an understood calling.

What I wish to lay out, as this writer ponders his journey, is that the reader do the same, taking on the work of looking more deeply at what it took to arrive at this point in one's life, while taking in the connections to be found between the evolution of the career and the recognition of the journey that developed from the time one was the age of one's current students. Since I asked, let me begin to address this strikingly intriguing parallel.

As an adolescent, I was taught by many competent teachers, but only one outstanding teacher of English. Majoring in history at Princeton, I would be blessed with memorable professors in that field as well as others, at least in so far as their teaching was experienced. So, the first point of reference was that my commitment to teach was laid by my intuitive desire to empower my brother, followed ten years later by watching professionals offer me their best—unraveling the material, making insightful connections across the historical landscape, and performing their theatre so well as to cause me to catch the fever.

If the cultural domain of the integrative system (number 3) set me up to reject not what I was learning, but what I might do with the learning, then it would take me a while to commit to the thought of teaching adolescents. Succeeding at learning was fine, only if . . . Because the world of my parents and almost all of my peers was that of "getting a job in one of those skyscrapers that we could see on the western horizon." For that would prove success—and validate the efforts of my parent's generation, second- and third-generation Americans, with my grandparents coming from either Brooklyn or the Bronx.

And so, this history major was supposed to go to law school. Thus, the honest conversation was impossible to begin—that I MIGHT want to teach. That is, making less money than a garbage man. Culturally, I was dead in the water. (Although I would find out a few years later than I had a grandmother secretly rooting for me.) It would take a couple of extraordinary conversations with a respected woman in the community, a classmate's mother, to invite me to "go for it."

Of course, this leads me to explain "why that age group?" Easy. My life just seven miles southeast of the world of Trump, just twenty miles south east of mid-town Manhattan was, to me, a world of immorality. "Sex, drugs, rock and roll" was our mantra. "Do whatever you want, just don't get caught, and you'll be fine" was the parents'. Deep within me, I knew there had to more to life. To be sure, and to this day, I am one of only a couple of my peers who felt that way. And who saw fit to leave to incorporate more spiritual to the mix. Even if it meant, making less money than a sanitation engineer! Point being, my own adolescence was fraught with achievement, the never ending cycle of success which begot even harder efforts, which triggered more success. And a complete lack of understanding of what I was really striving to learn.

As my budding career unfolded, becoming a high school teacher/coach/adviser/mentor in south Florida, it slowly became apparent that what I was doing was pouring my energies into the lives of the age group that was toughest in my own life—sixteen- to eighteen-year-olds. The mantra was "to save them from the ravages of MTV—and cocaine." I had no idea what they did on weekends. They actually sought to protect me from going anywhere where I could get into any trouble—and so, Coral Gables, South Beach, and certainly Coconut Grove were off-limits!

Interesting how these teenagers (and yes, it is most certainly the other larger half of the paycheck to enjoy strong friendships with some of them thirty plus years later) sought to keep me above board—as they told me they needed me to remain innocent so that could come back knowing I would be there, as Brother Kokol, to them, that they might confess their sins (as they hinted in their own way), but also to know that I was not tarnished, bruised or taken out by the craziness of 1980s Miami. In this sense, I was their priest after soccer practice, and during lunchtime, a bit of their therapist—whether or not they should "turn in their parents" for what I thought only they would be tempted by! Not a bad calling for a late twenty-something—to find meaning in this archetypal image! Teacher as philosopher would have to wait for another era when I would be more fully rounded in the cognitive domain, rather than connections in the physical and emotional worlds.

The commitment to these emerging young adults was the culmination of gainig the education and the experiences I would need to be of help—to go through my own pain, battle my own demons, question my very efforts —so that I might have legitimacy for their adolescence ten to fifteen years after my own. What happened next was an interesting shift, as I would no longer find commitment to the zip code in which I worked, even to the age group I was teaching in the first chapter of my career. It would be toward getting back into learning (I would head north to Cambridge/Boston for two forays at graduate work) so that my teaching (not even knowing where this would all lead me) would be rekindled, refocused, and reframed by my insistence that my attendance once per week to a house of worship was not enough. The commitment morphed into reinvesting in myself. It would require time, some money (although a full scholarship plus stipend certainly helped!), and letting go of knowing what would emerge from this investment. What a surprise awaited me.

To forge a commitment as a teacher, one must soon recognize that, as Parker Palmer reminded all of us in his seminal work *The Courage to Teach* (1997, 2007) we don't teach what we know, but rather who we are. I might add that, across a career, we might even share what we are becoming—and the journey that that requires. Stepping up into higher education, I found that my work as priest and sometimes therapist had to open up to additional roles. Stepping away from all teaching during the stretch of dissertation (and time away to replenish the bank account), I found myself retooling with a new discipline (Secondary Education), focusing not so much on the student, but on the subject.

As I stepped into the world of higher education, where I would teach, supervise, administrate, and read/write/publish, I didn't realize that the commitment was no longer to teaching—but to education—and that I would begin to teach through writing. As a slight extravert, this would be a relatively difficult assignment, but one whereby the discipline was healthy for me. The commitment was now not just to a work, but to a profession. Slowly, almost imperceptively, I found that my career was becoming a calling. Not just because I had become a Latter Day Saint (in an effort to combine the good works of my Jewish roots with the grace of God in my Christian faith), not just because I had moved to Salt Lake City to find a wife (just one, thank you!) and not just because my impressions when I taught were tinged with something larger than my cognitive ability, somewhere deeper than my ability to connect affectively.

I knew from the glorious moments that occurred on occasion that there was another force that was engaging all of us—as teacher and learner were sharing something even more significant than the normal ties that bind. Shared religious convictions certainly connects to the social roles domain (number 4), as the commonality not only reflects well to and from teacher and learner, but also strengthens the clan, those housed in the same theological container through which the content of any lesson could be viewed, experienced, even digested.

One thing was for sure—in this newly understood commitment to education (and to address fully my desire to assist, motivate and inspire those between sixteen and twenty-five)—my work was no longer as a secondary social studies guy. It was far more complex—as I came to understand, now in my forties, that my own life was strengthened with challenges but also fraught with peril at that age. And so, the calling (which I would come to realize, but really not completely accept until recently!) was extended to include not just high school students, but also undergraduates as then masters degree candidates as well. The commitment to education insured that I would make this arc my life's work. The calling occurred each time I tried to walk away from the profession, in order to try my hand at something far more remunerative. And so, not only once but twice in the next decade, I would find myself studying for the Series 7 exam in order to prepare to trade stocks and bonds, to buy puts and calls and naked puts and even understand straddles. But, it was not to be! No matter how much the ghosts of those skyscrapers from my own adolescence wooed me to join up.

Teaching undergraduates at two universities in Utah found my own work arriving into humility and compassion—humbled that I was the newcomer to these zipcodes, that I was the newcomer to this religious view—and in some ways, I was quietly learning from my students. Commitment to a work may be laudable—but I found that the greatest source of my happiness was to learn from them—and what drove them spiritually, many of whom had already "served" for eighteen months to two years—with the hope that they would teach others what it was they believed. And so, this experience, lasting a total of ten years, found me not teaching others how to teach, but sharing with others WHY they would teach in the public schools of Utah and America and what they could offer.

And in case it wasn't clear to me by then that I had learned all that I needed to learn from the successes of being a highly effective teacher, the mother of all mid-life crises hit just when I thought I was settling into fatherhood (with three daughters, aged nine, seven, and five). My life's journey would be interrupted by unfinished business. And like the teen/young adult who was only beginning to unfold their Eriksonian development regarding identity and intimacy, I had some work to do. And it apparently wouldn't wait.

So that I am not personal, bordering on the private, I will simply state that once one bounds into the mire of "calling," there are aspects of one's life that need to be polished—for the work that a calling takes on is, by definition, in need of upgrade, of polish, of completion in the mortal run. Any cracks in the plaster, any fissures in the glass, any unsureties in the foundation from which calling can be fully realized—the work within oneself must go on. Even if it means stepping away for a year or two.

Arriving at Teacher as Philosopher engenders pain and patience. And the beginning of wisdom—for it is as the Jewish tradition states, that the acquisition of wisdom begins somewhere around age forty. For me, it was forty-something. And it didn't come from a book. It came from a broken heart (in my personal life), an overloaded mind (tenure track woes), and a shattered spirit (loss of faith). Fortunately, I lived through it all, an extraordinary emergency room experience non-withstanding. The key is to accept loss, supposed failure, and even having hope challenged to the depths of despair.

Resurfacing in New York City, thanks to family, I found myself learning something really important about this stage of a career—that it is wise, if one hasn't already at fifty, to learn where one comes from before one heads off into the next chapter of life. I knew I had run away from the world I was raised in. That was no secret. "Go West, young man" was my high school English teacher's advice—and I had taken it seriously! So, who were the graduate students I would now teach at this wonderful new assignment? Young men and women (some even in their forties) who were from the city, not the suburbs like myself. Many were second generation Americans—like my father. Most all of them longed to do a good work for their community. I knew what they wanted.

What I could offer was simply some perspective for having travelled and lived west of the Hudson. And so, the entertainer emerged—as I took them on an I-80 tour, far beyond the bounds of New Jersey. Interactive theatre began here. Although when a bunch of young men arrived in my classes in the Spring of 2009, fresh from being fired from Wall Street jobs, I knew that I had to make it worth their while. For you see, I was teaching one block from Wall Street, a three minute walk to the statue of George Washington in front of Federal Hall, a two minute walk from Alexander Hamilton's grave—places that students had not even noticed until I decided that we had the ultimate field trip to take, for this class of Social Studies Education 7–12. It almost felt that I was in heaven. Really.

Alas, it had come to dawn on me from these extraordinarily heterogeneous classes that my efforts were now not just about the "how" of teaching, but of the "why" of teaching. Techniques and technology were not enough now. Intellectual hunger emerged with the economy's demise. What was the purpose of school anyway—at least in New York City? Was it to be the prophet of capitalism? Where was democracy to be found? And how could we find evidence that commitment was more important than ever, as their generation had watched many of their older peers teach for two to five years and then go off to graduate school. Bottom line: how could I help them take on "commitment" when their hearts were telling them to simply get this stint on their resume—and until the economy turned around?

Earlier in this seminal book by Professor Mayes, we find the following comment: "At the center of it all, a teacher and a student, face to face try to teach and learn. It is astonishing that they get anything of educational consequence done in the classroom. But, they do. And that is the miracle of it" (see p. 95 of this book). If we posit for just a moment that education must by definition secure a noteworthy, even a significant, consequence, could we teach this as well? Could our aims to secure a satisfactory outcome for our STEM curriculum, to open to a significant development for our arts, for our foreign languages, even for our sports teams? What would that look like? How would we detail such a success? How would we measure it? Would we need a new vocabulary, not just for the matters of the mind—whereby outcomes could be quantified—but also for habits of the heart—whereby inputs would have to be qualified? How would such an offering be secured? Or even acknowledged? Or even written up? If there is one place I have wanted to secure, if there is one area within education that needs to be tackled head on, at this point of the American journey, I would say it is here in this camp—that I would seek to secure a complete education.

What I propose can be started by offering the following overview. It is a napkin-sketch sized beginning that I use to address the basic areas of our lives that cry out for development:

Arena	*Problem*	*Desire and Cure*
Intellectual	Boredom	To develop career
Emotional	Loneliness	To develop friendship
Physical	Lethargy	To develop core
Spiritual	Emptiness	To develop sensitivity

What we do with it all is of serious import for not only teachers, but for students born in the twenty-first century, as well as for curriculum that shall be written when the time comes for another educational overhaul, going far beyond the call for job training. Finding commitment and even calling to and for a teacher's work is absolutely paramount in this age of ever increasing tensions impacting the work of the teacher. Over the past few years, one can easily find a multiplicity of articles all pointing to the very obvious situation we now face in this country regarding unhappy teachers that have recently been or are currently on strike, a situation that is also compounded by a teacher shortage that has been reported in respected news sources:

A. America has a teacher shortage, and a new study says it's getting worse: *Washington Post*, September 14, 2016
B. Why America's teacher shortage is going to get worse: *NYPost*, February 14, 2018

C. School's back in session, but many teachers aren't returning: *CBS News*, August 23, 2018

D. Teacher shortages worsening in majority of US states: *The Guardian*, September 6, 2018

If the teacher shortage, certainly coming a decade sooner than expected, was simply something to study, I found myself drawn to the world of secondary education as soon as I arrived in Jackson, WY. Given an opportunity to continue teacher full-time and on-line, I repositioned my life in this economically wealthy resort town, after the years teaching and supervising graduate students in New York City's public schools. Meeting with students on Zoom.us was to be done when they got home, after 5pm ET. And so, taking up the advice of one of the most intellectually gifted students I had taught, I visited the HR office of the local school district, with their one middle school, one high school and one alternative high school, and applied to become a substitute teacher. And that was when I found out what commitment might look like within me. For I would no longer be supervising all over New York City, and nor was I a longer a part of the college's administrative team that was preparing for the upcoming accreditation visit. And so, I had ample time to do something new.

Commitment to a new community is an easy decision. Commitment to a school district is simple. But, commitment to a student body and their teachers requires just a bit of reflection—not necessarily about whether or not the students were worth the time and the pay of a substitute teacher—but whether or not this teacher had the right stuff to make a difference, to fill the gaps, to offer something worthwhile. Commitment, then, can be considered a realization of self-worth and an invitation to examine whether I might make enough of a mark to warrant my time. What type of a mark? Simply that I had something to offer, even if it was once a month that I might see a particular student again, or teach the same subject in the same building once again.

My years teaching online would not carry me to the end of a career—something more fundamental was going to occur. It had come time for me to reconnect with adolescents, and actually reconvene with this new generation of "judges" who might see what I have to offer besides twenty-something energy and an Ivy League education—certainly fulfilling to both students and this teacher back when. But, now, was there a good work to be done exactly thirty years later? I was about to be given quite the surprise.

There is something quite interesting that developed those first few months in those three schools. To be sure, I got to be known rather quickly, as I had married a "local," someone whose family was well known by some in the community of 12,000. I quickly came to notice that my presence in a local supermarket, at the playhouse, or at a church was enough of a connection for the students to see me as a "real" person of the community.

Commitment was easy for me. The payoff was not the $104/day (mind you, I was able to sub at least two days/week), but rather the recognition and further curiosity on the part of the students and their parents outside the school building. Of course, this could cut both ways—offering stronger reason for commitment, but also inviting deeper examination for scrutiny. This would most probably play out in any town where anonymity would be practically impossible!

And so once commitment was secured within my own mind and heart, it was meant that I simply deepen the offer—which tends to happen when the work (once it is no longer measured by the economic token of appreciation) takes on far more value to the teacher. Such a feeling of belonging alongside of value adding becomes an instant winner within oneself—and the commitment is secured. But, then, what about calling?

It's one thing for an individual to declare to him/herself that the work they are doing has been "given unto them by God." That would make the calling of a teacher seem secure, with the pronouncement of such a statement. But, there must be some sort of tangible backing to reveal that such a work is not only ordained, but also deeply appreciated, even noted for its aid for members of the community. And thus, it belies even the most religious individual to come up with evidence that one's work has been brought forth with such an imprimatur, that one's efforts can be shown to offer a superior seal of approval by some measure.

That measure, that confidence in the invitation to offer oneself for the benefit of others, lay in the simple and deeply meaningful measure of satisfaction in the students' countenances—for it would not be found in the clarity of one's own voice, no matter how stimulating the lesson might be, but rather in the moment where the teacher realizes that most all faces have drawn strangely still—and that the focus is sharp, quiet, and coming straight on. This is the beauty of the calling—to recognize when connection is being forged at a very significant level. It might last anywhere from ten seconds on up—and its force can only be measured by a simple metaphor of "walking on sacred ground"—the realization that the class is not just listening to the fascinating words coming forth, but is also feeling and allowing the lines of connection that are being offered. For it is then that calling is recognized, with teacher and students now together on a course of deep effectiveness, planting the seeds for future mentoring if wanted, and even hinting at a couple of them awakened to wanting to continue conversations long after the school year, or even the chapter of their adolescence ends.

Calling, then, is not about how secure one can get in the work; it is when this type of connection is built, because one is not engaging only with student's minds, or even with their hearts. For the work of the mind is to secure knowledge. And this has nothing to do with calling. And the work of the heart is to offer understanding. And this is still not to do with calling (but rather a caring compassionate and even outstanding teacher). It is the work of the soul to introduce wisdom, to tap deep into the very being of the youth, adolescent or emerging young adult—that will be an indicator of calling, as it cannot be reproduced by intellectual acumen alone.

This then turns our attention to the education of the teacher—beginning with the years securing license, and my first invitation to look deeply into what is offered—from child and adolescent development, to multiculturalism to courses in special ed right on into student teaching. All very important in their own right. All foundational for successful entry into the classroom. But, this is just the starting point. Within X amount of years, successful mastery of what I call head, heart, social, and management work all must be clearly put into play. But, even with the lane name of Master Teacher, I will venture to say that there is still room for "calling"—the realization by not just students, or even administrators, but by the community itself, that this particular teacher has a gift that cannot be replicated. For it is special to that particular master teacher. For it bespeaks a moment when something both dynamic and foundational has become unearthed. Mind you, this calling is not all about arriving at some magical point in one's career—for I have seen teacher's callings come to an end—one reason being that the calling for doing the work for a particular community comes to an end. (I am currently living that myself at this time.)

But, by and large, the calling of a teacher cannot be quantified, and is only rarely arrived at qualitatively. The way to identify such a level (or rather a depth) or successful pedagogy is to use language of the believer—that something deep within a sensitive and spiritually attuned observer can recognize such a reality, and that something rare is being unearthed. Nowhere is any of this to be found in the work of the professionalization of teacher education —for example, examining the standards of the Council for the Accreditation of Educator Preparation (CAEP), looking at their six recommendations, as quality teacher education continues to center upon "professionalization." (See Educational Renaissance, by Katrina Norfleet (February 19, 2019)— we come up with continued insistence to whip teachers into some kind of level of expertise that would allow observers of the profession to shake their heads in agreement that deadwood, incompetents, and burned-outs would be more easily removed—and thus we are continually haunted by the unsightly spectacle of those that need to leave. But, rarely in my thirty years in public higher and secondary education do I find any reference to the beauty of the profession, rather than the beast—and that is, toward those who shine.

If we cannot fully engage with the identity of those called to teach, it may be best if we step away a bit and come to understand WHY we desperately need those called to teach in our midst. For what they offer, beyond being committed to the work, long after Step 14 offers no pay raises through the years heading toward retirement. (Well, that's Idaho for you.) Leaven for the loaf, as I would say. Knowledge would be the cognitive ingredient in the bread, Understanding would be the affective ingredient. Flatbread would certainly be edible. But, the delight comes when wisdom is added—the spiritual ingredient. The rise comes. Of course, in order to digest properly, water would be needed—and this would come in the form of sociability—for the adult to build connections for the child/adolescent/young adult.

From talking with a few hundred student teachers (as I have supervised them) to novice teachers, it does become obvious that teaching is not an interchangeable part—that ones calling is not just about subject matter, but also about target audience. Second grade teachers, even the most talented, do not make for a wonderful high school teacher. We all know that. I am convinced that the calling has a lot to do with when we ourselves developed through our own difficult times—and that whatever was unfinished in our lifetime (thinking Sternberg's Eight Ages of Man) can very well appear in the calling to teach. The gift is not just for the students—it is also for the teacher—that we might strengthen our own journey by teaching and mentoring others.

But this belies an unusual perspective that I don't believe has been captured from others—and that is that the call to teach might also stem from our own selves, rather than from any force outside of ourselves. We all ourselves because we find that it is indeed our work. That to find the greatest satisfaction in our professional lives, we choose this work. We commit to it. We call ourselves by the name of teacher.

Many years ago, I had what I thought to be a humorous description of my work to many of my peers, now safely entrenched in careers on Wall Street, the law or medicine. What I described was that I had been captured by the nine-month calendar similar to that of conceiving and ultimately birthing a child. And that it was my job to take the one hundred or so under my care and, with a particular type of script as guideposts (for me, it would be studying U.S. history or U.S. government), to deliver them to their next stage of life—perhaps infancy as a soon to be high school senior or as a soon to be emerging young adult as a high school graduate.

I must be clear that this metaphor certainly did not hold up with college students, whom I simply had the pleasure of steering through sixteen-week semesters. But, as a K-12 teacher, regardless of decade (for my work here has been in the 1980s and the 2010s), I was well aware that I had the unique privilege of steering them through, guiding them with and coaching them for the purpose of making it to the next level of growth. My passion, my determination in my entire career has been in the sphere of getting young people to successfully navigate their journey from fourteen to twenty-five, from the rages of the hormones to the completion of the brain functions—and whether I was given one slice of that time for one high school assignment or given another slice of that time with college students (along with novice teachers), I chose it.

Other lifelong friends have chosen end of life care—doctors who work with terminal patients; even others have gone with beginning of life arrival—doctors and nurses attentive to the start. Still others have gone with midlife frustrations—regarding legal, economic, or social matters. I have tried unsuccessfully to leave this work for financial reasons—but within weeks, three times, I came to realize that I was selling myself away, that the value of my work simply did not call for me to abandon it for the pursuit of a larger paycheck. That the original pursuit for happiness, for meaningfulness and for purposefulness was right after all. And that it was only a matter of time before I called myself back.

What was most attractive for me regarding this work? Can it be encapsulated by Sidney Poitier's final scene in *To Sir With Love* (1968), where he rips up the offer from an engineering firm, after a close encounter with a couple of frolicking future students? For this was my first encounter with calling. Or would I turn, for absolute security to the big screen once again with Robin Williams, to the sage on the stage in *Dead Poets Society* (1989) and to a guide on the side in *Good Will Hunting* (1997)? (See Kamenetz, August 12, 2014.) Relationship with the group or relationship with the individual?

What I have learned to be my work is that I see adolescents and emerging young adults as an ends, not as a means to other works. And that technology must be a means. And that even formal curriculum must only be a way to reserve context. And that even instructional strategies simply tease the recipient to open up so that student and teacher might connect. It is simply that human connection remains front and center, above all else.

There is one more piece of the puzzle I wish to mention before we sweep past the notion of calling—and that is the power, the energy, the intelligence that would be requisite for any teacher to utilize their calling for something substantial. What might the fruit of a calling look like, below the evidence of being one of a school's treasures? What might the fuel be to gain success in a calling? I can only remind the reader of Dana Zohar's work out of England right around the turn of the millennium—her book called SQ, that seemed to offer a goldmine, but which, sadly, I did not see catching on in the United States. The field of spiritual intelligence was about to be born, and it was coming perhaps from one intellectually popular source—Steve Covey's Seven Habits of Highly Effective People—a must read now for thirty years. But, it was his eighth habit that somehow didn't catch on, at least beyond the Wasatch Front of Utah. The habit—spiritual intelligence—was (he wrote "the central and most fundamental of all the intelligences, because it becomes the source of guidance for the others." The subtitle was clear: "from effectiveness to greatness."

Now fifteen years old, it would appear that the dominance of Google right around then brushed this hugely important find to the side ("When did Google become the number one search engine?," July 2018). Spiritual intelligence would become the work of the Dala'i Lama. And teaching as calling would slowly recede into the politics of education, with the post-Vietnam generation of teachers firmly in place, with the 2008 recession well on its way to freezing and cutting teacher's pay, and with the slow but steady erosion of seasoned teachers beginning to leave the profession. Indeed, just recently, it was noted that the connection between teaching and calling need to be sharply reexamined (Fenton, August 17, 2016).

For its years in the drivers seat, No Child Left Behind might very well have pushed education to the next level of federal government scrutiny, whereby the urban culture, left brained (how else would we measure anything?), and now much more technologically assessed insistence in having the right answer, was in charge. Calling is about as far away from left-brained measurement as we might fathom. And so, the quandary we now face (as we regain our footing with social/emotional learning) continues to be: "How do we define professionalism?" How could we possibly make room for something like this? Commitment to students could very well be shown with data ranging from amount of time assisting with extra-curricular activities, to creativity of classroom walls. But what shall we offer for calling, except for qualitative data from students, their parents and perhaps a principal—if even that?

One possible avenue for arriving at a teacher's calling might be in the world of mentorship—the continued need for a seasoned or more likely a master teacher to be assigned to the rookie or novice teacher for the express purpose of not only assisting with curriculum development, instructional strategy, local school culture and personal development—but also to offer something that we have really neglected for this work, that being an adult relationship in a sea of childhood or adolescence. If there is one thing that I have seen lacking in my thirty-seven-year career, it is the notion of camaraderie for the express purpose of support.

What would it take for someone designated the "master teacher," not just because of X number of years in the field, and even combined with X number of credits beyond the bachelors or even master's degree? How could we train such a treasure for the school? How might we offer an education—probably in the schools of education, but possibly in a philosophy class—that would invite the soon-to-be master teacher an opportunity to demonstrate what it means to be called, not only for him/herself, but especially for the express purpose of successful mentorship?

Now, suddenly, we have arrived at the precipice whereby we truly need to take on the development of the teacher ladder—something I will do in future writings—so that mentoring can finally secure its rightful place in the work of master teachers, and so that "calling" can finally be included in the developmental stages of a teaching career—something I had pondered over and co-authored over thirty years ago (along with my doctoral adviser Kevin Ryan at Boston University).

The calling of a teacher is really linked to the emotional and the spiritual quotient (and not just the cognitive) that must guide the student. To start, Chinese President Xi Jinping has gone on record and pointed out the primary importance of EQ as "important for adapting to society (although it should be used together with professional knowledge)." Why do I say that they are linked? Because I will venture to say that cognitive downloading is no longer the critical offering of a teacher. Google has replaced that primary drive in many of the traditional secondary school matters—at least as far as the students are concerned. And so, with the continued realization that these Smartphones have transformed this current Generation Z away from human interaction and towards technology, it becomes even that much more important that what the teacher can do to offset this imbalance, what the master teacher can offer to the teen students AND the twenty-something teachers is to reconnect emotionally. And to introduce the fundamental issues, the driving questions that are screaming for attention in this first quarter of the century—the need for the spiritual, as sentiments for matters larger than ourselves must offer.

Why then is mentoring a potential cornerstone of gaining of securing an emotional quotient? Because relationship is the critical ingredient that exists in a successful school—one reads about it all the time in how private schools brag about their community; and one understands, if only intuitively, what it is for the gems of teachers that stay in a welcoming community for a career.

The quality, even the existence of mentoring (and again, this is not to be confused with professional evaluation) between administrator and teacher is the cornerstone of what type of community is being built in each and every school. Whether the school is built on the factory model, meant to churn out product, or whether the school is built on the community model, meant to develop meaningful relationships—and we must not shove the former to represent secondary education, and only allow the latter to be offered in primary education. In a nutshell, how much of school is meant to contribute to capitalism's wants? How much of school is meant to contribute to democracy's needs? And how much of school's efforts are meant to contribute to individual happiness?

We have been seeking such a balance at almost every turn since the rise of the American public school some 120–170 years ago. The implications for K–12 education for 2020 is to balance these fundamental needs: intellectual growth with maturing relationships both interpersonal AND intrapersonal (thank you, Howard Gardner), where the intuitive AND the logical are welcomed. And ultimately, where the rational, the emotional and the spiritual can be found—somewhere along the X axis where man and machine are viewed, somewhere along the Y axis where humanity and divinity are pondered. It is then, and ONLY then, that commitment can be measured—and calling can be ascertained.

For this rising generation, the youth that cannot break from their screens, as for the young adults that might be wondering if they can continue on with this work beyond their novice years, one can only wonder whether or not the exploration of the possibility of being called to teach might help. And thus, we have looked at the possibility of being called—for securing such a confidence might very well continue to be one of the primary antidotes to teacher burnout in this generation. We have wondered from whence the recognition of being called might be ascertained—although the education of the master-teacher-in-the-making is now fraught with important additions for their success. We have connected the matters of the mind with the habits of the heart—and recognize that there is yet the third leg for this teacher and student chair, a leg only hinted at in the daily grind of American public education—the stirrings of the soul.

Of course, in the end, this might be simply too much of a stretch for where we are at our American educational journey. I realize that all this might become the province of the charter schools constructed and yet to be built. Head, heart and spirit. For many might take the third leg and house it simply in the primary religious tradition of the community. But, before we give up, might I offer this: First, using the head, the teacher motivates, the student performs; the result is achievement, satisfying the needs of the state. Second, using the heart, the teacher inspires, the student aspires; the result is dream construction, satisfying the wants of the individual. The intermediate problem here: unlocked precision is crushing; unbridled passion is destructive. The head MUST work in tandem with the heart. Commitment is the satisfaction that these two are now fastened to each other.

If the head and heart work together with the spirit (or, to look at it another way, one's deepest intuition), the calling is the joy that all three are now favorably stretching each other. As Parker Palmer said, We don't teach what we know. We teach who we are. May I add one small addendum: "in the end, we might also teach what we are becoming." If we can arrive here, we are really sharing our journey in the space between our humanity and our divinity—and thus, commitment along with calling now become secure.

References

Abrams, M. H. (1973). *Natural supernaturalism: Tradition and revolution in Romantic literature.* New York: Norton.

Adams, M. (1995). *The multicultural imagination: "Race," color, and the unconscious.* London: Routledge.

Adler, A. (1930). *The education of children.* (Tr. E. Jensen and F. Jensen). South Bend, IN: George Allen and Unwin, Ltd.

Adler, M. (1982). *The paideia proposal: An educational manifesto.* New York: MacMillan.

Ahlstrom, S. (1972). *A religious history of the American people.* New Haven, CT: Yale University Press.

Aichhorn, A. (1990). "The transference." In A. Esman (Ed.), *Essential papers on transference* (pp. 94–109). New York: New York University Press.

Ajaya, S. (1985). *Psychotherapy east and west: A unifying paradigm.* Honesdale, PA: Himalayan International Institute.

Almon, J. (1999). "From cognitive learning to creative thinking." In J. Kane (Ed.), *Education, information, and transformation: Essays on learning and thinking* (pp. 249–269). Columbus, OH: Merrill.

Anderson, R. (1977). "The notion of schemata and the educational enterprise." In R. Anderson, R. Spiro, and W. Montague (Eds.), *Schooling and the acquisition of knowledge* (pp. 415–431). Hillsdale, NJ: Erlbaum.

Anthony, E. (1989). "The psychoanalytic approach to learning theory (with more than a passing reference to Piaget)." In K. Field, B. Cohler, and G. Wool (Eds.), *Learning and Education: Psychoanalytic Perspectives* (pp. 99–126). Madison, CT: International Universities Press, Inc.

Anyon, J. (2001). "Inner cities, affluent suburbs, and unequal educational opportunity." In J. Banks and C. Banks (Eds.), *Multicultural Education: Issues and perspectives* (pp. 85–102). New York: Wiley and Sons.

Appel, S. (1996). *Positioning subjects: Psychoanalysis and critical educational studies.* New York: Garvey.

Apple, M. (1979). *Ideology and curriculum.* London: Routledge and K. Paul.

Aries, P. (1962). *Centuries of childhood: A social history of family life.* New York: Vintage.

Assagioli, R. (1965). *Psychosynthesis: A Manual of Principles and Techniques.* New York: Penguin Group.

The Atlantic. (October 2018). "Is Democracy Dying?" *The Atlantic* 322(3).

Au, K., and Kawakami, A. "Research Currents: Talk Story and Learning to Read." *Language Arts* 62(4) (1985): 406–411.

Augustine, Saint. (2008 ed.). *Confessions.* C. Chadwick (Ed.) (p. xxix). Oxford, UK: Oxford University Press.

Bair, D. (2003). *Jung: A biography.* Boston: Little, Brown.

Bandura, A. (1977). *Social learning theory.* Englewood Cliffs, NJ: Prentice Hall.

Banks, J., and Banks, C. (Eds.). (2002). *Multicultural education: Issues and Perspectives* (4th edition). Boston: Allyn and Bacon.

Barford, D. (Ed.). (2002). *The ship of thought: Essays on psychoanalysis and learning.* London: Karnac Books; New York: Wiley.

Barnes, J. (Ed.). (1997). *The Pre-Socratic philosophers.* London: Routledge; New York: HarperCollins.

Bateson, G. (1972). *Steps to an ecology of mind.* New York: Ballantine Books.

Beck, A., and Weishaar, M (1995). "Cognitive psychotherapy." In R. Corsini and D. Wedding (Eds.), *Current Psychotherapies* (pp. 229–261). Itasca, IL: Peacock Publishers.

Beck, J. (1995). *Cognitive therapy: Basics and beyond.* New York: Guilford Press.

Becker, C. (1966). *The heavenly city of the eighteenth-century philosophers.* New Haven, CT: Yale University Press.

Belenky, M., Clinchy, B., Goldberger, N., and Tarule, J. (1986). *Women's way of knowing.* New York: Basic Books.

Bell, D. (1976). *The cultural contradictions of capitalism.* New York: Basic Books.

Berger, P. (1995). "From the crisis of religion to the crisis of secularity." In S. Bruce (Ed.), *The sociology of religion: vol. 1* (pp. 636–646). Aldershot, UK: The International Library of Critical Writings in Sociology: An Elgar Reference Collection.

Berger, P. (1967). *The sacred canopy: Elements of a sociological theory of religion.* New York: Doubleday and Company.

Berger, P., and Luckman, T. (1963). "Sociology of Religion and Sociology of Knowledge." In S. Bruce. Aldershot (Ed.), *The Sociology of Religion.* Aldershot, UK: The International Library of Critical Writings in Sociology 1: 174–184.

Bergson, H. (1902). *Creative evolution.* New York: Modern Library.

Bernstein, B. (1996). *Pedagogy, symbolic control, and identity: Theory, research, critique.* London: Taylor and Francis.

Best, S., and Kellner, D. (1991). *Postmodern theory*. New York: The Guilford Press.

Bestor, A. (1953). *Educational wastelands: The retreat from learning in our public schools*. Urbana, IL: University of Chicago Press.

Bettelheim, B. (1976). *The uses of enchantment: The meaning and importance of fairy tales*. New York: Random House.

Bion, W. (1984). *Transformations*. London: Karnac Books.

Block, A. (1997) *I'm only bleeding: Education as the practice of social violence against children*. New York: Peter Lang.

Bloom, H. (1992). *The American religion: The emergence of the post-Christian nation*. New York: Simon and Schuster.

Boorstein, S. (Ed.). (1996). *Transpersonal psychotherapy*. Albany, NY: SUNY Press.

Bourdieu, P., and Passeron, J. C. (1990). *Reproduction in education, society and culture*. New York: Oxford University Press.

Bowles, S., and Gintis, H. (1976). *Schooling in capitalist America*. New York: Basic Books.

Britzman, D. (2001). *Freud and Education*. London: Routledge.

Brophy, J. (1994). *Motivating students to learn*. Boston: McGraw-Hill.

Broudy, H., and Palmer, J. (1965). *Exemplars of teaching method*. Chicago: Rand McNally & Company.

Brown, G., Phillips M., and Shapiro, S. (1976). *Getting it all together: Confluent education*. Bloomington, IN: Phi Delta Kappa.

Brubacher, J., and Rudy, W. (1997). *Higher education in transition: A history of American colleges and universities* (4th edition). New Brunswick, NJ: Transaction Publishers.

Bruner, J. (1996). *The culture of education*. Cambridge, MA: Harvard University Press.

Bruner, J. (1960). *The process of education*. New York: Vintage.

Buber, M. (1985). *Between man and man*. New York: Vintage.

Buber, M. (1965). *I and thou*. New York: Vintage.

Buendia, E., and Ares, N. (2006). *Geographies of difference: The social production of the east side, west side, and central city school*. New York: Peter Lang.

Bullough, R., Jr. (2001). *Uncertain lives: Children of hope, teachers of promise*. New York: Teachers College, Columbia University.

Bullough, R., Jr. (1989). *First-year teacher: A case study*. New York: Teachers College Press.

Bullough, R. (1988). *The forgotten dream of American public education*. Ames, IA: Iowa State University Press.

Bullough, R., Jr., and Gitlin, A. (1995). *Becoming a student of teaching: Methodologies for exploring self and school context*. New York: Garland Publishing, Inc.

Burke, K. (1989). *On symbols and society*. J. Gusfield (Ed.). Chicago: University of Chicago Press.

Burroughs, W. (1959). *The naked lunch*. New York: Grove Press.

Campbell, J. 1949. *The hero with a thousand faces*. Princeton, NJ: Princeton University Press.
Carier, C. (1976). "The ethics of a therapeutic man: C. G. Jung." *The Psychoanalytic Review* 3(1): 115–146.
Chardin, T. de. (1975). *The phenomenon of man*. New York: Perennial Library.
Chi, M., Feltovich, P., and Glaser, R. (1981). "Categorization and representation of physics problems by experts and novices." *Cognitive Science* 5: 121–152.
Chinen, A. (1989). *In the ever after: Fairy tales and the second half of life*. Wilmette, IL: Chiron Publications
Chodorow, N. (1978). *The reproduction of mothering: Psychoanalysis and the sociology of gender*. Berkeley, CA: University of California Press.
Chomsky, N. (2006). *Failed states: The abuse of power and the assault on democracy*. New York: Metropolitan Books.
Chomsky, N. (1965). *Aspects of the theory of syntax*. Cambridge, MA: MIT Press.
Cizek, G. (1995). "Crunchy granola and the hegemony of the narrative." *Educational Researcher* 24(2): 26–28.
Clandinin, J., and Connelly, M. (2000). *Narrative inquiry: Experience and story in qualitative research*. San Francisco: Jossey Bass.
Clark, E., Jr. (1991). "The search for a new education paradigm: The implications of new assumptions about thinking and learning." In R. Miller (Ed.), *New directions in education: Selections from Holistic Education Review* (pp. 16–37). Brandon, VT: Holistic Education Press.
Clift, R., Houston, R., and Pugach, M. (Eds.). (1990). *Encouraging reflective practice in education: An analysis of issues and programs*. New York: Teachers College Press.
Cobb, P. (1994). "Where is the mind? Constructivist and sociocultural perspectives on mathematical development." *Educational Researcher*, October 13–20.
Cohler, B. (1989). "Psychoanalysis and education: Motive, meaning, and self." In K. Field, B. Cohler, and G. Wool (Eds.), *Learning and education: Psychoanalytic perspectives* (pp. 11–84). Madison, CT: International Universities Press, Inc.
Comer, R. (1998). *Abnormal psychology* (3rd edition). New York: Freeman Press.
Conger, J., and Galambos, J. (1997). *Adolescence and youth: Psychological development in a changing world*. New York: Longman.
Conner, U. (1996). *Contrastive rhetoric: Cross-cultural aspects of second-language writing*. Cambridge, UK: Cambridge University Press.
Cortright, B. (1997). *Psychotherapy and spirit: Theory and practice in transpersonal psychotherapy*. Albany, NY: State University of New York Press.
Counts, G. (1932). *Dare the school build a new social order?* New York: John Day.
Coward, H. (1985). *Jung and Eastern thought*. Albany, NY: State University of New York Press.
Cremin, L. (1988). *American education: The metropolitan experience: 1876–1980*. New York: Harper and Row.
Cremin, L. (1980). *American education: The national experience: 1783–1876*. New York: Harper and Row.

Cremin, L. (1977). *Traditions of American education*. New York: Basic Books, Inc.
Cremin, L. (1964). *The transformation of the school: Progressivism in American education, 1876–1957*. New York: Vintage Press.
Croce, B. (1953). "The primacy of the symbol." In E. Vivas and M. Krieger (Eds.), *Theories of aesthetics* (pp. 234–256). New York: Reinhart.
Cuban, L. (1993). *How teachers taught: Constancy and change in American classrooms, 1890–1990*. New York: Teachers College Press.
de Unamuno, M. (1954). *The tragic sense of life*. New York: Dover Publications.
Deleuze, G., and Guattari, F. (1987). *A thousand plateaus*. Minneapolis, MN: University of Minnesota Press.
Devall, B. (1985). *Deep ecology*. Salt Lake City, UT: G. M. Smith.
Devine, D. (1995). Prejudice and out-group perception. In A. Tesser (Ed.), *Advanced social psychology* (pp. 467–524). New York: McGraw-Hill.
Dewey, J. (1916). *Democracy and education*. New York: Free Press.
Diekman, H. (1999). *Complexes: Diagnosis and therapy in Analytical Psychology*. Wilmette, IL: Chiron Publications.
Doll, W. (1993). "Teaching a Post-Modern Curriculum." In J. Sears and D. Marshall (Eds.), *Teaching and thinking about curriculum: Critical inquiries* (pp. 39–47). New York: Teachers College Press.
Dusek, J. (1994). *Adolescent development and behavior*. New York: Macmillan.
Edinger, E. (1985). *Anatomy of the psyche: Alchemical symbolism in psychotherapy*. La Salle, IN: Open Court Press.
Edinger, E. (1973). *Ego and archetype: Individuation and the religious function of the psyche*. Baltimore, MD: Penguin Press.
Egan, K., and Nadaner, D. (1988). *Education and imagination*. Stony Stratford, UK: Open University Press.
Eisner, E. (1985). *The educational imagination: On the design and evaluation of school programs*. New York: Macmillan.
Ekstein, R., and Motto, R. (1969). *From learning for love to love of learning: Essays on psychoanalysis and education*. New York: Brunner/Mazel Publishers.
Eliade, M. (1974). *Shamanism: Archaic techniques of ecstasy*. Princeton, NJ: Princeton University Press.
Eliot, T. (1971). *T.S. Eliot: The complete poems and plays: 1909–1950*. New York: Harcourt, Brace and World, Inc.
Epstein, M. (1995). *Thoughts without a thinker: Psychotherapy from a Buddhist perspective*. New York: Basic Books.
Erikson, E. (1980). *Identity and the lifecycle*. New York: W.W. Norton.
Fairbairn, W. R. D. (1992). *Psychoanalytic studies of the personality*. London: Routledge.
Fay, B. (2000). *Contemporary philosophy of social science: A multicultural approach*. Oxford, UK: Blackwell Publishers Ltd.
Fay, B. (1987). *Critical social science: Liberation and its limits*. Ithaca, NY: Cornell University Press.

Fenton, Dylan. (August 17, 2016). "Let's Stop Referring To Teaching As A Calling." *Huffington Post* [https://www.huffingtonpost.com/entry/lets-stop-calling-teaching-a-calling_us_57b48bd4e4b014a587fc02ab].

Ferrer, J. (2002). *Revisioning transpersonal theory: A participatory vision of human spirituality*. Albany, NY: State University of New York Press.

Ferrucci, P. (1982). *What we may be: Techniques for psychological and spiritual growth through psychosynthesis*. Los Angeles: Jeremy P. Tarcher, Inc.

Field, K., Cohler, B., and Wool, G. (Eds.). (1989). *Learning and education: psychoanalytic perspectives*. Madison, CT: International Universities Press, Inc.

Forbes, S. (2003). *Holistic education: An analysis of its nature and ideas*. Brandon, VT: Foundation for Educational Renewal Press.

Foucault, M. (1979). *Discipline and punish*. New York: Vintage Books.

Foucault, M. (1975). *The birth of the clinic*. New York: Vintage Books.

Fowler, J. (1981). *Stages of faith: The psychology of human development and the quest for meaning*. San Francisco: Harper and Row.

Fox, M. (1988). *The coming of the cosmic Christ: The healing of Motr Earth and the birth of a global renaissance*. Boston: Shambala.

Fox, M. A. (2005). *The accessible Hegel*. New York: Prometheus Books.

Freire, P. (2001). *Pedagogy and freedom: Ethics, democracy, and civic courage*. New York: Rowman & Littlefield.

Freire, P. (1970). *The pedagogy of the oppressed*. New York: Seabury Press.

Freud, S. (1923/1960). *The ego and the id*. (Tr. Joan Riviere. Ed. James Strachey). New York: W. W. Norton & Company.

Freud, S. (1915–1917/1970). *A general introduction to psycho-analysis*. (Tr. J. Riviere). New York: Simon and Schuster.

Friedman, T. (2000). *The Lexus and the olive tree*. New York: Anchor Books.

Gadamer, H. G. (1977). "The Western view of the inner experience of time and the limits of thought." In P. Ricoeur (Ed.), *Time and the philosophies* (pp. 33–48). Paris: UNESCO.

Gardner, J. (1999). "Are there additional intelligences? The case for naturalist, spiritual, and existential intelligences." In J. Kane (Ed.), *Education, information, and transformation: Essays on learning and thinking* (pp. 111–131). Columbus, OH: Merrill.

Gebser, J. (1985). *The ever-present origin*. Athens, OH: Ohio University Press.

Gee, J., Michaels, S., and O'Connor, M. (1992). "Discourse analysis." In M. LeCompte, W. Millroy, and J. Preissle (Eds.), *The handbook of qualitative research in education* (pp. 227–291). London: Academic Press.

Gellert, M. (2001). *The fate of America: An inquiry into national character*. Washington, DC: Brassey's, Inc.

Giddens, A. (1991). *Modernity and self-identity: Self and society in the late modern age*. Stanford, CA: Stanford University Press.

Giddens, A. (1990). *The consequences of modernity*. Stanford, CA: Stanford University Press.

Giddens, A. (1986). *A brief but critical introduction to sociology*. New York: Macmillan International.
Gilligan, C. (1982). *In a different voice: Psychological theory and women's development*. Cambridge, MA.: Harvard University Press.
Ginsberg, T., and Huq, A. (2018). *How to save a constitutional democracy*. Chicago: University of Chicago Press.
Girard, R. (1977). *Violence and the sacred*. Baltimore, MD: Johns Hopkins Press.
Giroux, H., and Myrsiades, K. (2001). *Beyond the corporate university: Culture and pedagogy in the new millennium*. Lanham, MD: Rowman & Littlefield.
Glazer, S. (Ed.). (1999). *The heart of learning: Spirituality in education*. New York: Jeremy P. Tarcher.
Goffman, E. (1997). *The Goffman reader*. C. Lemert and A. Branaman (Eds.). London: Blackwell.
Goldbrunner, J. (1965). *Individuation: A study of the depth psychology of Carl Gustav Jung*. Notre Dame, IN: University of Notre Dame Press.
Golomstock, I. (2011). *Totalitarian Art in the Soviet Union, the Third Reich, Fascist Italy and the People's Republic of China*. New York: Random House.
Goodlad, J. (1994). *Educational renewal: Better teachers, better schools*. San Francisco: Jossey-Bass.
Gray, R. (1996). *Archetypal explorations: An integrative approach to human behavior*. London: Routledge.
Greeley, A. (1974). *Unsecular man: The persistence of religion*. New York: Delta Books.
Greene, M. (1975). "Curriculum and consciousness." In W. Pinar (Ed.), *Curriculum theorizing: The reconceptualists* (pp. 299–317). Berkeley, CA: McCutchan Publishing Corporation.
Griffin, D. (1997). *Parapsychology, philosophy, a spirituality: A postmodern exploration*. Albany, NY: State University of New York Press.
Grof, S., and Grof, C. (Eds.). (1989). *Spiritual emergency: When personal transformation becomes a crisis*. Los Angeles: Tarcher.
Gutek, G. (2002). *American education: 1945–2000*. Prospect Heights, IL: Waveland Press.
Habermas, J. (1975). *Legitimation crisis*. Boston: Beacon Press.
Halliday, M. A. K. (2016). *Aspects of language and learning*. Berlin, Germany: Springer.
Hall, G. S. (1904). *Adolescence: Its psychology and its relations to physiology, anthropology, sociology, sex, crime, religion and education*. New York: Appleton Press.
Handy, W. (1963). *Kant and the Southern new critics*. Austin, TX: University of Texas Press.
Hanh, T. N. (1997). *Living Buddha, Living Christ*. Los Angeles: Riverhead Trade.
Hanh, T. N. (1987). *The miracle of mindfulness: A manual on meditation*. Boston: Beacon Press.
Harding, E. (1963). *Psychic energy: Its source and its transformation*. New York: Putnam Publishing.

Harris, M. (1991). *Teaching and religious imagination: An essay in the theology of teaching.* San Francisco: Harper Collins.
Hartshorne, C. (1984). *Omnipotence and other theological mistakes.* Albany, NY: State University of New York Press.
Hartung, C., and Widiger, T. A. (May 1998). "Gender differences in the diagnosis of mental disorders: conclusions and controversies of the DSM-IV." *Psychological Bulletin* 123 (3): 260–78
Hayek, F. (1944). *The road to serfdom.* Chicago: University of Chicago Press.
Heath, S. (1983). *Ways with words: Language, life, and work in communities and classrooms.* Cambridge, UK: Cambridge University Press.
Heidegger, M. (1964). *Being and time.* E. Robinson (Trans.). New York: Harper and Row.
Henderson, J. (2000). "The inner vision and social organization." In T. Singer (Ed.), *The vision thing: Myth, politics, and psyche in the world.* London: Routledge.
Hendricks, G., and Fadiman, J. (Eds.). (1976). *Transpersonal education: A curriculum for feeling and being.* Englewood Cliffs, NJ: Prentice-Hall, Inc.
Herberg, W. (1954). *Protestant, Catholic, Jew: An essay in American religious sociology.* New York: Doubleday.
Hergenhahn, B. (2006). *An introduction to the history of psychology.* New York: Cengage Learning.
Herrigel, E. (1971). *Zen and the art of archery.* New York: Vintage Book.
Hillman, J. (2004). *Archetypal psychology.* Putnam, CT: Spring Publication.
Hillman, J. (1990). *We've had a hundred years of psychotherapy—and the world's getting worse.* San Francisco, CA: HarperSanFrancisco.
Hobbes, T. (1651/2010). *Leviathan: Or the Matter, Forme, and Power of a Common-Wealth Ecclesiasticall and Civill,* Ian Shapiro (Ed.). New Haven, CT: Yale University Press.
Hoeller, S. (1982). *The Gnostic Jung and The Seven Sermons to the Dead.* Wheaton, IL: Theosophical Publishing House.
Homans, P. (1995). *Jung in context: Modernity and the making of a psychology.* Chicago: University of Chicago Press.
Huebner, D. (1999). *The lure of the transcendent: Collected essays by Dwayne E. Huebner.* V. Hillis (Ed.). London: Lawrence Erlbaum Associates.
Huxley, A. (1996). "The perennial philosophy." In R. Walsh and F. Vaughan (Eds.), *Paths beyond ego: The transpersonal vision* (pp. 212–213). Los Angeles, CA: Jeremy P. Tarcher.
Hyde, J. (September 2005). "The Gender Similarities Hypothesis." *American Psychologist* 60(6): 581–592.
Jasers, K. (1935/1996). *Reason and existenz.* Milwaukee, WI: Marquette University Press.
Jaynes, J. (2000). *The origin of consciousness in the breakdown of the bicameral mind.* New York: Houghton Mifflin.
Johnston, W. (1971). *Christian Zen.* New York: Harper and Row.

Johnstone, R. (1997). *Religion in society: A sociology of religion*. Upper Saddle River, NJ: Prentice-Hall.

Jones, M., Jones, B., and Hargrove, T. (2003). *The unintended consequences of high-stakes testing*. Lanham, MD: Rowman & Littlefield.

Jones, R. (2001). *Jung, psychology and postmodernism*. London: Routledge.

Joseph, P., and Burnaford, G. (1994). *Images of schoolteachers in twentieth-century America: Paragons, polarities, complexities*. New York: St. Martin's Press.

Jung, C. G. (1971). *Psychological types* (R. F. C. Hull, Trans.). (Volume 6 in the Collected Works). Princeton, NJ: Princeton University Press.

Jung, C. G. (1970). *Mysterium coniunctionis* (R. F. C. Hull, Trans.). (Volume 14 in the Collected Works). Princeton, NJ: Princeton University Press.

Jung, C. G. (1969a) *Aion: Researches into the phenomenology of the self* (R. F. C.Hull, Trans.). (Volume 9.2 in the Collected Works). Princeton, NJ: Princeton University Press.

Jung, C. G. (1969b). *The structure and dynamics of the psyche* (R. F. C. Hull, Trans.). Volume 8 in the Collected Works). Princeton, NJ: Princeton University Press.

Jung, C. G. (1967). *Two essays on analytical psychology* (Volume 7 in the Collected Works). (R. F. C. Hull, Trans.). Princeton, NJ: Princeton University Press.

Jung, C. G. (1954a). *The development of personality: Papers on child psychology, education, and related subjects* (R. F. C. Hull, Trans.). (Volume 17 in the Collected Works). Princeton, NJ: Princeton University Press.

Jung, C. G. (1954b). *The practice of psychotherapy: Essays on the psychology of the transference and other subjects* (R. F. C. Hull, Trans.). (Volume 16 in the Collected Works). Princeton, NJ: Princeton University Press.Kalsched, D. (1997). *The inner world of trauma: Archetypal defenses of the personal spirit*. London: Routledge.

Kamenetz, Anya. (August 12, 2014). "What Robin Williams Taught Us About Teaching." *NPR* [https://www.npr.org/sections/ed/2014/08/12/339735740/what-robin-williams-taught-us-about-teaching]?t=1572884578988].

Kane, J. (Ed.). (1999). *Education, information, and transformation*. Columbus, OH: Merrill/Prentice Hall.

Kant, I. (1781/1997). *The critique of pure reason*. Chicago: Hackett Publishing.

Kantor, H. (1979). "The great school warriors." *Social Policy* (1979, March–April): 54–58.

Kawai, H. (1996). *Buddhism and the art of psychotherapy*. College Station, TX: Texas A&M University Press.

Kelly, G. (1955). *The psychology of personal constructs*. New York: Norton.

Kesey, K. (1962). *One flew over the Cuckoo's nest*. New York: Signet Press.

Kliebard, H. (1986). *The struggle for the American curriculum: 1893–1958*. New York: Routledge.

Koestler, A. (1969). *The ghost in the machine*. New York: Macmillan.

Kniker, C. (1990). "Teacher Education and Religion: The role of foundations courses in preparing students to teach about religions." *Religion and Public Education* (17) 2: 203–222.

Kohlberg, L. (1979). "The meaning and measurement of moral development." Clark Lectures: Clark University.

Kohut, H. (1978). *The search for the self: Selected writings of Heinz Kohut, 1950–1978.* Madison, CT: International Universities Press.

Kohlberg, L. (1987). *Child psychology and childhood education: A cognitive-developmental view.* New York: Longman.

Krashen, S. (2003). *Explorations in language acquisition and use: the Taipei lectures.* Portsmouth, NH: Heinemann.

Kristeva, J. (1989). *Language—the unknown: An invitation to linguistics.* New York: Columbia University Press.

Kuhn, T. (1970). *The structure of scientific revolutions.* Chicago: University of Chicago Press.

Lacan, J. (1977). *Ecrits.* New York: Norton.

Laing, R. D. (1969). *The politics of experience.* New York: Ballantine Books.

Lakoff, G. (1987). *Women, fire, and dangerous things: What categories reveal about the human mind.* Chicago: University of Chicago Press.

Lakoff, G. (1981). *Metaphors we live by.* Chicago: University of Chicago Press.

Lasch, C. (1995). *The revolt of the elites and the betrayal of democracy.* New York: Norton.

Lickona, T. (1991). *Educating for character: How our schools can teach respect and responsibility.* New York: Bantam.

Linde, C. (1993). *Life stories: The creation of coherence.* New York: Oxford University Press.

Lipman, M. (1988). *Philosophy goes to school.* Philadelphia, PA: Temple University Press.

Lippa, Richard A. (2005). *Gender, nature, and nurture* (2nd edition). Mahwah, NJ: Erlbaum.

Lowe, M., and Yasuhara, Y. (2013). "The origins of higher learning: time for a new historiography?" In Mordecai Feingold, *History of Universities.* Oxford: Oxford University Press 27(1): 1–19.

Macias, J. (1987). "The hidden curriculum of Papago teachers: American Indian strategies for mitigating cultural discontinuity in early schooling." In G. Spindler and L. Spindler (Eds.), *Interpretive ethnography of education: At home and abroad* (pp. 363–380). London: Lawrence Erlbaum and Associates.

MacIntyre, A. (1981). *After virtue: A study in moral theory.* Chicago: University of Chicago Press.

MacLeod, J. (1987). *Ain't no makin' it: Leveled aspirations in a low-income neighborhood.* Boulder, CO: Westview Press.

Mailer, N. (1972). *Existential errands.* New York: Little, Brown.

Marty, M. (1987). *Religion and republic: The American circumstance.* Boston: Beacon Press

Marty, M. (1970). *Righteous empire: The Protestant experience in America.* New York: The Dial Press.

Maslow, A. (1968). *Toward a psychology of being* (2nd edition). Princeton, NJ: D. Van Nostrand.

May, R., and Yalom, I. (1995). "Existential psychotherapy." In R. Corsini and D. Wedding (Eds.), *Current psychotherapies* (pp. 262–292). Itasca, IL: F. E. Peacock Publishers.

Mayes, C. (2020, in press). *Archetype, culture, and the individual in education: The three narratives of teaching and learning*. London: Routledge.

Mayes, C. (2017a). *An introduction to The Collected Works of C.G. Jung: Psyche as spirit*. Lanham, MD: Rowman & Littlefield.

Mayes, C. (2017b). *Teaching and Learning for Wholeness: The role of archetypes in educational processes*. Lanham, MD: Rowman & Littlefield.

Mayes, C. (2017c). "Art as Individuation, individuation as art." *Quadrant: Journal of the C.G. Jung Society for Analytical Psychology* 46(2): 69–81.

Mayes, C. (2017d). "Jung's view of the symbol and the sign in education." *Psychological Perspectives: A Semi-Annual Journal of Jungian Thought* 59(2): 191–201.

Mayes, C. (2016). *Understanding the whole student: Holistic multicultural education*. Lanham, MD: Rowman & Littlefield.

Mayes, C. (2015). *The archetypal hero's journey in teaching and learning: A study in Jungian pedagogy*. Madison, WI: Atwood Educational Press.

Mayes, C. (2012). *Inside education: Depth Psychology in teaching and learning*. Madison, WI: Atwood Publishing.

Mayes, C. (2009a). "The psychoanalysts' view of teaching and learning: 1922–2002." *The Journal of Curriculum Studies* 40(2): 121–143.

Mayes, C. (August, 2009b). "Rhizome and the Curriculum: A Jungian Critique of Current Educational Reform." A paper presented at the Annual Conference of The Society of Jungian Studies at Cornell University. Ithaca, NY.

Mayes, C. (2005a). *Jung and education: Elements of an archetypal pedagogy*. Lanham, MD: Rowman & Littlefield.

Mayes, C. (2005b). *Seven curricular landscapes: An approach to the holistic curriculum*. Lanham, MD: University Press of America.

Mayes, C. (2005c). "Teaching and time: Foundations of a temporal pedagogy." *Teaching Education Quarterly* 32(2): 143–160.

Mayes, C. (2004). *Teaching mysteries: Foundations of a spiritual pedagogy*. Lanham, MD: University Press of America.

Mayes, C. (2002). "The teacher as an archetype of spirit." *Journal of Curriculum Studies* 34(6): 699–718.

Mayes, C. (2001). A transpersonal model for teacher reflectivity. *Journal of Curriculum Studies*, 35(2), 56–70.

Mayes, C. (1999). Reflecting on the archetypes of teaching. *Teaching Education* 10 (2): 3–16.

Mayes, C. (1998). "The use of contemplative practices in teacher education." *Encounter: Education for Meaning and Social Justice* 11(3): 17–31.

Mayes, C. (March, 1997). "Some contradictions of the postmodern curriculum." A paper presented at the American Educational Research Association. Chicago, IL.
Mayes, C., Grandstaff, M., and Fidyk, A. (2019). *Reclaiming the fire: Depth Psychology in teacher renewal*. Lanham, MD: Rowman & Littlefield.
Mayes, C., Cutri, R., Goslin, N., and Montero, F. (2016). *Understanding the whole student: Holistic multicultural education* (2nds edition). Lanham, MD: Rowman & Littlefield.
Mayes, C., and Williams, E. (2010). *Nurturing the whole student: Five dimensions of the curriculum*. Lanham, MD: Rowman & Littlefield.
McNiece, G. (1969). *Shelley and the revolutionary idea*. Cambridge, MA: Harvard University Press.
Merleau-Ponty, M. (2012). *The phenomenology of perception*. London: Routledge.
Merrell-Wolffe, F. (1973). *The philosophy of consciousness without an object: Reflections on the nature of transcendental consciousness*. New York: Julian Press.
Merton, T. (1967). *Mystics and Zen masters*. New York: Dell Publishing Co.
Messerli, J. (1976). *Horace Mann: A biography*. Cambridge, MA: Harvard University Press.
Miller, J. (1994). *The contemplative practitioner: Meditation in education and the professions*. London: Bergin & Garvey.
Miller, J. (1988). *The holistic curriculum*. Toronto, Ontario: The Ontario Institute for Studies in Education.
Miller, J. (1983). *The educational spectrum: Orientations to curriculum*. New York: Longman.
Miller, J., and Seeler, W. (1985). *Curriculum: Perspectives and practices*. New York: Longman.
Mocanin, R. (1986). *Jung's psychology and Tibetan Buddhism: Western and Eastern paths to the heart*. London: Wisdom Publications.
Moe, T., & Cubb, J. (2009). *Liberating learning: Technology, politics and the future of American education*. San Francisco: Jossey Bass.
Moffett, J. (1994). *The universal schoolhouse: Spiritual awakening through education*. San Francisco, CA: Jossey-Bass Publishers.
Morrow, R., and Torres, C. (1995). *Social theory and education: A critique of theories of social and cultural reproduction*. Albany, NY: State University of New York Press.
Murphy, M. (1975). "Education for transcendence." In T. Roberts (Ed.), *Four psychologies applied to education: Freudian, behavioral, humanistic, transpersonal* (pp. 438–447). New York: John Wiley and Sons.
Niebuhr, R. (1986). *The essential Reinhold Niebuhr: Selected essays and addresses*. R. Brown (Ed.). New Haven, CT: Yale University Press.
Nieto, S. (2002). *Language, culture, and teaching: Critical perspectives for a new century*. Mahwah, NJ: Lawrence Erlbaum Associates.
Nieto, S. (2000). *Affirming diversity: The sociopolitical context of multicultural education*. New York: Longman.

Nikola-Lisa, W. (1991). "On the education of wonder and ecstasy." In R. Miller (Ed.), *New directions in education: Selections from Holistic Education Review* (pp. 256–261). Brandon, VT: Holistic Education Press.

Noddings, N. (1999). "Stories and conversations in schools." In J. Kane (Ed.), *Education, information, and transformation: Essays on learning and thinking* (pp. 319–336). Columbus, OH: Merrill.

Noddings, N. (1995). "Care and moral education." In W. Kohli (Ed.), *Critical conversations in the philosophy of education* (pp. 137–148). New York: Routledge.

Noddings, N. (1992). *The challenge to care in schools: An alternative approach to education*. New York: Teachers College Press.

Nord, W. (1995). *Religion and American education: Rethinking a national dilemma*. Chapel Hill, NC: University of North Carolina Press.

Novak, J. (1990). "Concept maps and Vee diagrams: Two metacognitive tools to facilitate meaningful learning." *Instructional Science* 19: 29–52.

Nozick, R. (1994). *Anarchy, state and utopia*. Chicago: University of Chicago Press

Nussbaum, J. (1985). "The Earth as a Cosmic Body." In R. Driver, E. Guesne, and A. Tiberghein (Eds.), *Children's Ideas in Science*. Philadelphia, PA: Open University Press.

O'Reilley, M. (1998). *Radical presence: Teaching as a contemplative activity*. Portsmouth, NH: Boynton/Cook Publishers.

Ornstein, A., and Hunkins, F. (1998). *Curriculum: Foundations, principles, and issues*. Boston: Allynand Bacon.

Otto, R. (1958). *The idea of the holy*. New York: Oxford University Press.

Pagels, E. (1992). *The Gnostic Paul: Gnostic exegeses of the Pauline letters*. Philadelphia, PA: Trinity Press International.

Paglia, C. (1992). *Sex, art and American Culture: Essays*. New York: Vintage.

Pai, Y., and Adler, S. (2001). *Cultural foundations of education* (3rd edition). New York: Merrill, Prentice Hall.

Pajak, E., and Blase, J. (1989). "The impact of teachers' personal lives on professional role enactment: A qualitative analysis." *American Educational Research Journal* 26(2): 283–310.

Palmer, P. (1998). *The courage to teach: Exploring the inner landscape of a teacher's life*. San Francisco: Jossey-Bass Publishers.

Palmer, P. (1990). "'All the way down': A spirituality of public life." In P. Palmer, B. Wheeler, and J. Fowler (Eds.), *Caring for the commonweal: Education for religious and public life*. Macon, GA: Mercer University Press.

Parsons, T. (1951). *The social system*. New York: Free Press.

Patton, M. Q. (2002). *Qualitative research and evaluation methods*. Thousand Oaks, CA: Sage Publications.

Phenix, P. (1974). "Transcendence and the curriculum." In E. Eisner and E. Vallance (Eds.), *Conflicting conceptions of curriculum*. Berkeley, CA: McCutchan Publishing Corporation.

Phenix, P. (1964). *Realms of meaning: A philosophy of the curriculum for general education.* New York: McGraw-Hill.
Piaget, J. (1966). *The moral judgment of the child.* New York: Free Press.
Pinar, W. (Ed). (1998). *Curriculum: Toward new identities.* New York: Garland.
Pintrich, P., Marx, R., and Boyle, R. (1993). "Beyond cold conceptual change: The role of motivationalbeliefs and classroom contextual factors in the process of conceptual change." *Review of Educational Research,* 63: 167–199.
Plato. (1997). *The dialogues of Plato.* New Haven, CT: Yale University Press.
Polkinghorne, D. (1988). *Narrative knowing in the human sciences.* Albany, NY: State University of New York Press.
Posner, G. (1992). *Analyzing the curriculum.* New York: McGraw Hill.
Rama, S., Ballentine, R., and Ajaya, S. (1976). *Yoga and psychotherapy: The evolution of consciousness.* New Honesdale, PA: Kanzeon Press.
Rand, A. (1957). *Atlas shrugged.* New York: Random House.
Ravitch, D. (2000). *Left back: A century of failed school reforms.* New York: Simon and Schuster.
Ravitch, D. (1983). *The troubled crusade: American education, 1945–1980.* New York: Basic Books.
Rawls, J. (1971). *A theory of justice.* Cambridge, MA: Harvard University Press.
Reagan, T. (2003). *Non-western indigenous traditions: Indigenous approaches to education thought and practice.* Mahwah, NJ: Lawrence Erlbaum Associates.
Reinsmith, W. (1992). *Archetypal forms in teaching: A continuum.* New York: Greenwood Press.
Renfrew, C. (1984). *Approaches to social anthropology.* Edinburgh, UK: Edinburgh University Press.
Rickover, H. (1960). *Education and freedom.* New York: E. P. Dutton and Co.
Ricoeur, P. (1985). *Time and narrative.* Chicago: University of Chicago Press.
Ricoeur, P. (1991). *Freud and philosophy: An essay in interpretation.* New Haven, CT: Yale University Press.
Rieff, P. (1987). *The Triumph of the Therapeutic: Uses of Faith after Freud.* Chicago: University of Chicago Press.
Rieff, P. (1961) *Freud: The Mind of the Moralist.* Garden City, NY: Doubleday and Company.
Riegel, K. (1979). *Foundations of dialectical psychology.* New York: Academic Press.
Riordan, C. (1997). *Equality and achievement: An introduction to the sociology of education.* New York: Longman.
Roberts, T. (1985). "States of consciousness: A new intellectual direction, a new teacher education direction." *Journal of Teacher Education* 36(2): 55–59.
Roberts, T., and Clark, F. (1975). *Transpersonal psychology in education.* Bloomington, IN: The Phi Delta Kappa Educational Foundation.
Rogoff, B. (1990). *Apprenticeship in thinking: Cognitive development inn social context.* New York: Oxford University Press.

Rorty, R. (1992). *The linguistic turn: Essays in philosophical method*. Chicago: University of Chicago Press.
Rousseau, J. J. (1762/1979). *Emile, or on Education*. Trans. Allan Bloom. New York: Basic Books.
Rowland, S. (2005). *Jung as a writer*. London: Routledge.
Rummelhart, D. (1980). "Schemata: The building blocks of cognition." In R. Spiro, B. Bruce, and W. Brewer (Eds.), *Theoretical issues in reading comprehension* (pp. 125–167). Hillside, NJ: Lawrence Erlbaum Associates.
Rury, J. (1989). "Who became teachers?: The social characteristics of teachers in American history." In D. Warren (Ed.), *American teachers: Histories of a profession at work* (pp. 9–48). New York: Macmillan.
Russell, B. (October 1905). "On Denoting," *Mind*, New Series, 14(56): 479–493.
Salinger, J. D. (1951). *The catcher in the rye*. New York: Little, Brown and Company.
Salzberger-Wittenberg, I. (1989). *The emotional experience of learning and teaching*. London: Routledge and Kegan Paul.
Samuels, A. (1997). *Jung and the post-Jungians*. London: Routledge.
Samuels, A. (Ed.). (1992). *Psychopathology: Contemporary Jungian Perspectives*. New York: Guildford Press.
San Roque, C. (2000). "Arresting Orestes: Mythic events and the law." In T. Singer (Ed.), *Myth, politics, and psyche in the world* (pp. 105–121). London: Routledge.
Sardello, R., and Sanders, C. (1999). "Care of the senses: A neglected dimension of education." In J. Kane (Ed.), *Education, information and transformation: Essays on learning and thinking* (pp. 226–237). Columbus, OH: Merrill/Prentice Hall.
Sartre, J. P. (1960). *To freedom condemned*. New York: Philosophical Library.
Sartre, J. P. (1956). *Being and nothingness: An essay on phenomenological ontology*. New York: Philosophical Library.
Satir, V. (1967). *Conjoint family therapy: A guide to theory and technique*. Palo Alto, CA: Science and Behavior Books.
Schön, D. (1987). *Educating the reflective practitioner*. San Francisco, CA: Jossey-Bass Publishers.
Schopenhauer, A. (1819/2008). *The world as will and presentation*, trans. Richard E. Aquila in collaboration with David Carus. New York: Longman.
Schutz, W. (1976). Education and the body. In G. Hendricks and J. Fadiman (Eds.), *Transpersonal education: A curriculum for feeling and being* (pp. 104–110). Englewood Cliffs, NJ: Prentice-Hall.
Scotton, B., Chinen, A., and Battista, J. (Eds.). (1996). *Textbook of transpersonal psychiatry and psychology*. New York: Basic Books.
Segal, R. (1995). *The allure of Gnosticism: the Gnostic experience in Jungian psychology and contemporary culture*. Chicago: Open Court.
Selman, R. (1980). *The growth of interpersonal understanding: Developmental and clinical analyses*. New York: Academic Press.
Sendak, M. (1963). *Where the wild things are*. New York: Harper and Row.
Shamdasani, S. (2005). *Jung stripped bare by his biographers, even*. London: Karnac.

Shamdasani, S. (2003). *Jung and the making of modern psychology: The dream of a science*. Cambridge, UK: Cambridge University Press.
Singer, T. (Ed.). (2000). *The vision thing: Myth, politics and psyche in the world*. London: Routledge
Skinner, B. (1968). *The technology of teaching*. Englewood Cliffs, NJ: Prentice Hall.
Sklar, K. (1973). *Catherine Beecher: A study in American domesticity*. New Haven, CT: Yale University Press.
Smith, M. (1949). *And madly teach: A layman looks at public education*. Chicago: H. Regnery Co.
Smuts, J. (1926/1961). *Holism and evolution*. New York: Compass/Viking Press.
Snider, C. (1991). *The stuff that dreams are made on: A Jungian interpretation of literature*. Wilmette, IL: Chiron Publications.
Sovatsky, S. (1998). *Words from the soul: Time, East/West spirituality, and the psychotherapeutic narrative*. Albany, NY: State University of New York Press.
Spiegelman, J. M., and Mansfeld, V. (1996). "On the physics and psychology of the transference as an interactive field." In J. Spiegelman (Ed.), *Psychotherapy as a mutual process* (pp. 183–206). Tempe, AZ: New Falcon Publications.
Spiegelman, J. M., and Mokusen, M. (1984). *Buddhism and Jungian psychology*. Tempe, AZ: New Falcon Publications.
Spiegelman, J. M., and Vasavada, U. (1987). *Hinduism and Jungian psychology*. Tempe, AZ: New Falcon Publications.
Spindler, G., and Spindler, L. (1992). "Cultural process and ethnography: An anthropological perspective." In M. LeCompte, W. Millroy, and J. Preissle (Eds.), *The handbook of qualitative in education* (pp. 52–92). London: Academic Press.
Spring, J. (2000). *The intersection of cultures: Multicultural education in the United States and the global economy*. New York: McGraw Hill.
Spring, J. (1976). *The sorting machine: National educational policy since 1945*. New York: David McKay Co., Inc.
Steinbeck, J. (1986). *The grapes of wrath*. New York: Viking.
Sugg, R. (Ed.). (1992). *Jungian literary criticism*. Evanston, IL: Northwestern University Press.
Suzuki, D. T. (1964). *An introduction to Zen Buddhism*. New York: Grove Press, Inc.
Swatos, W., Jr. (Ed.). (1987). *Religious sociology: Interfaces and boundaries*. New York: Greenwood Press.
Taba, H. (1962). *Curriculum development: Theory and practice*. New York: Harcourt, Brace and World.
Tarnas, R. (2006). *Cosmos and psyche: Intimations of a new world view*. New York: Viking.
Tillich, P. (1959). *Theology of culture*. New York: Oxford University Press.
Tillich, P. (1956). *The essential Tillich*. New York: Macmillan Publishing Co.
Tomkins, S. (1979). "Script Theory: Differential Magnification of Affects." In Richard A. Deinstbier (Ed.), *Nebraska Symposium on Motivation*. Lincoln, NE: University of Nebraska Press.

Tremmel, R. 1993. "Zen and the art of reflective practice in teacher education." *Harvard Educational Journal* 63(4): 434–458.

Tyack, D. (1974). *The one best system: A history of American urban education.* Cambridge, MA: Harvard University Press.

Tyler, R. (1950). *Basic principles of curriculum and instruction.* Chicago: University of Chicago Press.

Tyson, L. (2006). *Critical theory today: A user-friendly guide.* New York and London: Routledge.

Underhill, E. (1961). *Mysticism: A study in the nature and development of man's spiritual consciousness.* New York: E.P. Dutton.

Valli, L. (1990). "Moral approaches to reflective practice." In R. Clift, W. Houston and M. Pugach (Eds.), *Encouraging reflective practice in education: An analysis of issues and programs* (pp. 39–56). New York: Teachers College Press.

Violas, P. (1978). *Training of the urban working class: A history of twentieth-century American education.* Chicago: Rand McNally

Veysey, L. (1969). "Toward a new direction in educational history: Prospect and retrospect." *History of Education Quarterly*, Fall: 343–359.

Wacks, V., Jr. (1987). "A case for self-transcendence as a purpose of adult education." *Adult Education Quarterly* 38(1): 46–55.

Wade, J. (2001). *Changes of mind: A holonomic theory of the evolution of consciousness.* Albany, NY: State University of New York Press.

Walsh, R., and F. Vaughan (Eds.). (1980). *Paths beyond ego: The transpersonal vision.* Los Angeles, CA: Jeremy P. Tarcher.

Washburne, M. (1994). *Transpersonal psychology in psychoanalytic perspective.* Albany, NY: State University of New York Press.

Watras, J. (2002). *The foundations of educational curriculum and diversity: 1565 to the present.* Boston: Allyn and Bacon.

Watson, L., and Watson-Franke, B. M. (1985). *Interpreting life histories.* New Brunswick, NJ: Rutgers University Press.

Wax, M., Wax, R., and Dumont, R., Jr. (1964). *Formal education in an American Indian community: Peer society and the failure of minority education.* Prospect Heights, IL: Waveland Press.

Weber, M. (1905/2002). *The Protestant ethic and the spirit of capitalism.* London: Routledge.

Weckowicz, T. (February 1989). *Ludwig von Bertalanffy (1901–1972): A Pioneer of General Systems Theory Center for Systems Research Working Paper No. 89–2.* Edmonton, AB: University of Alberta.

Wexler, P. (1996). *Holy sparks: Social theory, education and religion.* New York: St. Martin's Press.

"When did Google become the number one search engine?" (July 2018). *Quora* [https://www.quora.com/When-did-Google-become-the-number-one-search-engine].

White, M., and Epston, D. (1990). *Narrative means to therapeutic ends.* New York: W.W. Norton.

Whitehead, A. (1964). *The aims of education: And other essays.* New York: New American Library.

Whitmore, D. (1986). *Psychosynthesis in education: A guide to the joy of learning.* Rochester, VT: Destiny Books.

Wilber, K. (2000). *Integral psychology: Consciousness, spirit, psychology, therapy.* London: Shambhala.

Wilber, K. (1999). *Sex, ecology, spirituality: The spirit of evolution.* Boston: Shambhala.

Wilber, K. (1996). *A brief history of everything.* Boston: Shambhala.

Wilber, K. (1993). "The great chain of being." *Journal of Humanistic Psychology* 33(3): 52–65.

Wilber, K. (1983). *A sociable god: A brief introduction to a transcendental sociology.* New York: McGraw-Hill Book Company.

Wilber, K. (1980). *The Atman project: A transpersonal view of human development.* Wheaton, IL: Theosophical Publishing House.

Willis, G., Schubert, W., Bullough, R. Jr., Kridel, C., and Holton, J. (1994). *The American curriculum: A documentary history.* London: Praeger.

Willis, P. (1977). *Learning to labour.* Aldershot: Gower.

Wilson, W. J. (1987). *The truly disadvantaged: The inner city, the underclass, and public policy.* Chicago: University of Chicago Press.

Winnicott, D. W. (1992). *Psychoanalytic explorations.* C. Winnicott, R. Shepherd, and M. Davis (Eds.). Cambridge, MA: Harvard University Press.

Wittgenstein, L. (1953). *Philosophical investigations.* New York: MacMillan.

Wrightsman, L. (1994). *Adult personality development: Theories and concepts.* Thousand Oaks, CA: Sage Publications.

Yutang, L. (1949). *The Wisdom of Lao Tzu.* New York: Modern Library.

Zachry, C. (1940). *Emotion and conduct in adolescence. For the Commission on Secondary School Curriculum.* New York: Appleton-Century.

Index

2001: A Space Odyssey:
  HAL as metaphor of limits of "cold cognition," 117
ADHD:
  the new morbidity, 66; psychotropic medication, the use of on children, 67
Adler, Alfred, 69–70; *The Paideia Proposal*, 99
Adler, Mortimer, 99
adult education, 27
Age of Multiculturalism:
  twenty-first century as, 128
agency, 11, 26, 39, 101
Aichhorn, August, 60–61
Anglo-Germanic rhetorical patterns, 15–16.
  See also rhetorical patterns, Asian, contrasted with other patterns, Latin, Semitic
aperspectival madness, 11, 108
Apple, Michael, 30
Archetypal Forms in Teaching, 152
archetype(s), 18; morality as an, 18

the Aristotelian curriculum, 99
Arnold, Matthew, 40
Assagiolli, Roberto, 75

bad faith/good faith:
  Existentialist meaning of, 108–9
Bajer, Dustin, 145
Bateson, Gregory:
  double-bind, the schizogenic, 20
the Bauhaus Movement, 30
Beck, Aaron and Judith, 78–81
Beecher, Catherine, 94
Behaviorism, 50
Being and Nothingness, 106
Berger, Peter, 18
Bergson, Henri, 40, 135
Bettelheim, Bruno, 107; *The Uses of Enchantment*, 107
binaries, 19
Bion, Wilfred, 149; Bion's "O," 149
The Birth of the Clinic, 82
Blake, William, 139; Innocence, Experience, and Organized Innocence, 139

Block, Alan, 34, 67; education as the practice of social violence against children, 34
Bloom, Harold, 136
the body:
as curriculum, 47–48;
"body-subjects" (Merleau-Ponty), 51
Bohm, David, 149
Book of Mormon:
Mosiah, 2, 17
Bourdieu, Pierre, 71
Bruner, Jerome, 100
Buber, Martin, 19, 129–30, 153–56; "dialogical partnering" as ethical touchstone, 115; *I and Thou*, 19; "On Teaching," 129
the Buddha-Christ, 11
Buddha Nature, 150
Buddhistic spirituality, xviii; monistic, xviii
Bullough, Robert, 33

The Cardinal Principles of Secondary Education of 1918, 49–50
caritas, 29
Cash, Johnny, 77
catastrophizing, 96
The Catcher in the Rye, 74
Cathy Orte,ga's Private Vietnam, 83–87
Chardin, Pierre Teilhard de, 40, 101
"cheap grace," 109
Christianity and Buddhism in dialogue, 150
Chuangtse, 33
civic spirituality, 151–52
civil war, structural roots of, 21
Cognitive Therapy, 77–79
cold cognition, 75–76, 91–92
Comenius, John Amos, 48
complexes, 57:
as feeling-toned psychic clusters, 57;
origin of thought, as, 58
concepts:
the "imaginative basis" of "intellectual understanding," 146;
scientific, 119; secondary processes, as, 5, 28, 31, 55, 59, 77; varied pre- and trans-conceptual components of, 104
conceptual change theory, 4
consensual reality, 70, 91
Conservatism, 20–23
Coolidge, President Calvin, 94:
"The business of America is business," 94
Coriat, Isador H., 60
the corporate university, 88
Creative Evolution. See Bergson, Henri
credentialism, 88–90
Cremin, Lawrence, 33, 95, 97
Critical Social Science, 51
Croce, Bendetto, 122
cynicism:
avoidance of in educational processes with children, 107

The Dx2 Disadvantage, 38
Dante, 140
Dasein:
being-towards-death, 39
defamiliarization, education as, 131
democracy, xv, 10, 12, 20–22, 33, 54, 94–95, 98, 104–7, 111–16, 127, 146, 151, 156, 166, 175
despair:
danger of fusing at D5, 108
developmental models, 25–28; Erikson's model, 39; Freud's model, 25; holarchic solutions for problems in, 28–33; holistic solutions for problems in, 28; Jung's model, 27; Kohlberg's model, 27; non-Western, 100; Piaget's model, 26
devolution, 38–39

Dewey, John, xv, 6–7, 34–35, 38, 146
The Diagnostic and Statistical Manual of the American Psychological Association, 81–82
dialectic/dialectical tension, 12; crucial in democracy, 12
dialogical spirituality, xvii–xix, 147, 151–52.
See also monistic spirituality
dialogue, xvii; breakdown of, 19–20; central to democracy, 19
The Diamond Sutra, 149
Dickinson, Emily, 81; "Because I Could Not Stop for Death," 81; "I Heard a Fly Buzz When I Died," 124
Dinglichkeit, 124
discrete-unit taxonomies, xii
discursive spirituality, 151–52
The Doctrine and Covenants of the Church of Jesus Christ Latter-Day Saints, 136
Domain 1: *The Organismic Curriculum*, 45–52; neuroses and psychoses originating in, 47; Piaget's sensori-motor phase, 47; Wilber's "hatching of the physical self, 47
Domain 2: *The Emotional Curriculum*, 52–63; complexes, roots of in second domain, 57; primary narcissism, roots of in second domain, 52–53
Domain 3: *The Empirical-Procedural Curriculum*: 63–67; metacognition, roots in D-2, 63–64; role of mother in gender identity formation in D-3, 64; sign/symbol capacity begins, 63–64
Domain 4: *The Legal-Procedural Curriculum*, 67–101; Adlerian psychology suited to; conventional morality's origin in, 68; persona,

origin in D-4; upper-limit of most people's ethical development, 68–69
Domain 5, *The Phenomenological Curriculum*, 103–33; "going transpersonal," 103; good faith versus bad faith in; 108–9 hermeneutic capacities of, 105; roots of postmodern curriculum, 127; social deconstruction/reconstruction as foci of, 12
Domain 6: *The Immanent Curriculum*: 133–47: transpersonal realm, 134; Deep Ecology originating in, 141–43; Environmentalism versus Deep Ecology, 142–43
Domain 7$^{m/d}$: *The Ontological Curriculum*: 147–52; East-West dialogue having to occur here; twenty-first century, 147–48; teaching as ontological spirituality, 152–53; teaching as incarnational spirituality, 153–56; empirical reality epiphenomenon of ontological "fields" in both 7^m and 7^d, 149
double-hermeneutic, 24

E Pluribus Unum, 135
Eckhardt, Meister, 148
ecological education, 145
Edinger, Edward, 104, 132
Education as the Practice of Social Violence Against Children, 67
The Educational Imagination, 36
The Educational Spectrum, 36
egalitarianism: anti-democratic imbalance over gradation, 12; centrality of in holistic educational theory, xiii–xiv; democratic balance with gradation, 12

ego:
consolidation and growth of in Domains 1–4, 45–103; emergence and consolidation of as primary issue at D4, 67–70
ego-Self axis, 13, 104, 132
Einstein, Albert, 118
Eisenhower, President Dwight D., 94
Eliot, T. S., 101; *Four Quartets*, 137
Emerson, Ralph Waldo, 136; "Each and All," 137–39
Emile, 72
The Emotional Experience of Teaching and Learning, 60; the emotional domain of the curriculum, xvii
empirical-procedural domain of the curriculum, xvii
enantiodromia, 19–20
Encounter: Education for Meaning and Social Justice, 36, 143
epistemology:
cultural differences in, 16; importance of at Domain 5, 108, 114, 122, 127
The Ever-Present Origin, 45
evolution:
anxiety's inhibitory effects on, 39–40; epigenetic, 149; ethical imperatives implied by, 11; servant-leader as ethical apotheosis of, 29
existential intelligence, 131
existential project, 133

Fairbairn, W. R. D., 53
Fay, Brian, 18, 128; oppression as embodied and embedded, 51
Ferrucci, Paolo, 74
finite/steady-state systems:
versus non-finite/open-ended systems, 12–13
fixation, 39

Forbes, Scott, 97, 143; *Holistic Education: An Analysis of Its Ideas and Nature*, 97
"Form is emptiness. Emptiness is form," 149
"formal conversation," 99
Foucault, Michel, 82
free will. *See* agency
Freire, Paolo, 127; *Pedagogy of Freedom*, 127–28
Freud, Sigmund, 25, 73
Froebel, Friedrich, 48; effect upon Piaget, 48; holarchic curriculum, early example of, 48–49; Kindergarten Movement, father of, 48
fusion, psychological, 46, 60, 69; and defusion, 64; sociocentric and egoic causes of, 67

Gardner, Howard, 131
Gebser, Jean, 11, 108
Geworfenheit, 125
Gellert, Michael, 24–25; *The Fate of America*, 24–25
gender identity, the complex construction of, 64
Giddens, Sir Anthony, 18, 24, 87–90
Goffman, Ervin, 73–74; *facework*, 73–74
Grace, Divine, 41
gradation:
anti-democratic imbalance over egalitarianism, 12; centrality of in holistic educational theory, xiii–xiv; democratic balance with egalitarianism, 12
Greene, Maxine, 126; phenomenological approach to curriculum, 126

Habermas, Jurgen:
legitimation crisis, 20–21
habitus, 36, 71

Hall, G. Stanley, 100
Harris, Maria, 154–55
Harris, William Torrey, 55
Hartshorne, Charles, 40, 101
health and social services in the schools:
   history of, 50
Heidegger, Martin:
   being-towards-death, 39; *Dasein*, 39; *Geworfenheit*, 125; the "ontological" and "ontic" distinction, 116; propositional language, the limits of, 31, 59
Heraclitus, 19
hermeneutics:
   originating in D5, 106
the hermeneutics of hope/the hermeneutics of suspicion, 105–8; both necessary in a democracy, 111–14
the hero archetype, 90
Herrigel, Eugene, 152
hierarchical taxonomies, xi; dangers of, xiv–xv; legitimate uses of, xiv; structural problems, 19
Hobbes, Thomas, 71
the holarchic curriculum:
   essential features of, 37–39; research possibilities in education generated by, 13
holarchy:
   ability to hold tension between egalitarianism and gradation, 10–11; concentricity, 29; historical origins of, xv; interdependence of all domains in a holarchy 38, 47; *Px2* advantages, 9, 26, 29; permeability of domains, 10; permutability of domains, 10; problems in, 39
holistic education: xv, 3, 5, 26; history and tenets of, 33–37; its role in U.S. history, 136

Homans, Peter, 106
homeostatic balance, 31, 40
hook, in Jungian psychology, 89
hot cognition, 76–77, 117
Huebner, Duane, 131, 155;
   Education as "Ultimate Concern," 155; *The Lure of the Transcendent*, 131; Reconceptualist Movement in curriculum theory, founder of, 155
human capital approach to education, 34

the image, 4; basis of conceptualization, 4; generates systems, 31
immanent domain of the curriculum, xvii
Immanentism. *See* Transcendental Movement.
"immortality projects" as false consciousness, 109
implicate order, 149.
   See also Bohm, David
individuation, 72–73, 110
the in-group/out-group phenomenon, 53–54, 71
The Inner World of Trauma, 46
the instinct to learn, 35
"integrality," xiv
integrative curriculum, xi; differences from standard holistic curricula, 5–6; dysfunctions in integrative systems, 38–41
integrative historiography in education, 97
item-and-process taxonomies, xii; problems with, 24–25

John of the Cross, Saint, 148
Johnson, President Lyndon Baines, 71; the Great Society Program, 71; the War on Poverty, 71
Judeo-Christian spirituality:

dialogical, xviii
Jung, Carl, 18, 104–6; adult education, a cornerstone of, 27; against social engineering, 82; alchemy, 106; Jungian literary criticism, 124; Jungian theory as holistic, xviii–xix; the Self, 131–32; spiritual aristocracy, the existence of, 105; two hermeneutics at play in his alchemical studies, 109–11

Kalsched, Donald, 46; *The Inner World of Trauma*, 46–47
Kant, Immanuel: *The Critique of Pure Reason*, 3–4, 18, 59–60
karuna, 29
Keats, John, 137; "Ode on a Grecian Urn," 137; soul-making, 139
Kierkegaard, S., 111, 130; *Fear and Trembling*, 130
Kindergarten Movement, 48–50
King Lear, 75
Klein, Melanie, 20, 53
Kliebard, Herbert, 87
Koestler, Arthur, xv, 10
Kohut, Heinz, 52–53
Kokol, Martin, 161–76
Kuhn, Thomas, 4; paradigm shift, 4; *The Structure of Scientific Revolutions*, 4, 117–20

Lao Tzu, 19, 33
"law and order," 20–21
legal-procedural domain of the curriculum, xvii
Leviathan, 72
Liberalism, 20–23
liberatory theory and *praxis*, 51
the linguistic turn, 114
Lipman, Matthew, 99; *Philosophy Goes to School*, 99
Locke, John, 40

mana personality, 90
Mann, Horace, 94
Marx, Karl, 70–71; *The Eighteenth Brumaire of Louis Napoleon*, 71
Maslow, Abraham, 126, 132–34, 145; illness of the personal psyche without contact with transpersonal; *Notes Towards a Psychology of Being*, 132; religion with a little "r," 132; "self-actualization" as equivalent to Existentialist living in "good faith," 109
matter, 136; redemption of in medieval and renaissance Christian alchemy, 109–10
the mathetic versus poetic, 120–21
McLaren, Peter, 102
McMillan, Sylvia, 130–31,
the *medicina catholica*, in alchemy, 109–10
Merleau-Ponty, Maurice, 51; "body-subjects," 51
Merrell-Wolff, Franklin: *Consciousness without an Object*, 148–49
Merton, Thomas, 148
Mencken, H. L., 114
Metacognition, 63–64, 82–87
the military-industrial complex, 94
military-industrial-educational complex, 33, 57, 95, 123
"mind reading," as a script pathology, 96
monistic spirituality, xvii–xix, 147, 151–52.
See also dialogical spirituality
moral judgments in and of the curriculum: category errors in, xiv; evolutionary bases of, xiv; holarchic curricula, in, 38; lack of, relativism, 128; psycholinguistic processes involved in, xiv

Mormonism, 136; connection with American Transcendentalism, 137; theology, 49, 136–37
morphic field, 149.
   See also Rupert Sheldrake
Moses, 90
mother, 64
"Much Madness Is Divinest Sense," 81
mysterium tremendum et fascinans, 135

narcissism:
   primary, 52–53; secondary, 52–53
narcissistic wound, 53
Naumburg, Margaret, 60–61:
neural nets, 4–5
nihilism:
   somatic roots of, 46
Noddings, Nel, 61–62; teaching and care, 61–62; "formal conversation," 99
non-finite/open-ended systems, 12
Nurturing the Whole Student, 37

"object lessons," 48
objectivity, 4.
   See also subjectivity
Occam's Razor, 120
"Ode on a Grecian Urn," 139
Oedipus Complex/Electra Complex, 55, 60
omnipotence of thought, the child's, 56
"ontogeny recapitulates phylogeny," 49
ontological dimension of teaching, 151–52
ontological domain of the curriculum: dialogic foundations of, xvi; monistic foundations, xvi
Opera Didactica Omnia, 48
organismic domain of the curriculum, xvii
the "Other," 41
Otto, Rudolph, 132
The Oversoul, 136

Parker, Col. Francis W., 50
Parsons, Talcott, 71
Paul, St., 32;
   holarchic aspect of, 75; *First Corinthians* 12, 22–28; *Matthew* 22, 14; *Romans* 7, 75–76
pedagogy of liminality, 130
the Perennial Wisdom, 31
persona, 68; necessary for maintenance of social order, 73
Pestalozzi, Johann Heinrich, 48; object lessons, 48
phenomenological domain of the curriculum, xvii
Phenix, Phillip, 37
Philosopher's Stone:
   the *aurum non vulgi*, 109; the *aurum nostrum*, 109; Christian Gnosticism, 110; the *laphis philosophorum*, 109; the *medicina catholica*, 110
Plato, 48, 104, 139
political correctness, 99
Polkinghorne, Donald, 15; *Narrative Knowing and the Human Sciences*, 15
postmodern theory, 11
praxis, 13, 41
Preface to the Lyrical Ballads, 59
the Primal Mother:
   Primal Good Mother, 46; Primal Devouring Mother, 46
primary processes, 55–57
Process Theology, 40, 10; *Matthew* 22, 14
Progressive Education Movement, 97–99; conservative versus liberal, 98
the *puella* complex, 23–25
the *puer* complex, 23–25

radical pluralism, 38
Ravitch, Diane, 97
realia in teaching and learning, 48
Realms of Meaning, 37
Reinsmith, William, 152

relativism, ethical:
  aperspectival madness, danger of, 128
The Republic, 104
re-scripting, 97
Resistance Theory, 102
rhetorical patterns:
  African American, 17; Anglo-Germanic, 17; Asian, 17; contrasted with other patterns, 17; Latin, 17; Semitic, 17
Ricoeur, Paul, 105
role-shifting, 71; role transitivity, 42
Rorty, Richard, 11
Rosseau, Jean, 72
"run-away world," 18
Russell, Betrand, 125

Sartre, Jean Paul, 106
Schopenhauer, Arthur, xv
script theory, 77–79; problems with, 79; script pathology, 79
The Second Treatise of Civil Government, 40
secondary processes, 55–57
Sedlak, Michael, 50
Seeton, Mother Mary, 153
selective filtering, 96
the Self, 72–73
Self-object Psychology, 53–55
Sendak, Maurice, 107; *Where the Wild Things Are*, 107
Seven Curricular Landscapes, 37
the shadow, 75–76
Sheldrake, Rupert, 149
Shelley, Percy Bysshe:
  The Defense of Poetry, 118
Skinner, B. F., 50
social contract, 72
"social justice," 22
Social Darwinism:
  Dynamic Sociology, 21–22; *Social Statics*, 21–22; Spencer, Herbert, 21–22; Ward, Lester Frank, 21–22
sociocentric consciousness, 71
Solution-Focused Brief Therapy, 79
spatiality of privilege, 15
special education, 50
Spinoza, Baruch, xv
spiritual emergency, 81
Spock, Commander: as archetype, 117
Spring, Joel, 30
standardized education:
  negative consequences of, xv, 64
Steiner, Rudolf, 143, 145
Structural-Functionalism, 71
the structure-of-the-disciplines curriculum, 100
subjectivity, 4.
  See also objectivity
subpersonalities, 75
sub specie aeternitatis:
  human being as, 75, 108, 135, 147
surveillance in the Fourth Domain, 81
Suzuki, Daistezu, 148
symbol:
  sign different from, 65–66; 121–24

Taba, Hilda, 50
"talk story," 17
Tat tvam asi, 150
taxonomies. *See* hierarchical taxonomies; item-and-process taxonomies
teacher education, 76–77
teacher reflectivity, 128; teacher as civic prophet: political sense of calling, 151–52; teacher as mother: psychological sense of calling, 151–52; teacher as priest: incarnational sense of calling, 151–52; teacher as Zen master: ontological sense of calling, 151–52

technical rationality:
  Western dedication to, 17–18
teleological purposiveness, 28; Process Theology, 40, 101
temporality of privilege, 15
Tennyson, Alfred, Lord, 140; "Flower in a Crannied Wall," 140
tertium non datur, 22
the Theory of Relativity, 118
Thomas, Dylan, 140
Thoreau, Henry David, 77
Tillich, Paul:
  "Ultimate Concern," 155
Tolerance of ambiguity, 112
Totalitarianism:
  begins in a failed ideal, 38–40; Divine Grace as its ultimate enemy and undoing, 41; limits of, 40; narcissism, as, 40–41
transcendence:
  education as, 147; therapies of, 78
Transcendental Movement, 136
the Transcendent Function, 41
the transference:
  in the classroom, 60–61
transition/transaction/transformation, curricula as, 146
transpersonal psychology, 24–25, 133–34
Tremmel, Robert:
  "Zen and the Art of Teaching," 152
Tyack, David, 97
Tyler, Ralph, 50

the ultimate attribution error, 53
Understanding the Whole Student, 36
Unitarianism, 136
The Universal Schoolhouse, 13, 36
U.S. Supreme Court on education over last 70 years, 84

the *via negativa*, 148
vocational education:
  Dewey's holarchic vision of, 146; legitimation and reproduction of existing social order, 146

Wacks, V. Quinton, 147
Waldorf Schools, 60–61, 145–46
The War on Poverty. *See* Johnson, President Lyndon Baines
Whitehead, Alfred, 40, 101, 155; education as ultimately religious, 155
Wilber, Ken, viii–ix, xv–xvii, 10–11, 25, 26, 28, 47, 103–4
Willard, Emma, 153
Winnicott, Donald W., 53
Wordsworth, William, 59
"worker-citizen," preparing student to be, 35, 98

xenophobia, 72

Yeats, William Butler, 40

Zen in the Art of Archery, 152

About the Author

Clifford Mayes, PhD, PsyD, received a doctorate in the history of U.S. education from the University of Utah and a doctorate in psychology from the Southern California University for Professional Studies. Until his retirement, he was a professor of education at Brigham Young University and is now an adjunct professor of psychology at Pacifica Graduate Institute in Carpinteria, California. Mayes has authored ten books and forty scholarly articles in psychology, educational psychology, curriculum theory, and multiculturalism.

Lightning Source UK Ltd.
Milton Keynes UK
UKHW010634190120
357151UK00004B/368